Case Studies
in Spiritual Care

of related interest

Spiritual Care in Practice
Case Studies in Healthcare Chaplaincy
Edited by George Fitchett and Steve Nolan
ISBN 978 1 84905 976 3
eISBN 978 0 85700 876 3

Spiritual Care at the End of Life
The Chaplain as a 'Hopeful Presence'
Steve Nolan
ISBN 978 1 84905 199 6
eISBN 978 0 85700 513 7

Chaplaincy in Hospice and Palliative Care
Edited by Karen Murphy and Bob Whorton
Foreword by Baroness Finlay of Llandaff
ISBN 978 1 78592 068 4
eISBN 978178450 329 1

Critical Care
Delivering Spiritual Care in Healthcare Contexts
Edited by Jonathan Pye, Peter Sedgwick and Andrew Todd
ISBN 978 1 84905 497 3
eISBN 978 0 85700 901 2

Case Studies
in Spiritual Care

Edited by George Fitchett
and Steve Nolan

Jessica Kingsley *Publishers*
London and Philadelphia

First published in 2018
by Jessica Kingsley Publishers
73 Collier Street
London N1 9BE, UK
and
400 Market Street, Suite 400
Philadelphia, PA 19106, USA

www.jkp.com

Library of Congress Cataloging in Publication Data
A CIP catalog record for this book is available from the Library of Congress

British Library Cataloguing in Publication Data
A CIP catalogue record for this book is available from the British Library

ISBN 978 1 78592 783 6
eISBN 978 1 78450 705 3

Printed and bound in Great Britain

The editors are grateful to all who have contributed to producing this book. We want to acknowledge the honesty of the authors, who have shared their work so willingly and with such generosity to their professional colleagues. We are also deeply grateful to Kristen Schenk, who provided exceptional aid in preparing the manuscript for publication

Contents

Part 3 The Chaplain as Ritual Leader

Part 4 The Chaplain as Self-Reflexive Practitioner

Introduction

Autoethnography in Chaplain Case Study Research

Steve Nolan

Possibly the greatest value of case studies is their ability to take us into the intimacy of the bedside and allow fellow chaplains, healthcare colleagues and those who commission chaplaincy care, as well as the general public, to see what actually goes on in the private space of the chaplaincy/spiritual care relationship. In truth, little is known about the nature of spiritual care relationships. The lack of an agreed and plainly articulated definition for spiritual care means that, as a profession, chaplains struggle to explain clearly the nature of the work. But while, as yet, there may be no widely accepted definition of the chaplaincy/spiritual care relationship, as chaplains we do seem to know one when we see one! We talk about our own spiritual care relationships in terms of the people we have met, the things we said and did for them, the impact they had on us, and what happened (or may not have happened) as a result of our relationship with them. We tell stories, and we inspire others by the stories that we tell; and these stories are, in effect, case studies informally expressed.

This is not a frivolous point. It is necessary to underline that, however informally expressed, such case studies have the potential to provide rich data about the chaplaincy/spiritual care relationship. Yin has characterised case studies as having particular value when '"how" or "why" questions are being posed, when the investigator has little control over events, and when the focus is on a contemporary phenomenon within some real-life context' (Yin 1994, p.1). So to dismiss case reports that relate these encounters as 'mere stories' is to squander what could be significant information about spiritual care.

One reason why chaplains' reports of spiritual care relationships remain undeveloped into case studies is that, in the main, chaplains are under-equipped to do research. As Cobb observes, most chaplains have come into healthcare having been trained in theology and pastoral care, and lack any training in research methods, critical inquiry or analysis (Cobb 2006). As a consequence, as chaplains we tend not see ourselves as researchers.

So perhaps research needs demystifying. At its simplest, research is about finding answers to interesting questions. To that extent, everyone is a 'researcher'. For example, I may want to find an answer to a question as mundane as, 'What is the best laptop for under £500?' Or perhaps, 'Can I find a good vegan restaurant in Paris?' Or, a question more relevant to chaplains, 'What goes on in a chaplaincy/spiritual care relationship?' Each of these examples counts as 'research', because in each case the person asking the question needs to 'find stuff out'. The 'stuff' in each example may be very different, but in each the 'researcher' wants to find an answer to their research question. What distinguishes professional or academic research, and makes it more challenging than finding out about laptops or restaurants, is the requirement that the process of finding out 'stuff' follows a robust and logical methodology, so that other researchers can check that what has been found out is credible and valid. Because the stuff that needs to be found out varies so widely, the methods used to do research need to be tailored directly to the specific question that is being asked. So, for the novice researcher, there can seem to be a bewildering variety of research methodologies. However, research in the form of a case study is well within the reach of novice chaplain–researchers, especially those who enjoy telling stories of their spiritual care encounters and who are able to reflect on the stories they tell.

Here is one of my stories.[1]

---

1   The full presentation of this case is found below as Chapter 15, '"I'd like you to get to know about me" – Kristof, a 50-year-old atheist academic admitted to a hospice for palliative symptom control'.

Kristof

The immediate reason why 'Kristof' (not his real name) was admitted to the hospice was pain control. His cancer had been diagnosed about a year earlier, and initially he had been considered suitable for surgery but having agreed to undergo the painful procedure, Kristof contracted a virus and the operation had to be postponed. On recovering, Kristof reflected on his prospects, which he described as a lot of pain, followed by a long period of pain, with a 5–10 per cent chance of survival; or not much pain and a certain outcome. With the support of his family, he decided against surgery.

But a second, albeit related, reason for Kristof's admission to the hospice – at least as he explained it to me – was his recent attempted suicide by overdose. Kristof told me that he had taken what he thought would be more than a 'killer dose' of diamorphine but that it had been a slow-release formulation that just put him to sleep for 27 hours. With more than a hint of irony, he said it was the first time he had been out of pain in a year!

I'd been asked to visit Kristof on the basis that he would welcome all interventions (perhaps even the intervention of a chaplain). The man I met was charming, intelligent and pragmatic, and he spoke frankly about death and his dying: 'I've always been very logical about thinking about my death. It's going to happen, there's nothing I can do about it.' While he said that he welcomed my visit – 'I'm not going to turn down any offer of help' – he was clear with me that he did not see himself as religious. He had rejected religion while at school, due to an overly enthusiastic Christian teacher, who had 'scared everyone to death' with 'fire and brimstone sermons'. Nonetheless, Kristof acknowledged his respect for other people's religion: 'I'm not so arrogant as to say it's not true'; he admitted some belief in a higher power and welcomed a chaplain's help to confront his dying. Kristof told me that he wanted to understand who he had been in his life, what his life had meant and, for reasons he didn't expound, 'to do that in relation to Christianity'.

So we began to meet. Our meetings were not easy. Kristof was still having hospital appointments, which he found arduous and tiring, and which often took him out of the hospice for whole days. Also, the nature of his cancer meant that his diction was extremely poor and it was always difficult to discern his speech; indeed, towards the end of our relationship, Kristof had to write down the things he wanted to say. Despite these obstacles, we managed to meet reasonably regularly and Kristof was able to help me get to know him. He told me how his cancer had been discovered, the impact this had had on his family, and their decision that he would forego surgery; how he had been able to order his finances, write his will and prepare memories for his children, which included buying expensive presents that would 'last them for the rest of their lives'; and how he had come to regard his cancer as 'a tremendous gift', giving him time to get everything 'sorted out'. In effect, our meetings became an extended life review.

Kristof's observation that 'I've always wanted to be in control of things' resonated with his opinion that his logical side had always been stronger than his emotional side but he didn't deny that his emotions sometimes contradicted his logic: 'I've always been logical. So I've never been afraid of death; you live, you die. It's going to happen. But I don't want to die.' Perhaps his desire to live (not withstanding his attempt to end his own life) motivated his decision to accept palliative chemotherapy. Perhaps, too, despite expressing his preference for what he called 'analytic Christianity' – 'Christianity that you discuss and question and ask, "Do I believe that?"' – his openness to thinking about God was another indication that his emotions were contradicting his logic.

In that light, that Kristof's unexpected revelation that he believed in the Resurrection was likely instructive about his inner world, although to my regret I failed to pick up on its significance until I reflected on our work after he had died. If pressed, my defence would be that I was caught up in the immediacy of things but if I'm honest to myself, it is that I allowed myself to over-identify with Kristof's desire to make sense of his (my) experience 'in relation to Christianity'. Kristof and I shared similarities in our working-class backgrounds and academic aspirations, and I connected with his religious questions more than he knew, which meant that I was probably not as helpful to him as I imagined I might be.

Not that I was no use to him. Suicide remained Kristof's pain relief of last resort: 'No one here [in the hospice] sees it as suicide.

They understand that it's a way of ending the pain.' At our first meeting, he tested me about his overdose: 'I suppose that's technically a sin. But maybe Christianity is less harsh these days. Is it less harsh?' Although he didn't respond directly to my honest answer, he did open the door to our working together. And when the subject came up again, he affirmed that he found value in our relationship: 'What I really want to talk about is something more personal. It's about how I face my own death. I think we've hit it off – we seem to see things in the same way – I'd like to talk about how I face my own death.' Clearly, my openness to his questioning of religion, eschewing 'authorised' responses in favour of honest discussion, had been important to Kristof and had established a basis of trust between us.

From chaplain's 'story' to chaplain's case study

So this is my 'story' about my chaplaincy/spiritual care relationship with Kristof. What I've related is no more than I might have discussed in a good supervision session. The question is: what would be needed to modulate this 'story' of a chaplaincy/spiritual care relationship into a formal case study? I would suggest it needs four things: intention, method, analysis and writing.

Intention

The first thing needed to turn a chaplain's story into a case study is 'intention'. It is important to keep in mind that a case study is *research* and that, as such, it is an intentional process in which the chaplain–researcher wants to learn something new, find out some stuff they previously didn't know or understand. A case study, then, is not simply a formalised account of an interesting session or series of sessions written up after the event. A case study begins at the point where a chaplain becomes aware that there may be something in the relationship with this particular patient that, if processed, might offer some significant learning. Stake identifies two interrelated modes of intention, which he terms *intrinsic* and *instrumental interest* (Stake 1994, p.237). Intrinsic interest in a case is motivated by the intention to gain better understanding of this particular case; in a related way, instrumental interest in a case aims at developing insight into a specific issue or aspect of theory. Clearly, the two modes touch on each other: understanding this particular case is likely to deepen insights into specific issues or illuminate a particular theory, which, in turn, will almost certainly aid understanding of the particular case being studied. My reason for studying my relationship with Kristof was that I wanted to understand how I might be of use to someone who is dying (Nolan 2012) but I also felt that the nature of my work with Kristof may have the potential to contribute to the wider question of the value of chaplaincy/spiritual care. In that way, I had both an intrinsic and an instrumental interest in researching this relationship.

This said, the intention to study a relationship with a patient presents a chaplain–researcher with a significant ethical challenge. Intention necessarily changes the dynamics of the relationship. Leaving aside contested questions about how far what is known as the 'observer effect' impacts the validity of the research[2] (Monahan and Fisher 2010), a chaplain's intention to use their relationship with a patient as the object of research necessarily puts the chaplain into a dual relationship with the patient. The chaplain–researcher now becomes both a compassionate chaplain, offering spiritual care, *and* a detached dispassionate researcher, carefully observing a subject; a schizoid position that calls for the sort of passive dissociation that could jeopardise the relationship of pastoral care. For some chaplains, the potential for compromise will be enough to confirm that case study research is not for them – or worse, that it is always inappropriate to a chaplain's role since it contradicts the call to embody the compassionate love of the Divine. Against this, I would argue that a chaplain's intention to study the spiritual care relationship actually calls for no more than the high levels of pastoral skill one would expect in a professional chaplain, and that this level of skill should be

---

2   Also known as the 'Hawthorne effect', this is the idea that the researcher's act of observing may subtly, if unintentionally, affect the behaviour of the one being observed.

able to manage the dual relationship in such a way that the chaplain–researcher can observe and reflect on the relationship and at the same time avoid becoming detached.

Two things are helpful here: note-taking, including keeping verbatim records of conversations, and good supervision. If intention is what modulates a chaplain's 'story' into a case study, taking (field) notes and recording verbatim dialogue are the means of capturing data. The obvious challenge, for a busy chaplain, is that note-taking needs to be as contemporaneous to the encounter as possible, which is difficult if not nearly impossible given the demands on a chaplain's time. However, the benefit of near contemporary note-taking goes beyond its value for research. Reflecting on the encounter deepens a chaplain's understanding of the relationship, allowing them to notice what might otherwise be missed in the immediacy of the encounter. Additionally, it provides good material for use in supervision, which is the other essential means by which a chaplain–researcher can avoid becoming detached.

Method

To become a case study, a chaplain's 'story' needs to be constructed in relation to a method that gives the research direction and credibility. Problematic here is the fact that no single methodology has been recognised as definitive for case study research. However, one approach that seems to be particularly amenable is autoethnography.

As an approach to research, autoethnography emerged from sociology and cultural anthropology, in particular the field of ethnography (Anderson 2006), which is the systematic study of people [Greek *ethnos*] and cultures, including subcultures. But, whereas ethnography focuses on the researcher's observation of the 'other', researchers came to understand that the 'observer effect' implicated the researcher in her research. In response, 'researcher reflexivity' encouraged researchers to incorporate elements of their own experience into writing about the other, in what becomes a blend of ethnography and autobiographical writing (Scott-Hoy 2002, cited in Etherington 2004, p.139). This shift towards recognising that researchers are already implicated in their research has entailed a break with the traditional scientific requirement that obliged researchers to write in the third person and thereby give their work the (illusory) sense of researcher objectivity. Against this, the requirement of autoethnography that researchers should display their subjectivity by writing in the first person has troubled the familiar norms against which the quality of research has been judged (Etherington 2004, p.147).

Autoethnography, therefore, requires that chaplain–researchers make use of their subjective self (Etherington 2004; Wall 2006) in 'explicit and reflexive self-observation' (Anderson 2006, p.375), and thereby produce what is in effect a 'narrative of the self' (Holloway 2008, p.26). Swift has been among the first chaplain–researchers to use autoethnography as a way of researching 'chaplaincy and what is going on in the practice of spiritual care' (Swift 2009, p.97), and among the first to acknowledge that his research is 'fully implicated in the situations researched' (Swift 2009, p.104). Indeed, Swift goes further and acknowledges that, as the researcher, he may give rise to the situation he is researching. For this reason, I own that my story about Kristof is exactly that: *my* story of *my* relationship with Kristof as I sought to offer him spiritual care (doubtless *his* story would have been different, and who knows the degree to which I would have featured in it!). Autoethnography legitimises my writing myself into the case study, because, as Wall puts it, 'using self as subject is a way of acknowledging the self that was always there anyway' (Wall 2006, p.158).

Anderson (2006) identifies two main autoethnographic approaches. On the one hand, there is the approach of those researchers who are influenced by post-modern scepticism about the possibility of representing the experience of 'the other'. These researchers engage in 'evocative or emotional autoethnography' and make no claim to generalisability; instead, they aim to find resonance between their emotional response to 'the other' and those who read their personal narratives (Anderson 2006, p.377). To that end, evocative autoethnography depends on well-crafted prose, poetry and even artistic performances (for example, Richardson 1994; Ellis and Bochner 2000). However, this approach to autoethnography has been criticised for being 'self-indulgent, narcissistic, introspective, and individualised' (Wall 2006, p.155). In contrast, the reflexivity involved in 'analytic autoethnography' still requires 'an awareness of reciprocal influence between ethnographers and their settings and informants' (Anderson 2006, p.382) but entails the kind of self-conscious introspection that is 'guided by a desire to better understand both *self and others* through examining one's actions and perceptions in reference to and dialogue with those of others' (Anderson 2006, p.382, emphasis added). In other words, analytic autoethnography is less sceptical about the problem of representation and stresses the importance of 'dialogue with informants beyond the self' (Anderson 2006, p.378). In part, this is to overcome the solipsistic isolation that is a real and present danger for autoethnographic research. For chaplains, dialogue with informants beyond the self (in other words, with 'patients') is unavoidable and becomes an explicit part of case study research in the verbatim records that dramatise the narrative and form rich data for analysis. Verbatim reporting on chaplaincy/spiritual care encounters is a familiar part of many chaplains' supervisory practice. Incorporated with (self-)observations and (field) notes, verbatim records can form the core of a chaplain's case study. In studying my relationship with Kristof, I made extensive use of verbatim reporting as a way of capturing our encounters.

Analysis

According to Anderson, the aim of analytic ethnography is 'to use empirical data to gain insight into some broader set of social phenomena than those provided by the data themselves' (Anderson 2006, p.387). This generalised statement applies equally and directly to the aim of case study research. In other words, it is not enough simply to document personal experience. To become a piece of case study research, the chaplain's account of working with a patient must be analysed and interpreted, which means that the (self-)observations, verbatim records and (field) notes need to be seen as so much data.

Analysis is the intellectually demanding part of the work (Parahoo 1997, p.355). It is also the part that presents the greatest challenge, because, just as there is no definitive methodology for case study research, so there is no single, recognised method for analysing and interpreting case study data (Yin 1994, p.102; Holloway 2008, p.39). The goal is clear: analysis should 'treat the evidence fairly...produce compelling analytic conclusions, and...rule out alternative interpretations' (Yin 1994, p.103). But this still leaves chaplain–researchers with a good deal of freedom to work with the data according the qualitative approach they find most appropriate. This said, Yin proposes the best analytic strategy is to follow 'the theoretical propositions that led to the case study' (Yin 1994, p.103). By this he means the original ideas and objectives that shaped the research questions: the 'how' and 'why' questions that motivated the case study research, that shaped the data collection, and that can now suggest priorities for approaching the analysis (Yin 1994, p.104).

The ideas and objectives that shaped my study with Kristof were related to my interest in the intrinsic value of our work: I wanted to understand how I might be of use to someone who is dying. Directed by my previous research (Nolan 2012), I was intent on looking at how Kristof might have been helped by virtue of the quality of our relationship. So my analysis of the data – my (self-)observations, verbatim records and (field) notes – were, in part, directed by this question. I've already noted that I think certain parallels in our stories caused me to over-identify with Kristof's desire to make sense of his experience 'in relation to Christianity', which meant that I likely missed the significance of his unexpected confession of belief in the Resurrection. But despite this failure, Kristof nonetheless affirmed we had 'hit it off' and that he would continue using me as someone with whom he could talk about facing his own death.

But while my objectives in studying this relationship were shaped by an interest in its intrinsic value, I also felt that this piece of work might produce more general insights into the value of chaplaincy/spiritual care, in other words, that it might have instrumental value. On this basis, I analysed the data with regard to the same three issues George Fitchett and I asked the contributors to our case studies collection (2015) to describe and critically reflect on: 'their assessment of the patient, their interventions and the changes that did or did not occur as a result of the care they provided (outcomes)' (Fitchett and Nolan 2015, p.16). Put in question form, I asked myself these questions:

- How did I assess Kristof's spiritual needs?

- Why did I intervene as I did in response to his spiritual needs?

- How effective were my responses to his spiritual needs?

In analysing a particular case, it is important to remember that the case is *particular*, that it is tied to the specifics of a particular person, their situation and their relationship with a given chaplain. For this reason, as Holloway points out, 'this type of inquiry is even less readily generalisable than other qualitative research' and a chaplain–researcher should avoid making 'unwarranted assertions about *generalisability* on the basis of a single case' (Holloway 2008, p.40).

Writing

The final thing needed to develop a chaplain's account of spiritual care into a case study is writing. It is perhaps obvious to suggest that the work needs to be written up but this is the point at which so much research fails. Potentially, chaplains hold a wealth of rich data about the efficacy of spiritual care but, for whatever reason, we seem to be reluctant to commit to paper. The regrettable consequence of this is that our knowledge and wisdom is lost, not only to our profession but, perhaps more importantly, to the wider multi-professional team. Writing up our cases is a time-consuming and intellectually demanding task and comes with a set of ethical challenges, in particular with regard to patient (and colleague) confidentiality. Not every chaplain feels they have the necessary degree of literary skills to write for publication. However, we have good stories to tell, and if we don't tell them, who will?

But there is another reason for writing, which is that writing is itself a form of learning. As Richardson puts it, 'writing is not just a mopping-up activity at the end of a research project. Writing is also a way of "knowing" – a method of discovery and analysis' (Richardson 1994, p.516). Writing my account of working with Kristof enabled me to put into words what happened and in so doing to explain to myself what went on between us. As the person-centred psychotherapist Carl Rogers might have said, writing enabled me 'to experience my experience' with Kristof (Rogers 2004, p.76), and thereby to deepen my learning.

Fitchett first identified the lack of case studies from chaplains within the healthcare and pastoral care literature, and triggered the renewal of interest in chaplains' case study research by nurturing a case study project with a small group of oncology chaplains (Fitchett 2011). These chaplains had never previously published but they worked to support and encourage each other towards the goal of producing a series of publishable studies. Theirs is a model that could easily be replicated, and Fitchett offers the following framework for writing a good case study (Fitchett 2011).

BEGIN WITH BACKGROUND

The case study will include as much detail as confidentiality will allow about: a) the patient; b) the chaplain(s) (including their religious affiliation, theology and professional training); and c) the institutional context in which they met. This background will help readers to evaluate critically the spiritual assessment and the care delivered. Assuming an autoethnographic approach, the study will also cover the chaplain's awareness of their feelings about the patient and the role these feelings played in that relationship.

DESCRIBE THE CHAPLAIN–PATIENT RELATIONSHIP

The spiritual care relationship is the 'story' the chaplain has to tell. This description is effectively a 'history' of the chaplain–patient spiritual care relationship and it will detail all the salient points as the relationship developed over time. As such, the 'story' will include at least some verbatim reporting of chaplain–patient conversations.

INCLUDE A SPIRITUAL ASSESSMENT

The chaplain's assessment will help readers understand how the chaplain discerned and interpreted the person's spiritual needs; it will likely include the chaplain's care plan and any changes to the assessment made as their situation changed over time.

CLARIFY THE CHAPLAINCY/SPIRITUAL CARE INTERVENTIONS

Drawing out what the chaplain did, or didn't do, in response to the person's spiritual needs, *and why*, will give colleagues valuable insight into the processes of chaplaincy/spiritual care.

HIGHLIGHT THE OUTCOMES OF THE RELATIONSHIP

The case study will include any changes that occurred for the patient, particularly those changes that may be attributable to the chaplain's care. If necessary, it will be important that the case study is honest enough to admit that nothing changed, and explain why.

END WITH A SUMMARY

The case study will end with a summary that reminds readers of the key points of the case.

Chaplains' case studies and the development of the profession

It is not unreasonable to suggest that every chaplain will have one or more stories about people they have cared for that have affected them and informed the way they now offer spiritual care. All chaplains learn from those for whom we care, and these stories are our case studies, informally expressed. Potentially, these stories are rich data that could inform our profession and instruct our multi-professional colleagues; written up and published, they are available to be studied and used to develop research projects that may help establish the valuable (but contested) contribution chaplaincy/spiritual care is making to the health and wellbeing of our patients (Fitchett 2011).

Chaplaincy is at a critical point in its development as a profession. The evolution of healthcare is fundamentally changing the role of chaplaincy. The days when our religious identity bought respectful deference from hospital staff are gone. From the UK perspective, the ongoing application to have chaplaincy recognised as a healthcare profession is no less than the formal acknowledgement that that refuge is being lost forever, and the challenge confronting all chaplains now is to prove our value as healthcare professionals alongside other healthcare professionals. Telling our stories is an important part of proving our value; learning to tell our stories in a way that commands respect, in other words, formalised as case studies, will be an essential means of developing as a profession.

The cases presented in this collection add to the growing body of published chaplains' case studies[3] and further demonstrate the complexity of chaplaincy/spiritual interventions. This collection arose from an embarrassment of riches that followed a call for papers we, as guest editors, put out for submissions for a special issue of *Health and Social Care Chaplaincy*, which was to be given over to chaplains' case studies. The call was put out to experienced chaplains (with three or more years of clinical practice) who were able to reflectively think and write about their work. Potential contributors need not have had previous experience writing for publication, as we offered to support them through the writing process. We were looking for chaplains from any health and/or social care setting, including community locations, and the case studies could report on the work of an individual chaplain or teams of chaplains, or a chaplain's collaboration in a multi-professional team; they could also be a 'one-off' study or a study based on longer-term work. We wanted cases that would illustrate important themes in the work that chaplains do and we looked for diversity of case, of chaplain/patient faith group, and of nationality.

The response was strong and we had more cases submitted than we could include in the journal, so we decided to publish them as a book-length collection. It is important for readers to keep in mind that these cases were not chosen because either the authors or we as the editors considered them to be representative of chaplaincy in general or of chaplaincy in any specific context; nor were they selected because they offer examples of ideal chaplaincy care. However, we think the cases we

---

3   At the time of going to press, 19 cases are available. See Cooper 2011; King 2012; Risk 2013; Fitchett and Nolan 2015; Nolan 2016; Bassett 2017; Glenister, 2017; Murphy (JN), 2017; Murphy (K), 2017; Schmohl, 2017; Van Loenen *et al.*, 2017.

have included represent reasonably competent care, notwithstanding that, as editors, we have had our own debates about some aspects of several cases. Our central hope is that the cases and the responses will help readers identify issues that need to be discussed and debated in our profession.

The present collection is arranged in four parts. The first part focuses on two paediatric cases. In the first, Chaplains Bryson, Nash and Nash present work with 'Mark', a young boy who had recently become severely physically disabled due to a brain tumour. They report on how the chaplaincy team at Birmingham Children's Hospital National Health Service Foundation Trust (UK) uses what it calls 'spiritual play' as part of an interpretive spiritual encounter (ISE). In describing the work with Mark, the chaplains show through two spiritual play activities, one using beads and the other reflecting on the day, how such specially designed activities, chosen for their appropriateness to a child's age-related development, can be both an intervention and an assessment tool. The second case in this section reports on the work Chaplain Jinks undertook with the family of baby 'Sarah' prenatally diagnosed with trisomy 18. Prognosis and life expectancy for babies with this chromosomal abnormality is extremely poor but Sarah's parents were motivated to continue the pregnancy. Chaplain Jinks's work with this family and their newborn is exceptionally sensitive. As with the first case, he utilised childhood developmental theory to shape his age-specific interventions; but this case also demonstrates the way in which chaplains can find themselves fulfilling the pastoral role of faith leader to people who are either isolated from their faith community or who do not belong to any kind of spiritual community. Such was Chaplain Jinks's sensitivity that he was able to cross the boundaries of denominational and theological/ spiritual difference and be acknowledged as Sarah's pastor by her mother. His work highlights an important issue that concerns the continuity of spiritual support between chaplaincy and a person's faith community.

Critical response to these cases is offered, first by Hans Evers, a Dutch paediatric chaplain active in research. He helpfully identifies several areas of comparison and contrast across the work of these chaplains: what they do that an observer could notice; how they define themselves;

the critical concepts that characterise their interventions; the focus of their professional attention; their goals and outcomes. He concludes by reflecting on some wider chaplaincy/spiritual care issues raised by their work. Jennifer Baird, a paediatric nurse researcher who actively fosters research literacy among the chaplaincy staff members and trainees of her institution, takes each case in turn before identifying and examining parallels between them. Specifically, she discusses the chaplains' role as a source of non-aligned support, as they offer support to families who to some degree mistrust their healthcare team; the chaplains' role in providing continuity of care for long-stay patients and families; the chaplains' ability to engage with both the child and family, regardless of the child's developmental status.

Part 2 focuses on two cases with veterans. Coincidentally, there are a number of similarities between these cases: both were referrals to chaplaincy from mental health colleagues; both deal with issues of sexuality; both feature chaplains who work with acceptance and commitment therapy (ACT); and in both cases the veterans were Roman Catholics. In each case, the chaplain demonstrates the degree to which the principles that direct ACT might be integrated with chaplaincy care. Chaplain Hanson notes that this is 'because of its focus on acceptance of suffering as part of the human condition and living in the present while making choices to live out one's values in the world'. Again, both cases make clear a particular aspect of the chaplain's distinctive contribution to patient care outcomes insofar as the mental healthcare colleagues making the referrals recognised the chaplain's expertise in the spiritual aspects of their client's care needs. Specifically, Chaplain Hanson describes how, within the military, the chaplain has a valued role as confidant, which, in this case, enabled her to provide 'Vicki', a male-to-female transgender veteran, with a safe place to discuss her gender identity and faith formation. Important here was the chaplain's role as 'a benevolent moral authority', a role that allowed her to affirm that Vicki was loved by God, whatever the Church may think of her. Similarly, the dual qualification of Chaplain Sanders, as both chaplain – a figure of religious/spiritual authority – and licensed marriage and family therapist trained in ACT, enabled her to act as a bridge between the counsellor who had been seeing 'Mrs Helen', a survivor of military sexual trauma (MST), and the church from which Mrs Helen felt alienated because her abuser had been a priest.

Responding to these cases, Andrew Todd, a chaplaincy educator and researcher with practitioner experience, highlights differences that exist between North American models of reflective practice, which are rooted in clinical pastoral education, and British models that favour the use of the 'pastoral cycle' (essentially an action/reflection model). He also observes that British chaplains are likely to be less comfortable than their North American colleagues with the 'clinical' language of interventions and expected outcomes. To that end, he questions how the intentional language of interventions is squared with the intention of being person-centred, a question that speaks to the current debate about outcome-oriented chaplaincy. As a practical theologian, he also considers the chaplains' theological reflection, highlighting the 'lived theology' and 'lived religion' of those with whom the chaplains worked.

As a clinical psychologist who has taught and written about ACT, Jason Nieuwsma considers the chaplains' application of ACT principles. His detailed comments bring additional insight into the value of the therapy for chaplaincy care, adding detail to the arrangement of ACT's component concepts and their overarching domains. Interestingly, his response makes explicit Todd's observation about intentionality, and while Nieuwsma is able to go some way to showing how the intentionality of ACT can be squared with its person-centred intention, his response leaves open the question of how it can avoid being a form of soft-paternalism (Beauchamp and Childress 2013).

Part 3 presents four cases in which the chaplain acts as a leader of ritual. The cases show the chaplains' versatility with the form of ritual: one leads the formalised rituals of a christening and a funeral; another extemporises prayer in an informal blessing with a child; others work within the structures of formal ritual to create something that is highly personalised. In her work with ten-year-old 'Paul', Chaplain Bratt Carle saw beyond the urgent request for baptism to the deeper, underlying spiritual need, which was for connection and support. Responding sensitively to Paul's mother's request, Chaplain Bratt Carle shows how she was able to offer an alternative ritual that was more appropriate for Paul and his family, which was an extemporised blessing. Her account of the blessing, which was informal and allowed for laughter, and included Paul's stuffed animal toys, shows how skilfully she was able to build rapport with the child and his mother in what was a tightly time-limited pastoral encounter. On a broader note, she highlights the role of ritual at times of transition.

In contrast, Chaplain Ásgeirsdóttir, from Iceland, provides more or less formalised rituals for a dying man and his family. Specifically, the rituals include a christening and a set of funeral rituals: a private service for the family, a public funeral service, and an ashes burial service. Over a period of some time, Chaplain Ásgeirsdóttir provided pastoral and spiritual care in and through these rituals to a family that did not see itself as religious and did not practise any form of religion. Nonetheless, her work demonstrates the need many people feel, regardless of their religious convictions, to mark the times around birth and death with some form of ritual. Chaplain Ásgeirsdóttir was able to tailor the formal services of her Lutheran National Church of Iceland in a way that meaningfully addressed the needs of this non-religious family.

In a similar way to Chaplain Ásgeirsdóttir, Chaplain Roberts' case notes how she used the planning of a funeral of a former colleague as the vehicle for pastoral and spiritual care. As an 'aesthetic witness' to the dying 'Daisy' was living, Chaplain Roberts describes taking advantage of a series of serendipitous 'hallway' talks while Daisy was still working to build a relationship that led, eventually, to Daisy asking Chaplain Roberts to take her funeral. Of particular interest in this case is the fact that, although Daisy had grown to feel disconnected from the Methodist Church in which she had grown up, and although her 'lived theology/ lived religion' (to borrow Todd's phrase) inclined towards a form of reincarnation, her relationship with Chaplain Roberts was sufficient for her to reach out to the conventionally religious person of the chaplain. Perhaps the cases of Chaplains Ásgeirsdóttir and Roberts illustrate the way in which the felt need for ritual, particularly around birth and death, may map with the cultural memory of religion and point to what could be an emerging form of chaplaincy suited to the needs of a post-Christian spirituality. As Chaplain Roberts puts it: 'The chaplain's role is to meet people where they are in life and then create meaningful rituals of comfort or rites of passage.'

In the final case in Part 3, Chaplains Goodman and Baron echo a theme within Chaplain Jinks's case study – the idea of the chaplain as clergy to patients separated from their faith community. In the case they present, 'Rabbi Jacobs' serves as *shaliach tzibbur* (prayer leader) for 82-year-old 'Mrs Pearlman', a resident with Alzheimer's disease living in a skilled nursing facility. In their beautifully intimate case presentation, Chaplains Goodman and Baron show how a chaplain and their team work within formal structures (here, those of the Jewish High Holy Days) to create rituals that are appropriate to a patient's situation and condition, and in ways that support a person to maintain their connection with the spiritual tradition and community that has nourished them, sometimes over many, many years.

As the first respondent to these cases, Herbert Anderson writes from the perspective of practical theology. Considering the cases as two sets of pairs that focus on the beginnings (Ásgeirsdóttir; Bratt Carle) and endings (Goodman and Baron; Roberts) of life, he highlights how chaplains are challenged to listen to patients' stories, discern need, and draw from tradition or improvise responses that are appropriate to the situation, and he offers guidance in the form of principles drawn from a lifetime's experience. Mark Cobb, a senior chaplain and researcher holding academic appointments in the UK, prefaces his responses by highlighting the nature and form of ritual before commenting insightfully on each case in turn. Among other things, he reminds us that theological reflexivity is an area that needs to be kept as 'a lively feature of chaplaincy case studies'.

The final case in this collection records my work with 'Kristof', a 50-year-old man admitted to hospice for palliative symptom control. This case study is slightly unusual in that, rather than reporting on work with outcomes that, arguably, have been beneficial to the subject, this case reports work about which I remain somewhat ambivalent. In large part, I identify the reason for this ambivalence as my over-identification with Kristof. I worked with Kristof over a period of several weeks and the work we did together did have some good effect but that was largely in spite of me rather than because of me! Kristof presented as an atheist but as wanting to make sense of his life experience 'in relation to Christianity'. Reflecting on our work, I came to realise that Kristof was able to use me to do the work he needed to do. Positively, the case demonstrates the role and value of reflexivity for chaplains.

Cheryl Holmes, who leads the development and promotion of spiritual care services in hospitals across Victoria in Australia, picks up on my self-reflexive critique of 'over-identification', which she discusses in the context of three sets of binary opposites or dualisms: objectivity/subjectivity; logical/emotional; and process/outcomes. Linda Emanuel, a psychoanalyst, also considers 'over-identification', which she sees as an issue for chaplains as much as the psychotherapists and psychoanalysts who gave us the concept. She observes that candid self-reflection is critical for four important reasons: chaplains need to be able to admit mistakes; because chaplains make use of the self as a key instrument in the work, we need to know ourselves; equally, we need to know ourselves because ours is a self-regulating profession; and, because chaplaincy is relational, candid self-reflection is necessary to foster healthy relationships.

It takes a certain degree of courage to openly discuss one's work, and the chaplains who have contributed to this collection are to be commended (as are those who have previously published case studies) for sharing stories about their work. For each of them, the process of turning their chaplain story into a case study has been iterative; together with us as the editors, they have worked through several versions, responding each time to our critical feedback, and now they are opening the intimacy of their work for public scrutiny. In doing so, their aim as authors, and ours as editors, is both to help advance chaplaincy as a profession and to give insight into the nature of chaplaincy and spiritual care.

References

Anderson, L. (2006). 'Analytic autoethnography.' *Journal of Contemporary Ethnography*, 35, 373–395.

Bassett, L. (2017). 'Space, time and shared humanity: A case study demonstrating a chaplain's role in end-of-life care.' *Health and Social Care Chaplaincy*, 5, 2, 194–208.

Beauchamp, T.L. and Childress, J.F. (2013). *Principles of Biomedical Ethics* (7th edn). Oxford: Oxford University Press.

Cobb, M. (2006). 'Growing research in the practice of chaplains.' *Journal of Health Care Chaplaincy*, 9, 1/2, 4–9.

Cooper, R.S. (2011). 'Case study of a chaplain's spiritual care for a patient with advanced metastatic breast cancer.' *Journal of Health Care Chaplaincy*, 17, 1, 19–37.

Ellis, C. and Bochner, A.P. (2000). 'Autoethnography, Personal Narrative, Reflexivity: Researcher as Subject.' In N.K. Denzin and Y.S. Lincoln (eds) *Handbook of Qualitative Research* (2nd edn) (pp.733–768). Thousand Oaks, CA: Sage.

Etherington, K. (2004). *Becoming a Reflexive Researcher: Using Our Selves in Research.* London: Jessica Kingsley Publishers.

Fitchett, G. (2011). 'Making our case(s).' *Journal of Health Care Chaplaincy*, 17, 1–2, 3–18.

Fitchett, G. and Nolan, S. (2015). *Spiritual Care in Practice: Case Studies in Healthcare Chaplaincy.* London: Jessica Kingsley Publishers.

Glenister, D. (2017). 'I want to make it right' – A 46-year-old woman with end stage renal disease and her Australian Aboriginal partner make significant choices.' *Health and Social Care Chaplaincy*, 5, 2, 241–256.

Holloway, I. (2008). *A–Z of Qualitative Research in Healthcare* (2nd edn). Oxford: Blackwell.

King, S.D.W. (2012). 'Facing fears and counting blessings: A case study of a chaplain's faithful companioning a cancer patient.' *Journal of Health Care Chaplaincy*, 18, 1–2, 3–22.

Monahan, T. and Fisher, J.A. (2010). 'Benefits of "observer effects": Lessons from the field.' *Qualitative Research*, 10, 3, 357–376.

Murphy, J.N. (2017). 'The chaplain as the mediator between the patient and the interdisciplinary team in ethical decision making: A chaplaincy case study involving a quadriplegic patient.' *Health and Social Care Chaplaincy*, 5, 2, 241–256.

Murphy, K. (2017). '"I'm being swallowed up by this illness, so much pain deep inside" – Claire, a 40-year-old woman with cancer.' *Health and Social Care Chaplaincy*, 5, 2, 209–223.

Nolan, S. (2012). *Spiritual Care at the End of Life: The Chaplain as a 'Hopeful Presence'.* London: Jessica Kingsley Publishers.

Nolan, S. (2016). '"He needs to talk!" – A chaplain's case study of non-religious spiritual care.' *Journal of Health Care Chaplaincy*, 22, 1, 1–16.

Parahoo, K. (1997). *Nursing Research: Principles, Process and Issues*. Basingstoke: Macmillan.

Richardson, L. (1994). 'Writing as a Method of Inquiry.' In N.K. Denzin and Y.S. Lincoln (eds) *The Handbook of Qualitative Research* (pp.516–529). Thousand Oaks, CA: Sage.

Risk, J.L. (2013). 'Building a new life: A chaplain's theory based case study of chronic illness.' *Journal of Health Care Chaplaincy*, 19, 3, 81–98.

Rogers, C.R. (2004). *On Becoming a Person*. London: Constable.

Schmohl, C. (2017). '"You've done very well" ("Das haben Sie sehr schön gemacht") – On courage and presence of mind in spiritual issues.' *Health and Social Care Chaplaincy*, 5, 2, 281–296.

Scott-Hoy, K. (2002). 'The Visitor: Juggling Life in the Grip of the Text.' In A.P. Bochner and C. Ellis (eds) *Ethnographically Speaking: Autoethnography, Literature, and Aesthetics* (pp. 274–294). Oxford: AltaMira Press.

Stake, R.E. (1994). 'Case Studies.' In N.K. Denzin and Y.S. Lincoln (eds) *The Handbook of Qualitative Research* (pp.236–247). Thousand Oaks, CA: Sage.

Swift, C. (2009). *Hospital Chaplaincy in the Twenty-first Century: The Crisis of Spiritual Care in the NHS*. Farnham, Surrey & Burlington, VT: Ashgate.

Van Loenen, G., Körver, J., Walton, M. and De Vries, R. (2017). 'Case study of "moral injury": Format Dutch Case Studies Project.' *Health and Social Care Chaplaincy*, 5, 2, 281–296.

Wall, S. (2006). 'An autoethnography on learning about autoethnography.' *International Journal of Qualitative Methods*, 5, 2, 146–160.

Yin, R.K. (1994). *Case Study Research: Design and Methods* (2nd edn). Thousand Oaks, CA: Sage.

Part I
Chaplains' Care in Paediatrics

Chapter 1

'That's great! You can tell us how you are feeling'

– Mark, a recently severely physically disabled 11-year-old boy with a brain tumour

Liz Bryson, Paul Nash and Sally Nash

Introduction

One of the questions we most often get asked when offering training on paediatric spiritual care is: how do you work with patients who are severely disabled? This case study seeks to explore spiritual assessment and intervention with a severely physically disabled 11-year-old boy in a way that takes seriously the importance of patient-centred care. The core principles of patient-centred care are that care is personalised, coordinated and enabling, and that the person is treated with compassion, dignity and respect (Health Foundation 2014, p.7). One of the challenges we have sought to respond to at Birmingham Children's Hospital National Health Service Foundation Trust (UK) (BCH) is to engage in spiritual care that is appropriate to age, context and developmental level. Over one million children in the UK have some sort of speech, language or communication need (Allenby *et al.* 2015), thus a case study focusing on this issue is likely to have some transferable learning for other patients.

The chaplaincy team at BCH uses the shorthand term 'spiritual play' to describe what is often offered and done with patients. More formally, the team has developed spiritual play around the concept and objective of seeking an interpretive spiritual encounter (ISE). Creating the concept of ISE has been the work of the Rev. Paul Nash (Nash, Darby and Nash 2015) who has led on its development. It initially was developed as part of a spiritual care participation project with Kathryn Darby and Sally Nash and then progressed through our case study project, which seeks to reflect on our practice in conversation with spirituality, human development theories, good practice in work with children and young people, chaplaincy objectives and patient outcomes. Our previous research has also led to the discovery of principles for spiritual care (Darby, Nash and Nash 2014; Nash, Darby and Nash 2013). The Centre for Paediatric Spiritual Care at BCH has been established to research this further and to disseminate our practice (https://bwc.nhs.uk/centre-for-paediatric-spiritual-care). Sally Nash leads on our research and writing work, and has facilitated us in offering master's level continuing professional development courses in spiritual care and paediatric chaplaincy through her wider work with the Institute for Children, Youth and Mission (www.cym.ac.uk).

The chaplaincy team seeks to identify whether a need is religious, spiritual or pastoral and works with patients, their families and staff as appropriate in the context of day-to-day, life-limited/threatening, palliative or bereavement care. Typically, our chaplains arrive on a ward or to a bedside with a bag of activities. Each one has a personalised bag that contains a range of things patients can do; the chaplains will usually give the patients a choice of activities which are suitable (having identified any limitations or risks of particular activities for that patient). It is the participative nature of the encounter that creates the potential of time and space safely to explore spiritual needs, concerns or anything else they would like to share. That they have the option to say no to the encounter also offers a degree of agency not available with many other healthcare professionals. One of the underpinning concepts of ISE is to look for what lifts the spirits of a particular individual and to build on that; this often gets revealed through the choice of activity and the subsequent encounter. (For a description of a wide range of activities used in this way, see Nash, Darby and Nash 2015.)

Background

This case draws on two encounters between Liz Bryson, a volunteer lay chaplain since 2013 and the first chaplaincy team member to complete a university-accredited postgraduate certificate in paediatric chaplaincy offered by BCH in partnership with the Institute for Children, Youth and Mission, and 'Mark', a recently severely physically disabled 11-year-old boy with a brain tumour. The case is written in the first person, drawing on Liz's own recordings of her visits.

Liz has had a long-term interest in whole-person care. She has a background in education, pastoral care, mentoring and leadership in church communities. As a mother of four, Liz became a full-time carer for her eldest daughter following surgery for a brain tumour, the consequences of which left her disabled at the age of 10. Liz accompanied her daughter through the remaining years of childhood, teenage and young adult years as she was faced with physical, emotional, social and spiritual challenges. Through the years of walking alongside her daughter, continually processing loss and dealing with living bereavement, Liz witnessed the reality of spiritual growth despite physical regression in her daughter. Having supported her daughter through home-schooling and a part-time degree in art and design, Liz has experienced the value of creative arts activities which facilitated exploration and discussion of life and its challenges, with both her disabled daughter and her three other children. In her mid-20s, Liz's daughter developed another brain tumour and died within a few months. Some years later, aware of the potential for chaplaincy to enrich the lives of sick children and their families, and intrigued by the developing research regarding how to help them explore their own spirituality, Liz joined the chaplaincy team at BCH. She was convinced that children can find deep, inner resources despite physical deterioration when given a safe space in which to do so. She sees this unfold time and again as she delivers spiritual, pastoral and religious care as part of the chaplaincy team.

It is unique within the chaplaincy case study literature for a case study to focus on the work of a volunteer chaplain rather than an employed one. However, at BCH we have worked hard at offering chaplaincy volunteers the same training as staff, and Liz is very well qualified academically, having a postgraduate certificate in paediatric chaplaincy gained during her time at BCH, as well as having substantial chaplaincy experience. We have a thorough application and discernment procedure for volunteers, and it was clear during this and her induction that Liz had healthily grieved for her loss and had had an appropriate gap (two years) between her daughter's death and joining the team. When Paul and Liz discussed where the best fit for ward allocation would be, she suggested the oncology ward and, while we were concerned initially for her wellbeing, she has flourished. Liz is professional and highly skilled, and she now leads on our chaplaincy case study project.

Mark was 11 years old and resident on the Teenage Cancer Unit (www.teenagecancertrust.org) at BCH. This is a unit specially designed for adolescents which offers them an age-appropriate environment and specialist medical staff. Previously, a completely healthy, active 11-year-old, Mark had been admitted for surgery to remove a malignant brain tumour in early spring 2016. As a result of the surgery and two post-operative strokes, he became severely disabled, unable to talk or move his lower body. Liz met him in the oncology department while he was undergoing chemotherapy several months after his traumatic experience in intensive care. He could understand when spoken to but could not reply verbally. He communicated by nodding or shaking his head and had some movement of his hands and arms, though not enough motor control to be able to communicate via writing or keyboard. He was working hard with physiotherapy to increase the use/motor control of his unsteady (not dominant) left hand, using it as much as possible. His facial expression was minimal and it was difficult to read his mood or feelings from any body language, apart from nodding or shaking of his head.

Mark's background was Christian and his mum, Sarah, had been referred to the chaplain via a senior nurse. The senior nurse was aware that Sarah was struggling to have confidence in the medical and nursing staff. This limited their ability to help her begin to come to terms with the enormity of the changes in her son. It was considered that she would perceive a volunteer chaplain to be a safe confidante. Chaplaincy team members regularly find themselves in such roles and we do not necessarily notice a difference as to whether they are staff or volunteers. Liz's personal experience was not a factor in the decision to refer Sarah to her.

'Mark' is a pseudonym, and both Mark and his parents have read what we have written about our work with him and given us permission to publish. It was important to us that Mark was given the opportunity to assent to our use of his story, as he clearly had the capacity to do this, and best practice in work with children and young people is that they assent or give consent as well as parents. Mark has been on a national public broadcast television programme in the UK as well as in local newspapers, so his story is quite widely known outside his immediate context.

Case Study
Encounter 1

Mark had spent some weeks in the High Dependency Unit and had just moved back to the Teenage Cancer Unit when I visited with Michelle (a placement student). As we arrived at the bed space I could see that there was a lot of activity from Mark's mum and dad, and Mark was lying inactive on the bed. Mum and Dad were unpacking and setting up the bed space with pictures and familiar belonging to make it feel more like home for Mark. They were positive about the move but clearly everything was in a state of transition. A brief conversation with Mum (Sarah) established that she wanted to chat with me again but not at that time of relocation, so I decided to focus fully on Mark as Mum and Dad busied themselves with the removal jobs.

I introduced Michelle, and swiftly assessed that Mark was feeling the need for reassurance in the new space and wanted a sense of security and belonging. Mark was in need of oxygen, and was feeling particularly unsettled with the move. I sat beside Mark and asked him if he would like to do an activity, explaining the spiritual care beading activity as a possibility. He immediately nodded his head enthusiastically and seemed pleased to be engaged with someone. Michelle chatted to Mum and Dad as they unpacked, and slowly Mark and I went through the steps to make a bead keyring. Due to Mark's illness, he could only lie propped up in bed and look ahead. I was able to hold the spiritual care bead bracelet activity sheet directly in front of Mark and explain the choices he had, the first one being whether to make a bracelet or keyring.

With attention to detail, I talked through the different colours of beads pictured on the card and what each colour represented. In this ISE, each coloured bead represents something: green – peace; red – I matter; white – hope for the future; pink – strength; purple – faith in God; brown – honesty; blue – happiness; orange – to be able to help others; yellow – I belong; heart-shaped – I am loved/wanted. (For the full activity guide, see https://bwc.nhs.uk/spiritual-care-activities-and-resources.) Mark thought about each, one at a time, and nodded or shook his head according to which colours he wanted on his keyring. For each colour, I showed him the bead options from the bead box. If there were different shades of his chosen colour or varied textures or shapes, Mark chose which he preferred. I threaded the beads onto the elastic, holding it in front of Mark so he could see clearly the emerging keyring that he had designed. I fully engaged his focus and attention and made sure that he knew this activity was entirely his, asking his opinion and giving him choices at every point. Mark nodded or shook his head telling me his choices at every stage. It became apparent through the colour of the beads he had chosen that Mark needed strength and peace, hope for the future, to know he was loved and that he could contribute to the needs of others. I talked to him particularly about the way he hugely contributes to the family and how Mum and Dad value his presence, and about the courage and strength he offers to them through his determination. As a totally dependent, disabled 11-year-old, Mark needed to know that, although he felt disempowered in so many ways, his bravery, strength of character, cheeky smile and warmth were things that significantly helped those around him – parents, staff and other visitors.

I assessed that Mark needed to be reassured of how much he was securely loved by his mum and dad and by God, and how he belonged to his family and the hospital community. I clearly spoke about this and went over the colours he had chosen for his keyring. I then had enormous difficulty actually tying the elastic with beads on onto the metal keyring but eventually managed it! This caused great hilarity and drew assistance from Mum with some Blu-Tack (reusable adhesive putty), thus including everyone in the closure of the encounter. As we finished, Dad observed, 'You've really enjoyed that Mark, haven't you?' and Mark nodded in agreement. Helpfully, Mum said, 'We'll hang this [spiritual care keyring] on your stand so you can see it as a reminder.' Mum hung it on the stand and Mark nodded. We left reassuring the family of prayer. Mark seemed more relaxed than when we arrived.

Encounter 2

This second encounter came some months later, towards the end of Mark's stay at BCH. Having visited Mark regularly for some months and grown in understanding of his situation and physical, emotional, social and spiritual needs, I assessed that Mark was feeling very frustrated with his physical limitations: his cognitive ability was fully functioning yet he could not communicate verbally or in writing what he was thinking or feeling. Over the weeks, Mark had responded positively to affirmation and encouragement, and continued to need this. Few people, in addition to his parents, teachers and physiotherapists, gave him extended times of engagement with just him as a person, partly due to the communication challenges for Mark and for the visitor. Mark had a deep awareness of his inner being and a sense of the transcendence that needed nurturing and supporting. This had been evident in his responses to the activities he and I had engaged in and which had given him value and worth for who he was – his personhood and existence – regardless of his measurable human achievements. In this encounter, I used the 'Looking back on your day' lollipop stick activity (for the activity instructions, see Nash, Darby and Nash 2015, pp.192–194), sticker faces and written feeling cards glued on a poster, to identify and meet his needs. Because Mark could not communicate other than by nodding or shaking his head and using his unsteady left hand, I wanted to make sure he had as much choice as possible. I showed Mark a selection of stickers with faces that expressed different moods such as sad, happy, angry, frightened, for him to choose from. I then presented a wide selection of feeling words written on pieces of card, such as bored, frustrated, lonely, isolated, which Mark looked at thoughtfully and he nodded or shook his head to indicate which ones he wanted to be glued onto the sheet of cardboard. This poster with sticker faces and words summarised Mark's response to the 'Looking back on your day' activity. Usually this is done verbally but I had to find an alternative for Mark.

I was aware of the importance of continued affirmation and encouragement of his intrinsic value, and this activity was potentially an effective way for Mark to reflect on his day and communicate how he felt, despite being locked into his dysfunctional physical body. As usual I focused fully on Mark and talked to him directly. Dad and the nurse chatted completely separately. I began by talking to Mark about my recent visit to the north Cornish coast and showed him some pebbles I had collected. We talked about the way the pebbles were all so different and shaped by the crashing of the waves and hitting of each other against rocks and cliffs. Mark chose several pebbles to keep in his box of special things. I then showed Mark the card explaining the reflective 'Looking back on my day' activity and asked if he would like to do it. He was very keen. He chose a sad face to stick on one side of the stick boy and a happy face on the other as we talked about the importance of identifying things that make us both happy and sad in our days. I spoke about it being perfectly acceptable and necessary to be able to express both types of feelings. Mark could not use pencils, crayons or pens to draw or write on the stick figure but, with much effort, he could peel stickers from a sheet and place them onto something. I held the lollipop stick figure strategically so that, with enormous concentration and effort from Mark and careful angled manoeuvring by me, the faces were stuck in suitable places. Mark then had a lollipop stick boy with a sad face on one side and a happy one on the other.

I then opened an envelope of cards with numerous feelings written on them. Mark chose the ones he wanted and chose a range of sticker faces to place the feelings beside. I held a piece of card on to which he placed the faces, and using a glue stick I stuck the feeling labels Mark had chosen around the faces. The nurse came over and, pointing to the different emotions Mark had chosen to stick on the card, asked Mark how he was feeling. Mark shook his head over and over again as she rested her finger on each one, then he nodded at the label 'encouraged'. We finished the activity and talked about the frustration he found in being so immobile and unable to speak. Mark's mum arrived and looked at the activity with great interest. 'How are you feeling?' she asked Mark, pointing to each label. Again, he shook his head to many options but then nodded at the label 'hopeful'. 'That's great, Mark,' Mum said. 'You can tell us how you are feeling.'

Discussion

There are a variety of ways that spiritual needs can be assessed and, as discussed above, at BCH we do this in part through the activities described in the encounters. However, I also knew from a referral and lengthy conversation with the senior ward nurse that the family had been struggling with huge loss. Mark himself was cognitively aware but frustrated with his physical limitations, yet determined and making some very small, slow steps of recovery. The prognosis was unknown. From spending time with his mum, Sarah, I assessed that hope and resilience were running low in both Sarah and Mark. The move to the Teenage Cancer Unit was another unsettling factor for Mark; for example, his bed space was new and strange. In particular, I assessed that it was important to give Mark active attention, to communicate with him as a fully comprehending 11-year-old, and to create a safe space, empowering him to make choices and know that he was valued, cared for and loved, and belonged both to his family and the hospital community.

Assessment and interventions

I chose the beading spiritual play intervention because I felt it would engage Mark as fully as possible in decision making and expressing his feelings and needs without being able to speak or write. My assessment was that Mark was feeling unsettled and disorientated with the move – as evidenced by his unsteady breathing and need for oxygen support.

He needed the gift of time, to be valued as a unique individual, and given focused attention that would empower him to make some choices and have a sense of security restored. Mark's limited means of communication and inability to participate physically in activities were challenging. However, his comprehension was clear, and I made a decision to affirm him and empower him, creating safe space and time for him as a valued individual by making a spiritual care bracelet or keyring. This provided a framework for both assessment and intervention, and it enabled me to understand Mark's situation, his feelings and spiritual needs. In addition, it provided the opportunity for Mark to participate in an activity that gave him a safe context in which he could communicate his needs, desires and feelings through the choices he made.

I chose this activity to give Mark choice and empowerment. One of our best practice principles is that participation, empowerment and autonomy are core underpinning values of spiritual care (Nash, Darby and Nash 2015, p.19). Our strong focus on this in part derives from taking seriously good practice principles from the wider fields of work with children and young people (O'Connell 2013). The spiritual care beading activity enabled me to communicate respect and dignity, and to seek to build self-worth and value. It helped in building a sense of connectedness to the hospital community and offered hope and strength, while at the same time recognising loss. Mark was facing a huge amount of loss and was dealing with massive change. One of the elements of BCH spiritual care assessment is to name, identify and summarise the spiritual needs that emerge. Through Mark's very clear choices of coloured beads I was able to identify the need for love, security, hope, establishing identity, self-worth and value, and a sense of belonging, acceptance and connectedness. I was able to piece this information together with the knowledge I had acquired from the ward staff and from spending time alongside Mum. (One of our recording forms has a range of needs for chaplains to consider which has been developed through the department's research and review of the literature.)

From a brief conversation with Mum at the start of the second encounter, and from previous observations, I was aware that adults frequently spoke over Mark to his parents or the attendant nurse rather than engage him in conversations related to him. As a result, Mark was easily bored and frustrated. This was very lowering of his self-worth and value, and failed to recognise that Mark was a fully comprehending boy, who needed to be engaged with in discussions about his wellbeing and progress. Mum and Dad did their best to repeat things clearly to Mark so that he was included more effectively. In this second encounter, I was aware of Mark having to deal with huge ongoing limitations, and we were looking at how to develop strategies to communicate and deal with his frustrations and difficulties. (Communication in this respect is sometimes known as augmentative and alternative communication (see Beukelman and Mirenda 2013). The approach to the activity involved using alternative approaches for Mark to communicate his preferences.) I identified the need to establish identity, self-worth and value, and a sense of belonging, acceptance and connectedness.

Sarah had explained she felt Mark was struggling with the need to adapt to the long-term reality of his disabilities, which I assessed had huge implications for his identity, self-worth and acceptance. With Mark's limited means of communication, he needed to process his feelings, be understood more fully, find security, discover more effective ways to communicate, and find a sense of the transcendent. In addition to Sarah's insights, I found these needs became apparent through the spiritual play activities that Mark and I did together and also through Mark's increasing confidence in using his wobbly left hand and his facial expressions; for example, he had a wonderful, very lopsided smile and expressive eyes. I had a sense of a real lift in his spirit during and after an encounter. Vygotsky's concept of the 'zone of proximal development' (Vygotsky 1980) suggests that a child has areas of problem solving that are achievable only with the support and encouragement of another person (Meggitt 2006). It had become more important to consider this in the light of Mark's disabilities, and I was keen to find ways to help him achieve positive outcomes in new ways amid the frustration of no longer being able to do things he had very easily accomplished previously.

The activity for reflecting on your day is one of our regularly used activities, but it was adapted to be used within the limits of Mark's com-munication issues. We have found that this type of activity communicates respect and dignity as individuals are facilitated in making choices at whatever level they feel is right for them. It helps to build self-worth and value as the child's uniqueness is taken seriously. It gave Mark an opportunity to express himself and identify the positive and negative experiences of his day, empowering him to make choices and deal with some of his frustration. Particularly important with this intervention is the capacity to express feelings, both positive and negative emotions, through having a happy and sad face. Thus, in using the terminology from our taxonomy (Nash *et al.*, in press), I had identified clearly intended effects for the intervention I was proposing. The intervention was also designed to recognise that Mark had the cognitive ability of an 11-year-old, and the challenge was to help him to communicate. As the activity originates from a spiritual practice (the Ignatian 'examen'; for an accessible version, see Linn, Fabricant Linn and Linn 1995) there was also the option of discussing some of these roots and encouraging Mark in his awareness of the transcendent.

In considering a spiritual care plan for Mark there was a range of issues which this assessment and intervention highlighted. Mark needed encouragement, affirmation of his value and worth as a unique individual, with activities which would help him process loss. He needed to be treated with enormous respect and honour, and offered choice to empower him in the locked-in world that he had been thrown into through his medical experience. And he needed to be given opportunities to connect and find a deep sense of belonging and identity.

Outcomes

As I reflected on the first encounter, I felt one of the keys was the appropriate creative activity that empowered Mark to choose, to communicate, and to receive and give in a very profound way. From a place of limitation and insecurity, Mark and I connected and found the presence of the transcendent – the wounded healer himself – to be there in the midst of the encounter. I pondered on how communication and connectedness are easily misunderstood but so real, whether words can be spoken or not. From a place of vulnerability, Mark shared his longing to feel loved, and find a security and identity on the unwelcome journey he was now travelling. I felt the encounter had honoured Mark's alert mind and valued his personhood despite his physical limitations.

One of the ways we reflect on the effectiveness of the encounters is to identify which of our spiritual care principles have been demonstrated within it (Nash, Darby and Nash 2015, pp.19–28). With regard to this encounter with Mark, I believe a number of things took place, and he was able to:

- build a relationship with a trusted adult

- build a relationship with God/transcendent other

- feel connected and valued

- feel listened to and affirmed

- feel cared for

- be taken seriously, feel empowered

- be offered a non-medical experience of life

- explore feelings (worry, hope, fear, anger, guilt, joy)

- share fun, play

- gain a richness of experience

- have a sense of meaning and purpose.

I was able to gain a sense of what and who was important to Mark, and help to build his self-esteem and help him to feel good about himself. Together we could explore the sacred and nurture rituals and beliefs.

We particularly look for evidence of the transcendent and at one point there was a real sense of the transcendent presence of God, a moment of grace when Mark completely engaged in the creating of the spiritual care bead keyring, making choices at every point and responding to words of encouragement and affirmation.

As I reflected on the second encounter, I felt that one of the keys was the appropriate creative activity which empowered Mark to choose, to express his feelings and to take steps forwards in shaping and accepting his identity as a valued and whole person living with profound difficulties and limitations but with deep insight, sensitivities and contributions to make to his community and the world. Through the focus on the activity, Mark and I were able to touch real pain and yet real hope. Mark had the ability to think and know how he was feeling and yet had such limitations in the communication of those thoughts and feelings. This activity was a conduit for communication and connectedness. Mark was visibly thrilled with his stick doll and feelings card. There was a sense of transcendent hope that was very present in this encounter.

Again, the effectiveness of this encounter was in part measured by the way that our evidence-based spiritual care principles (Nash, Darby and Nash 2013, 2015) have been incorporated into practice, and in this second encounter the same principles as the first were embedded into what was done. Again, there was a real sense of the transcendent presence of God when Mark completely engaged in the activity looking back on his day and identifying his feelings, valuing the opportunity to express them. He loved to hold onto his lollipop stick doll, and I wrote 'You are loved however you feel' on it on both sides. The effectiveness of the encounter was also demonstrated by Mark's positive level of engagement; the feelings he expressed of encouragement and hopefulness; the keenness with which he used his very unsteady left hand to hold onto the stick man. It is also an ongoing activity, which can be used regularly, and I have been encouraged to see Mum using it with Mark when I have been there on subsequent visits. One of our principles is that concrete and visible expressions and reminders of spiritual care are important (Nash, Darby and Nash 2015, p.26); this activity did this very effectively.

Conclusion

In paediatric chaplaincy whole family care is sometimes the norm. It was helpful in the first encounter to have Michelle with me, as she was able to engage with Mark's mum and dad and gave me the opportunity to focus on Mark. Family members can have a profound impact on any encounter with a chaplain. In this instance, they were supportive, encouraging and helped draw out from Mark some of the learning from the activities. That Sarah carried on using the 'Looking back on my day' activity with Mark also highlights the significance of family members being present sometimes, as what we do with their child can act as a modelling experience for them and enable spiritual care to continue. Spending time with Sarah on her own at separate times from visiting Mark enabled me to gain additional insight and understanding of Sarah, Mark and the family dynamic and needs.

Initial and continuous assessment and intervention have been intertwined within this case study. Spiritual play activities, which have been designed to identify needs, are also in and of themselves an intervention. Having practice principles, such as participation and empowerment, creating space, meaning making, normalisation, support within the context of the family, building on existing spirituality or beliefs, which are in the mind of a chaplain as they encounter a patient (and their family), can add to the effectiveness and intentionality of an encounter, as our evidence suggests that there are several things which are important for sick children in hospital (Darby, Nash and Nash 2014; Nash 2016).

Mark seemed aware of his need to find redefined and restored identity and hope within the limitations of his now disabled body. In the future, he will have to struggle harder than many to forge a new identity in the light of his current situation. Erikson (1995) described this as the psychosocial developmental stage of transitioning between childhood and adulthood, when adolescents must re-examine their identity in order to discover who they will be. Mark's journey will be one of coming to terms with enormous loss and yet forging ahead to regain what physical ability he can, retraining brain pathways and forming new ones to work as well as possible. It will be a huge struggle, daily.

The importance of having someone who has time to listen and find ways of communicating with the patient is a significant learning point. The experience of this family was that not many healthcare professionals took the time to do this. There may be many reasons for this but one could be a lack of confidence in communicating with people who are profoundly physically disabled but whose cognitive development has not been impaired. Being aware of best practice from other disciplines and learning from multidisciplinary colleagues is important, and further reflection has led to realising the importance of the good communication standards adopted by speech and language therapists:

- There is a detailed description of how best to communicate with individuals.

- Services demonstrate how they support individuals with communication needs to be involved with decisions about their care and their services.

- Staff value and use competently the best approaches to communication with each individual they support.

- Services create opportunities, relationships and environments that make individuals want to communicate.

- Individuals are supported to understand and express their needs in relation to their health and wellbeing. (Royal College of Speech and Language Therapists 2013, p.4)

It has been important to acknowledge the impact of this encounter on me as a chaplain. Spiritual care often has an element of reciprocity. I felt the enormous privilege of sharing the journey of this family and connecting very profoundly with Mark, who was so locked in to a very challenging world of dependency and disability in so many ways. These encounters also led me to reflect on my own personal journey as a mother of a 10-year-old with a brain tumour, who then lived for 17 years with disabilities. I saw incredible struggle, loss and yet profound spiritual insight and development in my own child's journey. The involvement and faithfulness of a transcendent and very personal God in the human journey is an enduring reason for hope.

References

Allenby, C., Fearon-Wilson, J., Merrison, S. and Morling, E. (2015). *Supporting Children with Speech and Language Difficulties* (2nd edn). Abingdon: Routledge.

Beukelman, D.R. and Mirenda, P. (2013). *Augmentative and Alternative Communication: Supporting Children and Adults with Complex Communication Needs* (4th edn). Baltimore, MD: Paul H. Brooks Publishing.

Darby, K., Nash, P. and Nash, S. (2014). 'Understanding and responding to spiritual and religious needs of young people with cancer.' *Cancer Nursing Practice*, 13, 2, 23–37.

Erikson, E. (1995). *Childhood and Society*. London: Vintage.

Health Foundation (2014). *Person-Centred Care Made Simple*. London: Health Foundation. Available at www.health.org.uk/sites/health/files/PersonCentredCareMadeSimple.pdf, accessed 14 January 2018.

Linn, D., Fabricant Linn, S. and Linn, M. (1995). *Sleeping with Bread: Holding What Gives You Life*. Mawah, NJ: Paulist Press.

Meggitt. C. (2006). *Child Development*. London: Heinemann.

Nash, P., Darby, K. and Nash, S. (2013). 'The spiritual care of sick children: Reflections from a participation project.' *International Journal of Children's Spirituality*, 18, 2, 148–161.

Nash, P., Darby, K. and Nash, S. (2015). *Spiritual Care with Sick Children and Young People*. London: Jessica Kingsley Publishers.

Nash, P., Roberts, E., Nash, S., Darby, K. and Parwaz, A. (In press). 'Adapting the Advocate Health Care Taxonomy of Chaplaincy for a Pediatric Hospital Context – A Pilot Study.' *Journal of Health Care Chaplaincy*.

Nash, S. (2016). 'Message in a bottle: A comparative study of spiritual needs of children and young people in and out of hospital.' *International Journal of Children's Spirituality*, 21, 2, 116–127.

O'Connell, D. (2013). *Working with Children and Young People: Good Practice Guidelines for Healthcare Chaplains*. Birmingham: Red Balloon Resources.

Royal College of Speech and Language Therapists (2013). *Five Good Communication Standards*. London: Royal College of Speech and Language Therapists. Available at www.rcslt.org/news/docs/good_comm_standards, accessed 14 January 2018.

Vygotsky, L.S. (1980). *Mind in Society: Development of Higher Psychological Processes*. Cambridge, MA: Harvard University Press.

Chapter 2

'She's already done so much'

— Sarah, diagnosed prenatally with trisomy 18, and her family

Patrick Jinks

Introduction

This paediatric case study highlights the role and importance of the paediatric chaplain serving on a paediatric palliative care team. The study follows the roller coaster of experiences of one family who received a prenatal diagnosis of trisomy 18 (also known as Edwards' syndrome) from prenatal consultation, through the ups and downs of a neonatal intensive care stay. It examines how the family's spirituality impacted important milestones and decision points for intensive medical management along the way. The following reflection and assessment offer insight into the lived spiritual and emotional experience of this family, given a presumed lethal prenatal diagnosis, as well as how the family's faith informed and carried them into and through life-or-death decisions.

I had the opportunity to meet the 'James' family in my role as a chaplain serving as a member of the children's hospital paediatric palliative care team. The palliative care team was consulted during the 28th week of baby Sarah's gestation, after Sarah was diagnosed with trisomy 18, a severe genetic disorder. The James family was Caucasian and included Sarah's mother, Jessica (40s), her father, Steve (50s), and their three-year-old son, Jackson. Sarah was diagnosed prenatally as having trisomy 18 and a related congenital heart defect.

Trisomy 18

The prognosis and life expectancy for trisomy 18 is extremely poor, but there is growing evidence within medical literature of variable outcomes, which may be impacted by offering more aggressive medical interventions than have been historically offered (Haug *et al.* 2017). Trisomy 18 is a genetic defect defined by an extra replication of the 18th chromosome. This chromosomal abnormality leads to significant congenital birth defects often involving the heart, limbs, and, characteristically, severe neurological delays. The diagnosis is commonly made via prenatal genetic testing or when physical defects are noted during routine pregnancy ultrasound screening. The natural history of trisomy 18 is that most pregnancies will end in miscarriage or stillbirth, though the exact numbers of occurrence are not well defined (Burke, Field and Morrison 2013). Typically, a mother receiving a diagnosis of trisomy 18 might be offered options of pregnancy termination or carrying the pregnancy to term with a plan for comfort care (palliative or hospice care) after delivery. As studies have shown, however, there is a small percentage of the population of babies diagnosed with trisomy 18 that may survive through the neonatal period. This means that 5–8 per cent of babies diagnosed with trisomy 18 survive past one year, most requiring intensive medical management (Carey 2012; Nelson *et al.* 2016).

The possibility of survival is a powerful buoy of hope for some families receiving this diagnosis. This reality, the small but real possibility of long-term survival, has led some families with children diagnosed with trisomy 18 to become vocal public advocates for intensive management, arguing that medical experts should not think of children with trisomy 18 any differently from those with trisomy 21 (Down syndrome). A generation ago, it is argued, children with trisomy 21 had a poor long-term survival rate because we did not offer significant medical interventions such as respiratory support or cardiac surgery. The gap between the long-held opinion of medical doctors and more recent societal shifts in opinion over treatment have led to what neonatologist and biomedical ethicist John Lantos calls a moral 'stable grey zone' (Lantos 2016). 'In the age of social media', Lantos opines, '[p]arents share stories and videos, showing their happy 4- and 5-year-old children with these conditions. Survival, it turns out, is not as rare as once thought' (Lantos 2016, p.396). What Lantos highlights is that treatment decisions for children with a diagnosis of trisomy 18 will likely always involve a difficult balance of a patient-centric approach to decision making because the manifestations of the broad diagnosis can be so varied, from mild to severe, from few defects to many.

Background

At the time of diagnosis, the James family was presented with the option to terminate their pregnancy, given the poor prognosis of length and perceived quality of life. The family chose to continue the pregnancy. Their decision was based on several factors. Jessica and Steve began researching their baby's diagnosis on the internet. They quickly found several support group websites dedicated to providing a counter-balance to the 'conventional wisdom' that the diagnosis was fatal and any aggressive treatment was futile as almost all babies with trisomy 18 will die. Jessica and Steve also felt that their unborn daughter's specific challenges might not be as severe as her doctors predicted: she was small for her gestational age but she was on a steady growth curve, which is often not seen in babies with trisomy 18, who just stop growing or getting bigger; the significance of her heart defects was uncertain; and most importantly, she continued to survive week to week.

In searching for information, Jessica connected with another local family who had a school-aged child with the same diagnosis. They found the information to be helpful and it further underscored their own scepticism about the accuracy of genetic testing – and more importantly – their deep-seated, faith-informed desire and hope for baby Sarah to be born alive. Given the family's expressed wishes to continue their pregnancy, the hospital's paediatric palliative care team was consulted to meet with the family to offer support and to establish goals of care that would guide the hospital staff before, during and after Sarah's birth. The family's faith and expressed hope of God's healing intervention was foundational to ongoing decision making, support and care for the family.

I am a board-certified chaplain with the Association of Professional Chaplains and an ordained minister in the Presbyterian Church (USA), the largest Presbyterian denomination in the United States. It is a mainline Protestant Christian denomination, part of the Reformed tradition, known for its relatively progressive beliefs and doctrine. At the time of the encounters presented in this study, I was in my early 30s, having worked in paediatric chaplaincy with the paediatric palliative care team for three years and in professional chaplaincy for seven years. Concurrent with my work with the palliative care team, I also cared for other non-palliative care patients; my total assignments consisted of more than 150 patient beds, including a large neonatal intensive care unit (NICU), as well as paediatric intensive care, haematology and oncology services and a level II paediatric trauma centre. The children's hospital is located within a large, tertiary care academic medical centre in the south-eastern United States. The palliative care team consisted of physicians, a nurse practitioner, a nurse coordinator, child life specialists, and a child psychologist.

The patient's parents, Jessica and Steve, have given permission to share this case study as an expression of thanks and gratitude for the support and care they received throughout their hospital journey with Sarah. I have used pseudonyms, and some demographics or non-essential details of the case have been omitted or altered to provide privacy and respect to the patient and family.

Case study

One of the most compelling outcomes of a well-functioning palliative care team is the synergistic effect of care coordination through communication. This was particularly evident in my initial meeting with Sarah's mother, Jessica. Our first encounter was precipitated by an unplanned admission to the hospital for pregnancy complications at 30 weeks' gestation. The pregnancy complications resulted in Jessica being put on bed rest and having a foetal monitor to keep a close eye on Sarah's wellbeing. I was alerted to Jessica's admission during our normal daily palliative care team meeting. The nurse practitioner shared information about Jessica's earlier doctor appointments, the genetic diagnosis for baby Sarah and the parents' desire to continue their pregnancy. She further explained that the family clearly understood the statistics regarding the likelihood of a pregnancy miscarriage or stillbirth. The family had expressed a strong desire to carry the pregnancy to term and for Sarah to be born alive. They hoped to spend as much time with Sarah as they possibly could, beginning with the pregnancy itself and, it was hoped, extending beyond delivery.

An initial spiritual screening by the palliative care nurse practitioner had indicated that the family had a strong sense of faith, in the Christian tradition, which was a significant influence on their decision making. As a palliative team, we discussed that some medical providers had expressed concern about the degree to which the family understood the severity of Sarah's diagnosis. Jessica's obstetricians felt the family was either misinformed or in complete denial about the likelihood of the baby's survival. Jessica's doctors had re-addressed their concerns directly to Jessica the previous day, when she and Steve reiterated their desire for intervention and aggressive care if and when Sarah was delivered. Jessica was reportedly feeling a significant level of distress, worrying that her doctors might not respect or support the family's decisions around delivery and intensive management for baby Sarah.

As I prepared to visit Jessica in her room on the 'high risk' maternal-foetal floor of the hospital, I was particularly interested in assessing Jessica's identification as 'Christian' and to understand how she felt that her faith guided her decision making for baby Sarah. The geographic area in which the hospital is located is often colloquially known as 'the Bible Belt', a reflection of the region's higher degree of Christian religiosity as compared with other areas in the United States. In cases such as this, it is thus important to tease out the significance and importance of the specific religious or spiritual values of the particular person and family. For example, one might consider if the family expresses a tie to a particular community of faith; if the family is active in their faith; and how their faith is experienced and lived day to day.

Encounter 1: Jessica admitted to hospital

Jessica was admitted to the high-risk pregnancy floor for complications of pregnancy at 30 weeks' gestation. After the introductions, Jessica welcomed me to sit at her bedside and almost immediately expressed that she was fearful that medical staff would not support her and her husband's decision to maintain the pregnancy and seek aggressive interventions for Sarah. I invited Jessica to share her family's story of this pregnancy with me; my aim was to invite Jessica into self-reflective practice. In sharing her family's story in such an open-ended way, Jessica focused on their long-held desire to have a second child, her difficulty getting pregnant and the profound sense she and Steve shared that God had given them this pregnancy.

It was within the context of this narrative that Jessica began to share the importance of her faith tradition. Jessica explained that the family attended a church within the Christian Pentecostal tradition. For Jessica, this meant that she found a specific strength and hope in God's provision of care and her confidence in God's ability to deliver baby Sarah and allow her to 'beat the odds'. 'We know that Sarah might not be with us long,' Jessica said, 'but we hope that she will live long enough to be able to hold her here alive in this world.' Jessica's narration of her story underscored the importance of faith for comfort, meaning and purpose. Her fear was that the doctors would not attempt to resuscitate Sarah if she was delivered and did not breathe well, or that the doctors would not try hard to 'fight' for Sarah's wellbeing. She perceived this because the doctors kept revisiting Sarah's goals of care and reiterating the statistics that would indicate a poor outcome for Sarah.

I spent much of our first visit listening to Jessica's story. Jessica was quite animated as she talked about her fear that the doctors might not 'try hard enough' to help baby Sarah if she was born prematurely. She feared that she might be robbed of her chance to welcome Sarah into the world. We also talked about Jessica's 3-year-old son Jackson, particularly about what the family had shared with him about the baby's diagnosis and life expectancy. Jessica shared some uncertainty about how to talk to him. They had told Jackson that the baby was sick but nothing further, because they felt that Jackson was not able to understand. We discussed developmentally appropriate ways to talk to Jackson. We talked about the importance of using simple, concrete concepts to talk about the baby's body and what might happen during the pregnancy or after. We agreed that preparing Jackson for the possibility that Sarah might be born early would be prudent. Jessica's own sense of uncertainty about what might happen with the pregnancy also informed the limits of how she wanted to prepare Jackson.

We spent about 30 minutes together for our first visit. Jessica eventually brought the conversation back around to the importance of her church community for support. She lamented that she was not able to be closely connected to her church while she was admitted in the hospital. Sensing this conversation transition as an invitation, I enquired about Jessica's openness for prayer. My operating assumption was that someone who identified closely with an active and highly spiritual tradition would likely find prayer to be an essential element of faithful religious practice. She affirmed that prayer would be greatly appreciated, and together we prayed for baby Sarah's continued growth and wellbeing in the womb, as well as peace and patience for Jessica who was on bed rest for the indefinite future. I concluded the prayer by asking for understanding and compassion for all of the care providers, especially those working with and for Jessica and baby Sarah. Jessica's nurse entered the room as we concluded prayer, so I excused myself with a promise to visit again soon.

Following our first conversation together, I worked with the interdisciplinary team and palliative care nurse practitioner to advocate for Jessica's expressed concerns. The neonatal team responded by meeting with Jessica to hear her worries and express their support and commitment to follow the family's established plan of care to stabilise and support Sarah while they assessed her medical needs further. Jessica later reported a much-improved level of trust in her care providers, which led to a significant improvement in her mood and positive coping.

Encounter 2: Sarah's birth

Baby Sarah was born about two weeks after my initial visit with Jessica. She was delivered prematurely and emergently by caesarean section after foetal monitoring showed that Sarah was in distress with a low heart rate. Sarah required some respiratory assistance at delivery. I visited with Jessica, Steve and baby Sarah, in the NICU a few hours after her birth. As Jessica and Steve shared turns holding Sarah, they expressed themes of joy, thanks and relief for Sarah 'defying the odds' by surviving delivery. They attributed this unexpected time as a blessing and sign of God's care and provision for Sarah. At the time of our visit, Sarah was requiring respiratory support by continuous positive airway pressure (CPAP), a common need for many premature babies of her gestational age. Jessica and Steve described their observations of how several of the characteristic physical features of babies with trisomy 18 were either absent or not as prominent for Sarah. They expressed a renewed sense of hope that Sarah might even be able to come home one day. As we visited, Sarah was able to have a break from her CPAP mask, which allowed the family their first unobstructed glimpse of Sarah's face since her delivery, shedding tears in a moment that had been so deeply, immensely hoped for. Together we offered a prayer of thanksgiving for Sarah's safe arrival, specifically naming the unexpected delivery, survival and early medical stability as a way to honour and recognise the emotional struggle of the family's journey to date.

Encounter 3: Sarah, four months old in NICU

At about four months of age, Sarah continued to stay in the NICU where she had been since her birth. She was slowly growing and nearing a significant milestone of weight gain. As I visited the bedside, Jessica was holding Sarah and rocking her. I spoke directly to Sarah who was awake and alert, and seemed content. I talked to Sarah about her pyjamas, her family's love for her and the special story she was living. Jessica, however, was frustrated. She explained that the various doctors involved in Sarah's care could not come to an agreement on the plan of care and the next steps in her treatment. The question was whether or not Sarah needed to be sent to another hospital with a specialty heart centre to further evaluate her congenital heart defect. Jessica needed a plan to help ease her own worry and anxiety about Sarah's future and the possibility of her needing heart surgery. The heart centre was located in a city several hours' drive from their home. Jessica also noted that her husband Steve was working and on the road for work all week. Steve's work meant that he was unable to visit and so another important source of support was not always immediately present and available. There was a significant time of silence as I allowed the weight of Jessica's frustrations to be held in that moment, and then she asked, 'What do I do about Jackson?'

Jessica lamented the impossible challenge of being two places at once. She expressed grief and feelings of maternal inadequacy, because she felt she was not giving her son, Jackson, the time, attention and daily structure that he needed. Jackson was being cared for at home by his grandparents and was not seeing his parents during the week. Jessica expressed worry that Jackson was having a 'hard time' and had been 'acting out' a little with his grandparents. We explored Jessica's thoughts about why he might be having such a hard time, especially in light of his developmentally appropriate needs. In particular, I encouraged Jessica to be curious about his actions and what needs or distress Jackson might be trying to express through his actions. We talked about ways that Steve and Jessica could affirm Jackson by supporting his developmental and spiritual needs: his growing need for autonomy balanced by the comfort and assurance that he wasn't being abandoned; a need for structure and trust; and maybe even some confusion or self-created 'myth' about his sister's condition and medical challenges. Jessica decided that much of Jackson's 'behaviour' problem was related to missing his family, his supportive community.

Following our visit, I communicated with the other members of the palliative care team, sharing both Jessica's expressed frustration with the plan of care as well as her distress surrounding Jackson. Together, the team was able to assist the family in several strategies and interventions. Jessica and Steve made a plan to have Jackson spend more time with them at the weekends and to visit Sarah in the hospital. The child life specialists, who are trained to help children to understand illness in developmentally appropriate ways, also helped Jackson to feel more included in Sarah's care by having him draw pictures for Sarah and by sending notes from Sarah home to Jackson. In the midst of both internal and external stressors, the palliative care team worked to ease the burden of Sarah's prolonged stay in the intensive care unit. Sarah was transferred to the specialty heart centre for surgical evaluation shortly after this visit.

Encounter 4: Sarah five months old in NICU

Sarah returned from the heart centre about one month later. During this encounter, Jessica recounted her experience of being in a different city, with different medical providers. She expressed relief to be back closer to home, and with nurses and physicians with whom she was more familiar. Jessica was hopeful that Sarah would be able to be weaned from her respiratory support following the repair of her cardiac defect, which was thought to be causing some of her respiratory problems. Jessica was in good spirits, upbeat in her outlook for the coming weeks and thankful for the continuation of my spiritual care relationship with Sarah.

Over the next weeks, Sarah's doctors unsuccessfully attempted to wean her from respiratory support. Steve and Jessica were faced with their most difficult decision to date: whether or not to commit Sarah to a tracheostomy. This was a significant decision point in Sarah's care, and one that some nurses, doctors and other members of the medical team expressed concern about. Given a diagnosis of trisomy 18, was a tracheostomy and associated ventilator dependence ethically and morally appropriate? Was that too much of an intervention? What about Sarah's quality of life?

Ultimately, with the support and consultation of the medical and palliative care teams, Jessica and Steve decided that a tracheostomy would be more comfortable for Sarah and help her to breathe more easily, relieving suffering. In a joint conversation involving me and the nurse practitioner of the palliative care team, Jessica revisited 'the odds' against Sarah and noted that she had already lived nearly six months when most of her doctors hadn't expect that she would survive to be delivered alive. Sarah's parents expressed that they felt that her life was a gift from God and that she deserved every opportunity to not only survive but thrive. Steve and Jessica felt that a tracheostomy would allow for a better quality of life and a pathway to help Sarah get home.

Encounter 5: Sarah's death

Sarah continued to grow both physically and in personality. As she approached seven months of age, she would kick and wiggle playfully in her crib. I stopped by her bedside frequently, and on days when she was awake, we would sing children's songs together or play with toys in her crib. Sarah enjoyed it when I would help her clap her hands to the beat of songs. She could not vocalise like a typical infant because of her tracheostomy and ventilator, but she would communicate through smiles and frowns, and by clicking her tongue. Sarah was not developmentally a typical six-month-old baby, but she was able to interact, experience love and affection and be playful. My interventions regularly involved expressing care and presence through play, and joy through song, acting as an extension of her spiritual community.

However, in the matter of a few short days Sarah became acutely ill. One afternoon, I was called to Sarah's bedside by the medical staff in the midst of a life-threatening event. Jessica and Steve were at home, having just suffered the sudden and devastating death of Steve's adult child from a previous relationship. They were called and asked to come urgently to the hospital. I waited at the bedside as the physicians and nurses attended to Sarah. Jessica and Steve arrived a short time later, with several of their extended family members and church friends. The doctors explained the changes Sarah was experiencing, expressing their reality: they were running out of medical options to help Sarah, her body simply was not responding to treatment. Sarah was experiencing significant heart problems, and she was in imminent danger of cardiac arrest. They asked the family to consider agreeing not to resuscitate Sarah if her heart were to stop.

With the request for a 'Do Not Resuscitate' order, the medical team stepped out of the room and allowed Jessica and Steve to hold Sarah who was struggling to maintain her oxygen saturation. Jessica and Steve both cried quietly as all of the family stood in silence around them. I remained present, silently in the corner, feeling and allowing the weight of the moment to simply be. Sarah was dying. After some time, I knelt beside the chair where Jessica sat holding Sarah and asked if it would be okay with them if I prayed for Sarah. They eagerly agreed. In my prayer, I prayed for comfort and protection from suffering for Sarah. I also prayed for the medical team as they tried to make the best decisions for Sarah and especially for Jessica and Steve. I recalled Sarah's birth and many of the experiences we had shared along their journey. I gave thanks for Sarah and her family and asked for comfort and peace as the family considered impossible decisions. Following our prayer together, and a substantial time of tears, Jessica expressed: 'She's already done so much. She wasn't supposed to be here. No one thought she'd be here. But she's tired. You're so tired aren't you, sweet girl? I don't want you to go but I don't want you to suffer. It's okay, Sarah, you can go if you're ready. You can go home. You can go to be with Jesus.' With that, the family decided not to attempt resuscitation if it was needed. A short time later, Sarah's condition declined further and she died, peacefully, in her mother's arms.

Jessica called me two days later to ask if I would be willing to speak at Sarah's funeral service. Her request underscored what, to me, is one of the many aspects of the value and importance of the chaplain in the hospital setting. Sarah did not know a church pastor, as she had lived the entirety of her life within the NICU. She and her family were not able to have extensive visitation from their community of faith. The role and function of the chaplain stood as an extension of their community, a buoy of hope, and an incarnational assurance of God's presence in the midst of their hospitalisation. 'You were her pastor,' Jessica said.

Discussion

The complete, patient-centred care of Sarah and her family required that I, as the chaplain, worked together with Sarah's nurses and doctors as well as the paediatric palliative care team. In team meetings and individual staff conversations, I was able to share important pieces of the family's faith and the ways in which they found meaning in Sarah's life. These insights into the family's emotional and spiritual worlds also helped the staff have a greater sense of understanding and sensitivity for the family's goals of care for Sarah. This interpretation and explanation was also essential in helping to discuss and navigate times of ethical or moral uncertainty among the various care teams involved in Sarah's care.

Assessment

I typically use a spiritual assessment modelled after a simple five-part framework: Love, Faith, Hope, Virtue and Beauty. The framework is envisioned and described by paediatric chaplain Mark Bartel (2004), who suggests that human experience is best described as being lived on a spectrum, always in motion from spiritual fulfilment (satisfaction, strength) to spiritual suffering (need). My assessment considers each of these five broad categories and seeks to gauge where one might be found on the spectrum at any given moment by listening and watching for answers to questions such as these:

- (Love) Who loves you? Who or what are your communities of support?

- (Faith) What brings you meaning? When do you feel most connected to the transcendent?

- (Hope) What helps you get through hard times?

- (Virtue) What informs your sense of morality? How do you define right versus wrong?

- (Beauty) What restores your soul? What evokes a sense of awe and wonder in your life?

Hence, spiritual strengths and needs will ebb and flow over time as situations change and new strengths or stresses are encountered. My goal is always to identify where one might be located on a continuum at any given moment and to facilitate shifts that help to engage the spiritual needs and distress that are being expressed or lived. I find Bartel's framework exceptionally helpful, because it can be applied across age groups and developmental levels. One can equally anticipate and assess the age-specific needs of an infant just as easily as an elderly adult, across the span of religious and spiritual backgrounds and socio-economic experience.

However, Bartel's assessment model is limited because, unlike other leading, robust spiritual assessment models, such as Fitchett's 7x7 model (Fitchett 2002), it does not provide the chaplain with a detailed framework which prompts considerations such as how medical concerns or other cultural dimensions impact medical care. A chaplain utilising Bartel's assessment model must recognise the importance of this information and integrate it into their assessment on their own accord.

Interventions

I approached my initial visit with Jessica with a desire to begin building a relationship with her and to better understand how Jessica's faith informed her world view, in particular, how it informed the decisions that she and her husband had made for their pregnancy. Jessica's immediate invitation to pull up a chair and sit at her bedside indicated to me that she welcomed the visit and wanted to engage in talking about her worries. I purposefully encouraged Jessica to talk about her pregnancy story in the hope that it would not only help me to understand her values but also offer an outlet to help relieve some of her building distress. As she shared her story and the importance of her faith, I learned that she was very active in her Pentecostal church community (*faith, love*) and that her faith was a significant spiritual strength, a vital aspect of her coping and meaning making (*hope*). For Jessica, prayer was a way for her to re-centre herself and to find peace and God's presence in the midst of her worry and anxious waiting. Our prayer together was both a request for God's presence to be known and experienced, and an attempt to reframe Jessica's perception of the medical team by praying for them and their work together with Jessica and her husband. Finally, in my work with the palliative care nurse practitioner, I was advocating for Jessica's rights as a patient and parent.

My initial spiritual assessment in the NICU focused on baby Sarah's spiritual needs to be held and bonded with (*love*), as well as her family's profound joy and hope in seeing Sarah 'do better than expected' (*hope*). In their expressions of living in the moment, Jessica and Steve were also expressing a growing sense of purpose and meaning for Sarah's life. The interventions of this visit included the provision of spiritual presence, or the combination of a non-anxious presence and an embodied assurance of the presence of God. I also engaged the family in the processing of their thoughts and feelings, and provided prayer in order to support the family's pre-existing spiritual practices and integrate those practices into the life of their new baby (*faith*). As we celebrated Sarah's arrival, we also named and affirmed the commitment this family held to, and the joy they experienced in, the creation and birth of new life (*beauty*). My goals of care for future encounters included exploring what and how the family was finding meaning in the midst of Sarah's hospitalisation.

The third encounter was marked by significant expressions of distress from Jessica: isolation from multiple communities of support (family and church), disagreement about a plan of care (and thus her hope for Sarah's continued wellbeing), feelings of guilt and inadequacy, as well as a loss of control (grounded in the sacred moments). My interventions for this visit focused on using curiosity to explore Jessica's feelings and the sources of her significant spiritual distress in order to support normalisation of the family's experience and evolving needs. As our conversation evolved, I recognised that Jessica was in spiritual distress due to being isolated from her community (*love*) and her inability to care equally for both of her children (*virtue*). I also recognised Jessica's spirit was down due to her diminished hopefulness (*hope*). A significant portion of this conversation revolved around Jessica's own sense of guilt and responsibility for Jackson's emotional and behavioural struggle (*faith*, *hope*). I offered Jessica spiritual counsel around the spiritual needs of a 3-year-old, including Jackson's need to feel safe and secure, and to be able to cultivate his own relationship with his sister, which had been very limited to that point. I worked together with the palliative care team to make plans with Jessica to address and alleviate her distress by better incorporating whole-family support.

This particular conversation, and several others in and around the topic of a tracheostomy, underscored the importance of the patient-centred approach and incremental decision-making process that this family found to be most helpful and supportive. At each milestone, the family paused to reflect on the benefits and burdens of the given treatment. From their perspective, Jessica and Steve perceived that

Sarah had a significant and worthy quality of life: that she was a child with disabilities who experienced relationship, love and affection; that she was a child who was able to express personality and to engage in play through little games to garner desired attention (*love, beauty*). The family demonstrated particular spiritual strength and integration of their belief system and world view for the decisions that they were being asked to make (*faith, hope*). Their expression of faith, and how that should inform their decisions, was also supported by their sense of family connectedness and purpose (*love*). These characteristics, they felt, outweighed the burden that surgery might entail.

My final encounter with Sarah and her family was profoundly sad. The medical team was all but certain that Sarah was nearing the end of her life. They had expressed as much when they asked me to be present at the bedside, and they expressed as much when they spoke with the family. In the moment, there were very few words that were necessary. The gathered friends and family, many of whom had never been able to visit Sarah, understood the gravity of the situation. I stood silently present in the room, observing the family as they held and loved Sarah, and continued to embody the assurance of God's presence in that moment. The family had longed and hoped for, even dared to imagine, the day that Sarah might be ready to come home from the hospital. In the long silence of the gathering at Sarah's bedside, Jessica and Steve were once more weighing the benefits and burdens of Sarah's medical care.

The intervention of prayer in this encounter embodied my sense of the rapidly evolving shift in Jessica and Steve's own hopes and dreams. As they contemplated how best to care for Sarah now, in her current state, they were also actively re-imagining what the future might look like (*love, faith, hope*). In my prayer, I attempted to recount and honour their story in a style of life review, naming all that Sarah had accomplished as well as acknowledging that the family's hopes were shifting from going home to not suffering – a theme they had consistently considered throughout Sarah's life.

Outcomes

Sarah spent nearly seven months in the NICUs of two large academic medical centres. Those seven months were marked by Sarah reaching important milestones in a setting of restricted visitation, far away from her supportive communities. Any hospital admission will create a host of spiritual needs and distress for the patient and their family. They are isolated from their communities of support – be that immediate family, friends or spiritual/faith communities. Families with a child in neonatal intensive care face exceptional burdens of extended hospitalisations while trying to manage life (paying bills, caring for other children, maintaining homes and working) and being present and caring for their loved ones. Those needs are only further amplified when the family is also trying to hold their daily burdens in tension with the reality of their child's own mortality. Jessica's statement that I, as chaplain, was Sarah's pastor demonstrated both the reality of the isolating effect of a prolonged hospitalisation and a unique opportunity for the chaplain to reclaim sacred and holy ground for both the patient and their family.

In reflecting on this case, and many others that are similar in nature, I continue to be curious about the ways in which the care team might be able to further explore or assist the family in being more closely connected to their 'home' communities during their hospitalisation. Perhaps this is not the primary task of the chaplain but certainly chaplains have a unique opportunity and authority to encourage maintenance or strengthening of those supportive ties. The isolating nature of the neonatal intensive care environment is not conducive to maintaining close relationships with home communities – particularly for families that are a significant distance from home. Are there ways that we can assist families and patients to stay engaged with their supportive communities? How can we facilitate and encourage families to lean into the strength of their pre-existing supports given limitations such as distance, visitation restrictions and the emotional exhaustion of having a sick child in the hospital for an extended period of time?

Conclusion

Over the course of dozens of visits, I attempted to monitor and assess the evolving spiritual needs of the James family using the simple spiritual elements of love, faith, hope, virtue and beauty. I sought to help Sarah and her family experience and be connected to their broader spiritual community by frequent bedside visits and the extension of spiritual practices that brought comfort, hope and meaning making. I also sought to help them engage with their own inner spiritual resources and strengths through prayer and conversation. Utilising my knowledge of childhood developmental theory and age-specific spiritual needs, I offered play, song, prayer, reading and presence as tangible interventions to facilitate Sarah's experience of the sacred and holy (Fowler 1981). I sought to help Sarah, even in her infancy, experience joy and happiness, and to encounter the holy by introducing her to rituals of her family's faith tradition in partnership with her parents and brother. Caring for Sarah's spirit also meant caring for her family. In this case, most of my encounters were with Jessica as she was most often at the bedside. I often extended spiritual community through presence and conversation. Occasionally, the conversation took the form of spiritual counsel but equally important were the countless interactions that were limited to a few words of greeting and a smile. Those simple interactions were just as much an extension, reminder and symbol of the sacred and transcendent that dwelt in the midst of ventilators and medicines and incessantly beeping monitors. I believe both were essential elements to the overall care of Sarah and her family.

References

Bartel, M. (2004). 'What is spiritual? What is spiritual suffering?' *Journal of Pastoral Care & Counseling*, 58, 3, 187–201.

Burke, A., Field, K. and Morrison, J. (2013). 'Natural history of fetal trisomy 18 after prenatal diagnosis.' *Archives of Disease in Childhood. Fetal and Neonatal Edition*, 98, F152–154.

Carey, J. (2012). 'Perspectives on the care and management of infants with trisomy 18 and trisomy 13: Striving for balance.' *Current Opinion in Pediatrics*, 24, 672–678.

Fitchett, G. (2002). *Assessing Spiritual Needs: A Guide for Caregivers.* Lima, OH: Academic Renewal Press.

Fowler, J.W. (1981). *Stages of Faith: The Psychology of Human Development and the Quest for Meaning.* New York, NY: Harper Collins.

Haug, S., Goldstein, M., Cummins, D., Fayard, E. and Merritt, A. (2017). 'Using patient-centered care after a prenatal diagnosis of trisomy 18 or trisomy 13.' *JAMA Pediatrics*, 141, 4, 382–387.

Lantos, J. (2016). 'Trisomy 13 and 18 – Treatment decisions in a stable gray zone.' *JAMA*, 316, 4, 396–398.

Nelson, K., Rosella, L., Mahant, S. and Guttmann, A. (2016). 'Survival and surgical interventions for children with trisomy 13 and 18.' *JAMA*, 316, 4, 420–428.

Chapter 3

Critical Response to Paediatric Case Studies

A Paediatric Chaplain's Perspective

Hans Evers

The cases by Chaplains Bryson and Jinks illustrate exemplary models of chaplaincy in a paediatric setting. In mentioning the characteristics, I hope to do justice to the well-considered and elaborated practices and their descriptions. I conclude with some notes about contemporary challenges for professional practice and presentation.

What is visibly done by Chaplains Bryson and Jinks?

Chaplain Bryson describes a rule-based approach. First, she observes a situation and estimates Mark's psychological condition. She then has an idea about his request for help and the effective and efficient interventions. Next, she gives information about the possibility of spiritual care and the activities. After Mark's consent, she goes through the steps of the chosen activity. She repeatedly checks whether he can participate optimally and that he feels that he is in charge. Finally, she summarises what Mark has expressed and, in strong words, gives him her positive feedback. Chaplain Bryson explains her assessment conclusions, and once again estimates Mark's condition. She leaves the room after she promises to pray for the family.

Chaplain Jinks visited his clients in various ways, dozens of times, and participated in the palliative team's discussions. What are the details? In the accompanying presence, he ensures that his involvement is visible to Sarah's parents. Concerning the conversations with her mother, he provides information about the themes discussed. In his direct approach to the child, he plays and tells a story. When Chaplain Jinks prays at the end of a conversation, he asks if it is appropriate. The content of the prayer is the grateful repetition of what has been discussed, accompanied by wishes and more or less advice or an opinion. He reports to the palliative team about the content of his conversations and the client's reaction. All in all, after reading his description of the case, we know what he is doing and little about how he does it.

It is highly plausible that a passer-by or a new nurse sees Chaplain Bryson as a rehabilitation therapist and Chaplain Jinks at first sight as an authoritative visitor.

How do the chaplains introduce themselves?

Chaplain Bryson presents herself as a volunteer chaplain, academically well qualified. She is an experienced expert in the general and spiritual care of a child with a non-congenital brain disorder. She is familiar with the loss of a child and is intrigued by the developing research in her profession. Chaplain Jinks presents himself as a well-educated chaplain and ordained minister. As a member of a team, he contributes to the common goals. The chaplains differ from each other because of the qualities mentioned and jargon they use: she is a care expert and he an integrated minister.

What are the chaplains' critical concepts?

Chaplain Bryson testifies about the importance of patient-centred care. It is essential for her to offer a large degree of agency. The client is the protagonist in the process. This experience of autonomy is both the means and the purpose of her intervention in which Mark can safely explore spiritual needs, concerns or anything else he would like to share. She looks for what empowers him to make choices and know that he is valued, cared for, loved and belongs, both to his family and the hospital community. The intertwining of initial and continuous assessment and intervention is a distinctive aspect of a therapeutic approach.

Chaplain Jinks appreciates care coordination through communication and a patient-centred approach to decision making. Foundational for him is the family's faith, which is essential for comfort, meaning and purpose. He knows about his unique opportunity to encourage maintenance or strengthen ties with the home community. Prayer plays a particular role as a way to honour and recognise the emotional struggle of the family's journey to date.

Chaplain Bryson's critical concepts are mainly about autonomy and empowerment, while that of Chaplain Jinks is connectedness.

Special methodological remarks by the chaplains

Chaplain Bryson uses treatment plans that are also used by speech therapists and pedagogical staff. What distinguishes her use? She uses treatment plans for facilitating and enriching communication as assessment and intervention tools for spiritual care. She considers Mark's choice as an invitation to share, reveal and strengthen what lifts the spirit. Mark's participation enables her to understand and assess his spiritual needs. The playing together can give the client connectedness to the hospital community and can offer hope and strength.

Chaplain Jinks provides a spiritual presence, in which he distinguishes the combination of a non-anxious presence and an embodied assurance of the presence of God. He primarily gives meaning to communication and prayer. When he speaks with his client, he explores thoughts, feelings and values and tries to alleviate distress. He distinguishes many functions in his prayer. His prayer is meant to re-centre; to experience peace and God's presence; to redefine the perception of the medical team; to support and integrate the pre-existing spiritual practices into the life of a newborn; to formulate the rapidly evolving shift in a situation; and to recount and honour the family's story in a style of life review.

For both chaplains, direct contact with their clients has a transcendent meaning.

What is the focus of the chaplains' professional attention?

Chaplain Bryson focuses on 'spiritual needs'. As such, she considers the primary human motives for self-development and connectedness with the other. She is especially interested in her client's need to find redefined and restored identity and hope within the given limitations. The mother also confronts the chaplain with her struggle with what has happened to her son and her incomplete trust in practitioners and caregivers.

Chaplain Jinks focuses on connection with the family's 'home' community and the integration of the neonate in this tradition. He investigates the family's identification as 'Christian' and the function of their particular religious or spiritual values in decision making. He sees a role for the care team in assisting the family in being more closely connected to their home communities during their hospitalisation. The mother also asks his attention to what concerns her: her insecurity and scepticism about medical policy and her worries about her older son. The chaplains' attention is drawn, respectively, to facilitating the daily struggle of the client and experiencing the faith 'in exile'.

What about goals and outcomes?

Chaplain Bryson mentions her achievement of many goals. She identified intended effects for her proposed interventions. She gave Mark the opportunity to make decisions and communicate his feelings and spiritual needs. She delivered affirmation and encouragement of his intrinsic value. She assessed what was essential to give spiritual care. Together, they were able to touch real pain and yet find real hope. They connected, and found the presence of the transcendent in their activities.

The outcome reported by Mark, his mother and Chaplain Bryson is that Mark can tell what he is feeling.

Similarly, Chaplain Jinks lists many goals achieved. Some served his cooperation with the palliative team. By interpretation and explanation, he helped the staff have a greater sense of understanding and sensitivity about the family's goals of care. On behalf of the hospital, he hosted the spiritual needs and distress of the patient and her family, who were far away from their supportive communities. He listened to the mother and assisted her in the care of her son. But his primary goal was to provide a spiritual care relationship with the neonate. He acted by presence and attention as an extension of the home community, 'a buoy of hope' and an incarnational assurance of God's presence in their hospitalisation. The outcome reported by both Chaplain Jinks and the mother is that he had created and continued a spiritual care relationship as pastor with the neonate.

Both chaplains give a summary of the goals they have achieved. It is striking that each only mentions one outcome that is explicitly confirmed by the parents and the patient. I do not know what the parents think about achieving the other goals. Can you talk about an outcome if you are the only one who sees it this way?

Challenges for contemporary professional practice

How Chaplains Bryson and Jinks are operating as chaplains is rooted historically in times and communities where, successively, the ecclesial community and science have been, or still are the dominant sources of identity and morality. Chaplain Bryson represents the pastor as a therapeutic healthcare provider and Chaplain Jinks represents the ambassador of the church in the medical world. The role of religious institutions as sources of identity and morality and the chaplain as their representative is no longer self-evident. The cases illustrate that. Chaplain Bryson focuses on spiritual need without a visible religious framework and gains trust because she presents herself as a chaplain out of passion and not as a professional in paid employment.

The parents confront the chaplains with scepticism about academic, technical medical thinking and acting. The general reserve regarding institutions may also affect Chaplain Jinks. The question is whether he was a pastor for the parents. The case shows, on the ethical level, no direct interaction between him and the parents. He is mainly observer and interpreter. His case delivers no information about the home community, the level of church participation or the personal faithfulness of the parents. Chaplain Bryson does not mention anything about this either.

As a stimulus to further discussion about chaplains' professionalism, I make five notes.

The children's and parents' involvement with church

Chaplain Bryson asks Mark if and how he wants the contact with the chaplain. In this line, the chaplain can 'problematise' her presence for the patient and his family. If she informs them about her support, she can ask whether and how they want it, and what the results should be. This question can lead to very different intended outcomes to those that are common in the church and the care sector. For example, the client may ask the chaplain to listen carefully to him in search of what is essential and necessary and to expressly refrain from advice and judgement, even if the words are contrary to tradition or science. The chaplain is then not ambassador or care provider but spiritual accompanier of the soul.

The chaplains' communicative approach

Chaplains can explicitly determine which forms of intervention are appropriate for the assignment they receive from the patient. Every conversation technique has its own implicit goal. Personal exploration requires different verbal responses to those of an educational interview. Chaplains can also routinely check with patients every time to clarify if their approach fits the patient. I also consider all techniques for coaching as possible forms of intervention, as well as traditional rituals. It all depends on how clients express their spiritual need.

The chaplain as moral counsellor

Conversations about a child's ethical interests have to be conducted mainly with parents. A child is autonomous but not fully able to oversee everything for a long time. That certainly applies to neonates. Besides shepherd, the chaplain can be 'a teacher' who gives his clients the opportunity to reorient themselves concerning their convictions and to become more mature in their faith, depending on what life demands. Chaplains can provide information about the broad spectrum of thoughts in the sacred books about life, sickness, suffering, dying and parenting. They can also tell parents about the medical ethical principles and their roots in general and religious morality. Chaplains can familiarise parents with the balancing of many values and norms by care providers and parents. The role of moral counsellor to the parents requires a great deal of discretion towards other practitioners and caregivers.

Problem-solving and pastoral care as solace

Chaplains may be less preoccupied with wellbeing and the quality of the feeling. Consolation and happiness do not necessarily match. The one who, after mature consideration, does what they consider to be their private duty, may, at the same time, inevitably and irreversibly suffer. Chaplains can help distinguish what makes life bearable and tolerable by their acceptance of ambivalence.

The chaplain's position as deviation from 'normal'

Chaplains can claim a specific place within the hospital organisation and as members of teams. They are 'in but not of the world' when, as critical facilitators, they serve the quest for the appropriate treatment for both the patient and the professionals involved. The chaplain is not the privileged owner of the faith and the wisdom of life, who knows in advance how to do it; but the chaplain can be an expert in communication, where people alone or together formulate for themselves what ultimately matters.

Chapter 4
Critical Response to Paediatric Case Studies

A Paediatric Nurse's Perspective

Jennifer Baird

My reflections on these case studies stem from my professional identification as a paediatric nurse health services researcher, which is informed by my formal training in nursing, social work and public health. I currently work as a nurse scientist at an urban paediatric academic medical centre and collaborate with, mentor and provide research-related education to clinicians from an array of professional backgrounds. I am a member of the hospital's spiritual care advisory board and work closely with our institution's spiritual care department. My clinical background is in paediatric critical care, and my programme of research centres on healthcare delivery for children with complex chronic conditions.

Case study I

In the first case study, Chaplain Bryson reflected on her work with Mark, an 11-year-old boy with severe physical disabilities who was unable to communicate verbally after experiencing two strokes related to the removal of a brain tumour. Mark and his family were referred for chaplaincy services when difficulties with the medical team arose. Although the authors did not go into detail about the source of the problem, it seems likely that these difficulties were due at least in part to the medical team's inability to communicate effectively with Mark as a result of his non-verbal status. I found it interesting that the chaplaincy referral was made by a senior nurse specifically for Mark's mother Sarah but that Chaplain Bryson's interactions focused largely on communication with Mark.

Chaplain Bryson employed several important strategies to establish rapport and engage in therapeutic interventions. First, she demonstrated a willingness to jump right in, not allowing the chaos of Mark's recent move back to the Teenage Cancer Unit to distract her. When Mark's parents requested an alternate meeting time, this provided Chaplain Bryson with the perfect opening to focus her attention specifically on Mark, whom she quickly assessed to be in need of individualised attention. I would have liked additional information about her assessment strategy, particularly since so many clinicians struggle with how to interact (and by extension assess) non-verbal and/or cognitively impaired patients.

Second, Chaplain Bryson used this assessment to select an activity with which she could quickly engage Mark, capturing his interest and generating a quick 'win' that helped establish her as a trustworthy and valuable member of the care team. She was also thoughtful about selecting activities that matched the timeline of their therapeutic relationship. The bead bracelet activity, for example, enabled her to get to know Mark and to conduct a deeper assessment of his psycho-spiritual needs, and was therefore an appropriate activity for their initial visit. The lollipop stick activity built on the knowledge she had gained from her visits with Mark and was reflective of the type of activity appropriate for a more developed therapeutic relationship. Chaplain Bryson was also purposeful about selecting activities that could be adapted to facilitate Mark's participation in spite of his physical limitations and non-verbal status, which further fostered his engagement and helped to reaffirm her message that he was a valued part of his community.

Finally, Chaplain Bryson worked to involve Mark's parents in her interactions with Mark. Although she was clear that Mark was the primary focus of her interventions, she also welcomed his parents' input and supported their engagement with him. Presumably, her visits with Mark and his family were a combination of individual sessions with Mark and whole-family visits, and I would have liked additional insight into her strategy around how and when to engage Mark by himself versus the whole family. I was also struck by the potential for engaging members of the nursing staff in these types of activities as a means of helping to establish better communication and rapport with Mark and his parents.

Case study 2

In the second case study, Chaplain Jinks described his work with the James family. Chaplain Jinks identified several factors that helped to explain the conflicting goals of care for Sarah. Survival rates for trisomy 18 have historically been extremely poor but the development of new technologies and the standardisation of clinical care have enabled survival for many conditions once considered universally lethal. Unfortunately, practice change in healthcare is notoriously slow: one oft-cited statistic suggests a 17-year lag between the discovery of a research finding and its translation into clinical practice (Morris, Woodling and Grant 2011). As a result, healthcare teams often deliver care that is inconsistent with the best available evidence, and wide practice variations are noted across the healthcare system. At the same time, the ready availability of information on the internet has enabled patients and family members to become consumers of healthcare information (Pehora et al. 2015), and the advent of social media has fostered geographically diverse support networks for those dealing with relatively rare conditions (Sira et al. 2014; Kirk and Milnes 2016). Bolstered by information gained from the internet and these support networks, families have been empowered to advocate for care that is not supported by, or that may be in direct contradiction to, that offered by their medical team.

With an awareness of these dynamics at play, Chaplain Jinks suspended judgement about what 'should' happen and sought instead to understand Jessica's perspective, with a focus on the ways in which the family's faith traditions had informed their decision making. I was struck by how quickly Chaplain Jinks was able to assume the role of a trusted confidant. Jessica was clearly in need of an ally and she identified Chaplain Jinks in this role, sharing her mistrust about the healthcare team's planned response to Sarah's birth.

The trust and rapport that Chaplain Jinks developed with Jessica served multiple purposes. First, it allowed him to explore and attend to Jessica's other psychosocial stressors, including her concerns about how to address Sarah's condition with her young son, Jackson. In a beautiful example of interprofessional teamwork (Jessup 2007), that is the hallmark of highly functioning healthcare teams, Chaplain Jinks was able to provide this psychosocial support, which might otherwise be considered the domain of the team social worker or psychologist, in the midst of his chaplaincy visit because it was what Jessica needed most at that moment in time. Second, and perhaps most importantly, Chaplain Jinks's rapport provided him with the insight necessary to understand Jessica and Steve's priorities and to then communicate those priorities to the medical team on several occasions throughout Sarah's hospital stay. Serving as a liaison between Jessica and Steve and the medical team, Chaplain Jinks was able to help the team make sense of the family's requests in a way that allowed them to be honoured at the time of Sarah's birth and throughout her short life.

Chaplain Jinks's use of prayer helped to foster his connection to the James family. During their first visit together, he correctly discerned that prayer was a meaningful practice for Jessica and he used prayer to help communicate an understanding of Jessica's concerns by offering specific prayers for the understanding and compassion of her care providers. This was a smart therapeutic strategy: he communicated understanding and alignment with her without explicitly taking sides, thus maintaining a sense of neutrality critical to an effective role as liaison. Continued use of prayer throughout his relationship with the James family helped to solidify the connection he had built and provided an effective means of spiritual support for the family.

One additional strategy Chaplain Jinks employed was his demonstration of respect and affirmation of Sarah's worth as an individual, despite her young age and limited cognitive and physical development. He saw her as a person in need of spiritual development and worthy of his time, and he took the time to visit regularly and to interact with her. These actions may have provided a counterbalance to the dehumanisation that can often occur in the highly medicalised critical care environment and likely also helped to solidify his relationship with Jessica and Steve. Collectively, Chaplain Jinks's actions played a key role in helping to re-establish broken trust between the James family and their medical providers, which in turn allowed Jessica and Steve to advocate and care for Sarah during her short life and to make the difficult decision to withdraw further care when the limits of medical intervention had been reached.

Parallels between the cases

The most exciting part of reading these two cases was discovering several important parallels between two seemingly disparate narratives. The following themes were reflected in both cases and represent important takeaways for paediatric chaplaincy practice: 1) the chaplain's role as a neutral or unaligned source of support when the family is mistrustful of the healthcare team; 2) the chaplain's role in providing continuity of care for long-stay patients and families; and 3) the importance of engaging both the child and family, regardless of the child's developmental status.

In both cases, the family expressed mistrust and/or dissatisfaction with the medical team. As a result, each family was in need of a source of support – someone with whom they could share their concerns and frustrations and from whom they could receive guidance and strategies for coping. For Jessica, this meant sharing concerns with Chaplain Jinks about the medical team's willingness to provide treatment-focused care to Sarah after her birth; for Mark, this meant working with Chaplain Bryson to find ways to communicate his wishes, needs and concerns. Both chaplains served a unique role – their familiarity with the medical system gave them an 'insider' perspective but their roles as chaplains allowed them to be sufficiently distanced from the medical team to provide the type of unaligned support the family needed. Paediatric chaplains are often called on to enter highly charged and difficult situations, and their perceived neutrality in these instances can facilitate the development of a powerful therapeutic relationship that can, in turn, help to create a bridge between the family and the medical team.

Both cases also involved patients and families who were enduring an extended hospitalisation. During these long-stay admissions, families often need a stable, familiar team with whom they can develop a trusting relationship and on whom they can rely to provide consistent care. The realities of hospital staffing make this challenging. Physicians and nurses typically work inconsistent schedules (Baird *et al.* 2016), and medical trainees are on service for only short periods of time with limitations on their work hours (Antiel *et al.* 2011). As a result, families may feel their medical care is being delivered by an ever-changing cast of characters with whom they have no established relationship. Chaplains can help address this concern by providing a source of consistency.

Finally, both cases demonstrated the importance of providing care to both the child–patient and the family. In each case, it would have been easy for the chaplain to overlook the child–patient: Sarah was a developmentally delayed infant with limited ability to interact; Mark was non-verbal and also had severe physical limitations. In spite of this, both chaplains understood their role was to provide spiritual care to the entire family. Chaplain Jinks appropriately directed much of his attention to Sarah's mother but he also recognised a responsibility to provide for Sarah's spiritual development in the absence of an external faith community. Chaplain Bryson quickly identified that her therapeutic interactions needed to focus on Mark, particularly since the medical team was having difficulty engaging with him. Knowing how to navigate the child versus parent focus of their interventions enabled the chaplains to establish and maintain strong relationships with each family, which in turn fostered therapeutic and developmentally appropriate paediatric spiritual care delivery.

References

Antiel, R.M., Thompson, S.M., Hafferty, F.W. *et al.* (2011). 'Duty hour recommendations and implications for meeting the ACGME core competencies: Views of residency directors.' *Mayo Clinic Proceedings*, 86, 3, 185–191.

Baird, J., Rehm, R.S., Hinds, P.S., Baggott, C. and Davies, B. (2016). 'Do you know my child? Continuity of nursing care in the pediatric intensive care unit.' *Nursing Research*, 65, 2, 142–150.

Jessup, R.L. (2007). 'Interdisciplinary vs multidisciplinary care teams: Do we understand the difference?' *Australian Health Review*, 31, 3, 330–331.

Kirk, S. and Milnes, L. (2016). 'An exploration of how young people and parents use online support in the context of living with cystic fibrosis.' *Health Expectations*, 19, 2, 309–321.

Morris, Z.S., Woodling, S. and Grant, J. (2011). 'The answer is 17 years, what is the question: Understanding time lags in translational research.' *Journal of the Royal Society of Medicine*, 104, 12, 510–520.

Pehora, C., Gajaria, N., Stoute, M., Fracassa, S., Serebale-O'Sullivan, R. and Matava, C. (2015). 'Are parents getting it right? A survey of parents' internet use for children's health care information.' *Interactive Journal of Medical Research*, 4: e12.

Sira, N., Desai, P.P., Sullivan, K.J. and Hannon, D.W. (2014). 'Coping strategies in mothers of children with heart defects: A closer look into spirituality and internet utilization.' *Journal of Social Service Research*, 40, 5, 606–622.

Part 2
Chaplains' Care for Veterans

Chapter 5

'He is disappointed I am not the son he wanted. I tried and tried to deny I am a girl'

– Vicki, a male-to-female transgender veteran

Janet Hanson

Introduction

This case describes my spiritual care for Vicki, a transgender veteran in her 50s. Spiritual care with lesbian, gay, bi-sexual and transgender (LGBT) persons, and especially with transgender persons, is an area of growing need. LGBT health disparities are well documented, and the health risks experienced by LGBT veterans are even larger (Kauth and Shipherd 2016). Depression, anxiety, post-traumatic stress disorder and other mental health problems affect transgender veterans at higher rates than non-transgender veterans. These conditions may be connected to the higher rates of intimate partner violence and aggression and military sexual trauma that transgender veterans experience. Transgender veterans are also at an increased risk for heart and kidney disease because of hormone use, diabetes, smoking, obesity, high blood pressure and stress. These concerns and others raise opportunities for professional chaplains to develop spiritual care theories and practices to directly address the theological issues raised by the lived experiences of this population.

Within the past decade, several historic legal changes have taken place impacting LGBT persons within both the civilian and military worlds. The US Department of Defense (DOD) repealed the 'don't ask, don't tell' rule (DADT) in 2011, allowing gay and lesbian persons to serve openly in the military. Prior to the repeal, thousands of service members discovered to be gay or lesbian were discharged, frequently dishonourably, under DADT. Those receiving a dishonourable discharge because of their sexual orientation were unable to receive benefits within the Veterans Affairs (VA) system. Only a few veterans are now applying to upgrade their discharge to honourable to become benefit-eligible. To do so requires willingness to open paperwork referencing sexual orientation and potentially old wounds (McDermott 2017). In June 2016, the DOD began allowing transgender personnel to serve openly in the military. In August 2017, President Donald Trump signed an order that reversed this policy. The implications of his action for transgender service members and their potential discharge into the VA system remains unclear. For now, the VA remains committed to providing healthcare to transgender veterans based on its 2012 national directive.

Other important changes affecting LGBT people have taken place in federal and state law and policy. In June 2016, the Supreme Court of the United States ruled that same-sex couples have the right to marry in all 50 states. At the state level, in part due to the advocacy of Army veteran Jamie Shupe, Oregon recently became the first state in US history to offer more than two gender options on identity documents, including driver's licences, thus recognising non-binary, intersex and agender people on legal documents. Residents will have the option to choose among three gender categories when applying for driver's licences or state ID cards: male, female and 'X' for non-binary or unspecified. Soon, the VA will be adding a self-identified gender identity (SIGI) demographic field to the medical record system. Clinical reminders for health screening will be linked to the birth sex field, but the SIGI field will aid staff in using appropriate salutations and gender references (Kauth and Shipherd 2016).

Alongside increased legal rights for LGBT persons, a greater awareness of healthcare discrepancies has emerged. Minority stress research has demonstrated that both distal stress (external experiences of rejection, prejudice and discrimination) and proximal stress (internalised self-hatred and anxiety, often byproducts of distal experiences) accrue over time and cause poor health outcomes (Meyer 2007). It is to be hoped that the recent legal changes will reduce these stressors for LGBT persons, but our cultural norms and attitudes are rooted in values and beliefs and are not necessarily altered by new rules. Even so, there are some examples in the research literature and popular culture indicating increased visibility of LGBT persons who now feel safe to live openly in their communities. For example, teen suicide rates have decreased since same-sex marriage became legal (Raifman *et al.* 2017). Bruce Jenner's public transition to Caitlyn Jenner greatly increased awareness and perhaps a growth in overall acceptance of transgender persons.

Despite these gains, medical access to healthcare for transgender persons is not equal throughout the US. According to the Movement Advancement Project, an independent think tank that provides research and analysis related to equality for LGBT people (www.lgbtmap.org), currently only 12 US states and the District of Columbia have state Medicaid policies explicitly covering healthcare related to gender transition for transgender people. The Veterans Health Administration has a directive for providing medically necessary healthcare for transgender and intersex veterans, including hormonal therapy, mental healthcare, pre-operative evaluation, and medically necessary post-operative and long-term care following sex reassignment surgery. Sex reassignment surgery is currently not performed or funded by the VA.

Churches and faith groups have for years been working through theological stances on sexuality, homosexuality and, most recently, gender identity. Within Christianity there exists a wide range of acceptance, tolerance and rejection of persons who identify as LGBT. Individual Christian denominations subscribe to doctrines and beliefs containing varying degrees of welcome and inclusion of LGBT persons. For professional chaplains, this can provide unique challenges in supporting persons in their individual faith practice, when their organised religious group rejects them. It is important, then, for chaplains to examine their own experience and understanding of sex and gender identity to find a place of spiritual authority (grounding) from which to meet others in their individual and unique journeys.

This case demonstrates how a chaplain can effectively provide transgender veterans with a safe place to discuss gender identity and faith formation. The valued role of chaplain as confidant in the military contributes to the positive relationship many veterans expect with a VA chaplain. This gives the chaplain a role distinct from other disciplines: to act as a benevolent moral authority. My previous research and knowledge of community religious resources allowed me to be a referral resource for LGBT-welcoming congregations in the large urban area where the veteran in this case lives. This case outlines my spiritual care with the veteran incorporating principles of acceptance and commitment therapy (ACT) (Nieuwsma, Walser and Hayes 2016). ACT involves developing psychological flexibility through six core processes: acceptance, defusion, present-moment awareness, self as context, values, and committed action. Sometimes these are simplified as 'Are you open? Are you aware? And are you doing what matters?' I find that ACT integrates well with spiritual care because of its focus on acceptance of suffering as part of the human condition and living in the present while making choices to live out one's values in the world.

An initial version of this case was developed during my participation in the Mental Health Integration for Chaplain Services (MHICS) programme. MHICS is a training programme designed to help VA and military chaplains apply evidence-based principles in their spiritual care (www.mirecc.va.gov/mentalhealthandchaplaincy/MHICS.asp).

Background

Vicki (a pseudonym) is a transgender male-to-female veteran in her 50s. She is single and lives in an apartment in a large metropolitan area. Her family consists of two brothers and a father, all who live nearby. Vicki is a post-Vietnam era veteran who served in the Army reserve and then the Army for two years. She was discharged from the military early due to drinking problems but quit drinking 20 years ago after 'nearly drinking herself to death'. She is being treated at the VA for gender dysphoria, attention deficit and hyperactivity disorder and depression. Vicki gave me permission to use her case with the hope that it may provide insight to ministers helping transgender persons.

With Vicki's approval, her mental health social worker put in a referral to Chaplain Services after discussing in a therapy session her 'family's reaction to her transition... The family is Catholic and her father has openly expressed that he believes her transition is "wrong" and she shouldn't do it'. The on-call duty chaplain received the consult [referral] over the weekend and spoke with Vicki on the phone regarding her 'struggles with the Catholic Church and finding community'. The on-call duty chaplain charted providing support around 'struggles she is experiencing in her transition from M to F [male to female], such as new emotions in her life as well as difficulties with family's acceptance'. I received the referral to provide follow-up care.

I am an ordained elder in the United Methodist Church, an Association for Clinical Pastoral Education Certified Educator, and a chaplain currently working in the Veterans Health Administration system. I am also a member of the LGBT community, serving on an LGBT interdisciplinary work group within the medical centre addressing healthcare needs of this veteran population. I have compassion for the complex concerns transgender veterans raise as they struggle with theological questions of incarnation, embodiment and integration of mind, body and spirit.

My relationship with Vicki took place in the context of a large Veterans Administration (VA) hospital with a total of 248 operating beds, which provides over 950,000 outpatient veteran visits each year. The Veterans Health Administration (VHA) is likely the largest provider of LGBT healthcare in the world. Exact figures are not available, because sexual orientation and gender identity of veterans are not currently tracked in the VHA. However, given an estimated one million LGBT veterans in the United States and current rates of VHA use, more than 250,000 VHA patients are potentially LGBT veterans (Kauth and Shipherd 2016). The VA hospital where this case took place was given 'Leader' status in The Human Rights Campaign Foundation's Healthcare Equality Index for the fifth consecutive year, reaching benchmarks in meeting non-discrimination policies, practices and training criteria.

My spiritual care for Vicki consisted of one visit. This visit took place in my office in Chaplaincy Services, which shares space with two other departments. My office provided a confidential space with comfortable chairs for a 50-minute session. We have a VA-sponsored welcoming sign at the check-in for our offices that reads: 'We serve all who served', with a rainbow logo and military ID tag on it.

Case study

Each morning, our chaplaincy department meets for the overnight, on-duty chaplain to report any significant spiritual needs in the hospital and relay ongoing spiritual concerns for the unit chaplains to address that day. This consult for a transgender veteran was from a mental health social worker I know from our joint membership on an LGBT interdisciplinary work group at the medical centre. This work group fields consults from staff and provides education regarding care of transgender veterans to ensure adherence to VHA guidelines. The consult came in over the weekend and was responded to with a phone call from the on-duty chaplain. She reported speaking with the veteran on the phone and listening to her distress concerning family and spiritual issues. The veteran asked for a follow-up call Monday morning with a chaplain who could set up a meeting. As one of the chaplains assigned to outpatient mental health, I received the consult.

I called the veteran that afternoon and spoke with her on the phone as she was on the bus to the VA to have an appointment for voice therapy with the speech-language pathologist. This is a service offered at the VA for persons transitioning to help them learn to monitor and modulate the pitch of their voice and learn other behavioural methods to express congruence with their identified gender. I complimented her on her efforts in this process and she said to me, 'Oh, I am committed to this process.' We agreed to meet and scheduled an appointment the following week. The day of that appointment, she called and asked if she could come in early for our time, as she was trying to schedule a manicure. I could meet earlier that day and so easily accommodated her request. When the veteran arrived, she was wearing women's attire, including a dress and wig, and carrying a purse. She appeared at ease sitting in our public lobby area for a few minutes before I was ready to see her. I invited her into my office, which has two comfortable chairs and a living room-like sitting area. She expressed gratitude at my willingness to adjust the time and was excited to get her nails done. She told me of a salon that regularly does her nails, where she is welcomed and seems to know several of the technicians.

The following conversation happened after initial greetings:

Chaplain: Tell me how I can support you today?

Vicki: Well, like I have been talking with my therapist, my family doesn't accept me. Of course, they are Catholic, and the Church doesn't accept me either.

Chaplain: I am sorry. I think all of us long for acceptance.

Vicki: It has taken me a long time to accept and figure out my gender identity. My dad always tried to get me to play baseball with him, but really, I was never interested. I wanted to be good at it and enjoy it, because of course I wanted to hang out with my dad. I sucked at it and it wasn't fun for either of us, so finally he just quit trying. He is disappointed I am not the son he wanted. He still tells me that.

Chaplain: Am I hearing grief and disappointment for both of you not having the father–son relationship you hope for?

Vicki: (Nods with a sad expression)

Chaplain: I also heard you say that you have, after all these years, figured out and accepted yourself and your gender. Is that right?

Vicki: Oh yes. I tried and tried up until I was about 8 to deny I am a girl. I would sneak down to the corner drugstore and buy some cheap make-up to try to put it on. I would borrow my sister's clothing from the laundry basket and wear it in my room, just pretending to be a girl. Then I felt bad about what I was doing and threw away all the make-up and returned the clothing. Only to go back and do it again:

buy more make-up, keep dressing up in private, and really enjoying the feeling of the clothing, and imagining what my life would be like as a girl.

Chaplain: You had strong feelings about who you were that didn't go away.

Vicki: Nope, they only came back stronger, like a weed.

Chaplain: Weeds can be annoying and persistent. Is there another way to describe your feelings that might sound a bit more positive?

Vicki: How 'bout like grass, a perennial grass that grows back every year?

Chaplain: That seems truer to your delight in who you are.

Vicki: Yeah, now I get to dress up like a girl every day. I love it!

Chaplain: I can tell you enjoy your femininity. (*Pauses*) Do you have people in your life now who accept you?

Vicki: You know the Church believes it is a sin. I am so fed up with the Catholic Church and all the crap they have done in my lifetime with priest scandals and abuse. They hardly seem an authority of sexuality, when they can't keep it in their pants.

Chaplain: That's some strong feelings about the Church, I can understand. They have had immoral scandals reported, but of course all Church denominations are imperfect. The Church is not God, you know. I think at best it can be a place where God is experienced and known. At worst, there is brokenness and wrongdoing. (*Pauses*) What impact does all this have on your personal belief in God?

Vicki: I believe. I do. Jesus is the model for me...really who I want to be like. I mean, he was loving to everybody, wasn't he? Prostitutes, lepers, outsiders? I think we should be more loving and accepting like Jesus.

Chaplain: Jesus modelled the values of love and acceptance that you hope to follow.

Vicki: I had a really powerful spiritual experience with my dead mother a few months ago.

Chaplain: Really? Do you want to tell me about it?

Vicki: I don't know if you believe this but I felt my mother come and visit me through a disabled youth who is a volunteer at my workplace. I was overshadowed with a feeling of love and acceptance through this girl who was my mother's spirit. I had a strong feeling of assurance from my mother telling me, through this disabled kid, that she loves me.

Chaplain: I believe you. That sounds very powerful, having your mother's spirit tell you she accepts and loves you.

Vicki: It was. I still feel my mom's presence whenever I see this girl at work. Also, I have a few of my nieces and nephews who are fine with me. They have adjusted from having an uncle to an aunt and think I am kind of cool. One of my brothers is also okay with me and at least talks with me on family holidays.

Chaplain: So, many members of your family do accept you, or are in the process of developing new relationships with you as female.

Vicki: They are. It just takes time I guess.

Chaplain: It may help to think about your own coming-out process. How many years it has taken you to come to the point of accepting who you are and transitioning? Families and friends go through a similar coming-out process. It takes people time to adjust – and everyone does it at their own pace.

Vicki: That makes sense. I am about halfway through this process with my therapist. I would like to find a church though, one where I can go as myself, and meet some friends.

Chaplain: What have you tried?

Vicki: Well I used to go to the Q Center and hang out. I think they have some social groups or activities posted I could try and join.

I know the Pride parade is happening in a couple of weeks. I haven't been to one yet, so I thought I might try that.

Chaplain: Those are great ideas! I also know that several faith communities that are welcoming of LGBT folks will march in the parade.

Vicki: Really? Church groups?

Chaplain: Oh yes, many church groups march. It might be a really good place to see how many Christians actively support gay and transgender folk. I think there are also a couple of Catholic churches in town that are openly affirming. I can give you the website if you want to do some research.

Vicki: Sure, I would love to do that. I guess all Catholic churches aren't the same.

Chaplain: No, all churches in any denomination aren't the same. I encourage you to visit several and try them out. It can help to call first and speak with the pastor or priest. Tell them who you are and what you are looking for, and that way you can tell if it is an accepting place, and you will know someone when you visit. Next month we are having an event here in the auditorium to celebrate Pride month and LGBT veterans. You are welcome to come to that if you like. I will be there helping.

Vicki: Thank you. I will see if I have an appointment that day, so I am on campus already. I think I am ready to go back to church now, or at least try. *(Pauses)* Do you really think God loves me like this?

Chaplain: Yes, I really do.

Discussion

Assessment

My spiritual assessment model is based on the Great Commandment in the Christian tradition:

> Jesus replied: 'Love the Lord your God with all your heart and with all your soul and with all your mind. This is the first and greatest commandment. And the second is like it: Love your neighbour as yourself. All the Law and Prophets hang on these two commandments.' (Matthew 22.37)

This commandment teaches the importance of a relationship with self (intrapersonal), relationships with others (interpersonal), and a relationship with God/Holy (transpersonal). Through my 30 years of direct ministry and work as a chaplain educator I have discovered that these three focuses are found in most every major religious tradition. They also have corresponding spiritual needs: self-worth (intrapersonal), belonging (interpersonal), and meaning and direction (transpersonal). Addressing these needs happens through the chaplain's intentional engagement based on the veteran's need for self-worth (blessing/affirmation), belonging (reconciliation/forgiveness), or meaning and direction (universal awareness, call to service). I was first exposed to this model during my clinical pastoral education by my supervisor, Dennis Kenny. The model, now known as the Spiritual Assessment and Intervention Model (AIM), was further developed by Michele Shields (Shields, Kestenbaum and Dunn 2015).

Vicki personally felt relief and celebration about her transition (intrapersonal). She had grief related to her family and their judgement of her new gender identity (interpersonal). This grief was mixed with anger at the Roman Catholic Church, around not only her personal gender identity but the Church's past stands on sexuality and abuse scandals (transpersonal). She challenged the practices of Roman Catholicism that she felt were opposite to the core Christian beliefs of love and acceptance she was attempting to follow. Vicki was seeking a faith community where she could experience congruence between her beliefs and her embodiment in the world.

Interventions

I used ACT in listening and responding to Vicki during this session. My plan included demonstrating acceptance of Vicki as worthy, drawing on her own inner sense of 'rightness' about her gender, which is consistent with the ACT principle of *acceptance* of inner experience. She reported knowing she was female from the age of 8 after several instances of trying to deny it, after which her feelings only returned stronger, 'like a weed'. When I asked her if there was another word with a more positive connotation to describe her inner knowing, she smiled and said, 'How 'bout like grass, a perennial grass that grows back every year?' From a spiritual perspective as well as the ACT understanding, language has great power to both define and reshape our reality. I often invite people to consider the words they use to describe themselves and their experience as a way of empowering them to define their own experience.

Through an ACT-based approach to *perspective-taking*, Vicki was able to give her family more room to have their own experiences without as much judgement. She acknowledged that, as a male, relationships were not well developed in her family, especially her with father, whose expectations of her as a son were never realised; this gender transition embodied that loss for them both.

Using the ACT core process of *self as context,* Vicki deeply grieved her loss while maintaining a sense of the continuous 'self' that had been present since her earliest remembering. Her spiritual experience – meeting her mother through a disabled youth – may be thought of as a transcendent encounter with self, spirit, or even Jesus embodied in the youth. Vicki's deep recognition and embrace of her spiritual self fostered her resilience and courage in the transitioning and coming-out processes.

In speaking about her conflicted feelings about the Roman Catholic Church and its stances on sexuality, I invited Vicki to consider separating her personal faith in God from the institutional Church through *defusing* rule-based assumptions. Whereas 'rules, in contrast to values, reflect directions or imperatives about what actions are appropriate or inappropriate...religious and spiritual traditions often include moral expectations...attached to religious figures that epitomise the essence of the religion's value system' (Farnsworth 2016, pp.114 and 116). Vicki's understanding of Jesus as one who welcomed the poor and outcast gave her hope that she too was accepted by God. It also provided clarity about her own religious values of love and acceptance.

Outcomes

During our session, I used ACT principles in addressing Vicki's intrapersonal and interpersonal needs for *self-compassion* and *perspective-taking* with herself and family. In responding to transpersonal needs with her faith, I drew on the concepts of *defusion* and *committed action based on her values*. She personally felt an inward sense of rightness with her gender expression after years of attempting to deny or change it. Vicki had already invested a great deal in her gender transition and self-presentation in the world. She left our session hearing she was blessed in God's eyes. She had a greater understanding of the coming-out process for herself, which allowed for greater acceptance of her family's process of adjusting to her new gender identity. Vicki embraced a broader view of her faith as rooted in her understanding of Jesus and spiritual experiences not tethered to any organised religion. She left with resources that could help her to engage in communities for friendship and faith renewal, living out her values of love and acceptance.

Conclusion

One of the transformative gifts transgender Christians give to the body of Christ is a reminder of God's promise to make all things new (Lowe 2017). Co-creation with God, physically, emotionally, mentally and spiritually, is something I have been both challenged by and witness to in ministry with transgender veterans. I have had the privilege of seeing co-creation emerging and embodied slowly over months through their transitions.

Transgender persons live out a faithfulness to themselves that is radically challenging to many of us who struggle with self-worth. Vicki reminded me that the cost of being true to oneself and one's calling can be family rejection. In the Christian tradition, Jesus understood this well and reminds us to 'shake the dust off your feet' (Matthew 10.14) and consider 'Who is my mother, and who are my brothers?' (Matthew 12.48) when choosing values of love and acceptance. The desire to belong is a core spiritual need that Vicki was seeking in understanding her relationship with her father and with the Roman Catholic Church. She remains in an ongoing process of acceptance and reconciliation with her family that also means living her life even at the risk of losing those relationships. I may have missed an opportunity to help her grieve this relationship more, as it was her stated concern coming into the visit. While offering her resources to seek out welcoming faith communities, I affirmed her experience of a visit from her deceased mother through another marginalised person as confirmation of her spiritual connection. My personal theology and professional practice has been stretched to consider the unity of mind-body through the lives of transgender persons. I believe that duality, of any kind, is a false way of categorising. Duality helps us to understand, control and define our experiences but it is not authentic and embracing of the paradoxical reality of life.

References

Farnsworth, J. (2016). 'Enhancing Religious and Spiritual Values through Committed Action.' In J.A. Nieuwsma, R.D. Walser and S.C. Hayes (eds) *ACT for Clergy and Pastoral Counselors: Using Acceptance and Commitment Therapy to Bridge Psychological and Spiritual Care* (pp.109–125). Oakland, CA: Context Press.

Kauth, M. and Shipherd, J. (2016). 'Transforming a system: Improving patient-centered care for sexual and gender minority veterans.' *LGBT Health*, 3, 3, 1–3.

Lowe, M. (2017). 'From the same spirit: Receiving the theological gifts of transgender Christians.' *Dialog: A Journal of Theology*, 56, 1, 28–37.

McDermott, J. (2017). 'Few veterans expelled under "Don't Ask" policy seek remedy.' Available at www.military.com/daily-news/2016/06/25/few-veterans-expelled-dont-ask-policy-seek-remedy.html, accessed 14 January 2018.

Meyer, I.H. (2007). 'Prejudice and Discrimination as Social Stressors.' In I.H. Meyer and M.E. Northridge (eds) *The Health of Sexual Minorities: Public Health Perspectives on Lesbian, Gay, Bisexual and Transgender Populations* (pp. 242–267). New York, NY: Springer.

Nieuwsma, J.A., Walser, R.D. and Hayes, S.C. (eds) (2016). *ACT for Clergy and Pastoral Counselors: Using Acceptance and Commitment Therapy to Bridge Psychological and Spiritual Care.* Oakland, CA: Context Press.

Raifman, J., Moscoe, E., Austin, S.B. and McConnell, M. (2017). 'Difference-in-differences analysis of the association between state same-sex marriage policies and adolescent suicide attempts.' *JAMA Pediatrics*, 171, 4, 350–356.

Shields, M., Kestenbaum, A. and Dunn, L.B. (2015). 'Spiritual AIM and the work of the chaplain: A model for assessing spiritual need and outcomes in relationship.' *Palliative and Supportive Care*, 13, 1, 75–89.

Chapter 6

'I was able to go to confession'

– Mrs Helen, a survivor of military sexual trauma perpetrated by a religious leader

Valerie C. Sanders

Introduction

The reality of sexual assault in the military has received more attention since the early 1990s when military service members were encouraged to report any incidents of sexual harassment or rape to their commanding officer. Reports of sexual assault and harassment among active duty personnel and cadets have informed public law and increased research specifically focused on the potential traumatic stress associated with these experiences. The Department of Veterans Affairs has adopted the term military sexual trauma (MST), defining it as psychological trauma resulting from a physical assault of a sexual nature or sexual harassment which occurred while the veteran was serving on active duty, active duty training, or inactive duty training.

Although the term MST was coined some decades ago, the history of sexual harassment and assault extends back to the early years of the US military (Hyun, Pavao and Kimerling 2009). Efforts to estimate the prevalence of MST among veterans indicates that 41 per cent of women and 4 per cent of men reported MST (Barth *et al.* 2016). Under-reporting incidents of MST has skewed the statistical data. The reluctance to report MST continues to be rooted in fear, specifically the fear of the unknown, expressed in the question, 'What would happen next?' Barriers to reporting have included embarrassment or stigma, fear of a negative career impact, and confusion about what behaviours constitute sexual harassment or assault. Other barriers included lack of consequences for the perpetrator, negative reactions from peers, and uncertainty about confidentiality. The widespread fear of reporting sexual assaults is well grounded. Many women have come forward with their stories of sexual assaults and experienced mistreatment by the military and the subsequent destruction of their military careers (Cook *et al.* 2005).

Although there is data regarding sexual assault of adults by both Protestant and Catholic clergy, much of the data that has been gathered over recent decades regarding priests has been focused on minor children or adult survivors of childhood sexual abuse. Less is known about the sexual assault of adults by clergy, either in a one-time sexual encounter or in repeated sexual encounters over a prolonged timeframe, which often implies a consensual relationship (Frawley-O'Dea 2004). Evidence suggests that religious authorities have not responded appropriately to reported cases of adult sexual encounters with priests. 'Catholic church [*sic*] spokesmen point out that priests are only human, subject to irresistible passion, even as they invoke the holiness of church rules and their institution's special treatment under the First Amendment' (Schneider 1993). During court proceedings involving two priests serving the Roman Catholic Diocese of Madison, Wisconsin, the Diocese maintained that it had dealt adequately with the misconduct of two priests who both admitted to having sexual relationships with women in their parish. The two women involved accused the priests and sued them for violating a fiduciary trust as counsellors and priests. The emotional and psychological damage the women suffered was exacerbated by the Church's refusal to take their claims seriously and its unwillingness to provide support to them once the violations were exposed (Schneider 1993).

Background

This case study reports my care for 'Mrs Helen' (a pseudonym), a 65-year-old married, Caucasian veteran and a devout Roman Catholic. The case describes the use of acceptance and commitment therapy to help Mrs Helen begin viewing the events of her life without being overwhelmed by thoughts and feelings that accompanied her past memories of sexual violation. My work with Mrs Helen focused primarily on her desire to confess formally the anger she felt towards the priest who molested her while she served as a nurse in the Navy during the Vietnam era of the early 1970s. Since that time, Mrs Helen kept the incident a secret from both her family and her friends, primarily because of shame, guilt, judgement and self-condemnation. Although MST is a significant focus of this case, more significant and of greater impact on Mrs Helen was the abuse of power and sexual molestation that was perpetrated by a military chaplain, a Roman Catholic priest who was the trusted leader of her faith community. Consistent with her current desire to have her story told, Mrs Helen extended her consent and was grateful that part of her experience would be shared in this clinical case presentation.

I am an African American and an ordained itinerate elder in the African Methodist Episcopal Church. I have served as a spiritual care professional for over 20 years. I currently serve as a staff chaplain in a large healthcare system in the south-eastern region of the United States. I am also a licensed marriage and family therapist and have established a pastoral counselling clinic in an outpatient clinic, about four miles from the primary medical centre campus. I was referred to work with Mrs Helen as a chaplain but the complexity of her situation required the integration of both counselling skills and pastoral care. My sessions with Mrs Helen engaged the six core processes of ACT (Hayes and Lillis 2012). ACT is client-centred and based on the premise that clients are whole and complete individuals who possess everything that they need to move forwards and grow. In ACT, clients set their course in the counselling relationship. The psychological changes that need to occur are more like learning to embrace oneself than repairing something that is broken (Hayes and Lillis 2012). In these ways, ACT principles and processes are conducive to integrating with pastoral care.

Case study

Before contacting the Chaplain's Office, Mrs Helen had participated in group therapy with mental health providers in the MST clinic, followed by 19 weeks of individual psychotherapy with a psychologist using cognitive processing therapy (CPT), a specific type of cognitive behavioural therapy often used to treat post-traumatic stress disorder. Mrs Helen was referred to the Chaplain's Office because her psychologist identified Mrs Helen's understandings of her faith as 'barriers' to her recovery. Mrs Helen had not responded well to CPT, because she felt that she was being challenged to identify what her role was in the molestation and felt she was being blamed.

The referral to a chaplain was informal, and Mrs Helen was given the pertinent information in order to contact a chaplain on her own. The psychologist informed her that 'maybe a chaplain could help' her sort out the issues that evolved during their counselling. After she had collaborated with the psychologist, the initial treatment plan was to meet with the chaplain and work through the 'barriers' and then, if therapy was still indicated, to return to the referring psychologist for additional CPT. After scheduling an initial appointment with Mrs Helen, I reviewed her chart and contacted the referring psychologist to discuss her work with Mrs Helen. The psychologist shared that she believed Mrs Helen was stuck due to some of her spiritual understandings.

In lay terms, ACT is utilised to encourage clients to 'hold and move' (Nieuwsma 2016) – holding their pleasant and pleasurable experiences along with the daunting and devastating, yet simultaneously moving, experiences. In spite of the more common reaction of becoming stuck either in wanderlust or sadness, moving forwards in the direction of our values is the desired goal of ACT. Following the ACT model, the goal of Mrs Helen's care was to enhance her ability to exhibit signs of cognitive flexibility, no longer condemning herself for the actions of others and beginning to live out her values more consistently. Although many of Mrs Helen's values were strongly evidenced in her life, some had been compromised for decades due to living and suffering privately with MST. At the point at which Mrs Helen sought pastoral counselling with a chaplain, the pain of her private suffering was unbearable. Another primary goal of ACT is to move towards 'transforming unbearable pain into liveable disappointment' (Meador and Nieuwsma 2016) by achieving psychological flexibility. This flexibility is evidenced by one's ability to adapt behaviour to varying contexts and situations in the pursuit of one's core values (Nieuwsma 2016). Mrs Helen described the pain caused by her suffering as deep and often overwhelming. I will describe some of our key sessions and the ACT core processes associated with them.

Session 1: Confiding her story

Mrs Helen arrived promptly for her appointment and appeared relieved to finally have an opportunity to share her story. During this session, she described her time of military service and her fulfilling nursing career. She shared that as a young adult in the military, serving in Europe, it was important to her that she continued to live out the faith that she was baptised and confirmed into. To that end, she attended Mass regularly. She knew all of the priests who served on the military base where she was stationed and respected each of them, also experiencing a few of them as friends.

While on a bus excursion with military personnel and some military chaplains, she was the last one to board the bus and had to take the last remaining seat next to one of the priests. Mrs Helen had enjoyed this priest because of the way he led Mass and also because he was very personable. She shared that she was a little bit excited to sit beside him during their extended trip. They shared good conversation, reflecting on the richness of the tour that they had experienced and life in general. Eventually, Mrs Helen drifted off to sleep, only to be awakened by the priest fondling her breasts. She was mortified and very confused as she remained silent for the remainder of the bus ride back to the base. Her shock and confusion kept her silent about this significant violation. She spoke to no one about the incident, not even her closest friends. She continued to hold on to the anger that she felt towards the priest and had a strong desire to confront him, while also acknowledging that she had no idea where he was residing. In this first encounter, I explored the possibility of Mrs Helen writing a letter to her perpetrator as a means of venting and releasing some of her anger. She thought that it would be extremely difficult but said she would consider it.

As Mrs Helen continued to share her narrative, she revealed that prior to the molestation by the priest she had been raped by a fellow service member with whom she worked. She described that she and a group of other service members had been out together to attend a special concert in a nearby town. The comrade, who offered to give her a ride home after the concert, forced himself on her and raped her in her own home. After the rape, Mrs Helen continued to see the perpetrator on a regular basis while performing her normal duty functions. After a short period of time, Mrs Helen told one of her closest friends about the rape, but they did not believe a sexual assault could be reported without experiencing retaliation. Mrs Helen understood that there were no vehicles for reporting sexual assault at that time, but she continued to carry guilt for remaining silent.

During her time in the military, after the acquaintance rape and priest molestation, Mrs Helen met her husband. He also worked in the medical field and was also a devout Catholic. Mrs Helen never mentioned either violation to him, believing these incidents to be secret parts of her life that were never to be revealed. They were married within a year of beginning their courtship and had a son and daughter within the first five years of their marriage. The couple always lived a very modest lifestyle, consistently living out their faith by attending Mass weekly as a family and participating in activities and events in their local parish. Mrs Helen shared that, although the rape had been difficult and traumatic, the greater damage had been experienced as a result of the molestation by the priest. She expressed that she had 'gotten over' the rape but struggled with anxiety and depression because of the molestation.

Session 3: Present-moment awareness

In this session, I made efforts to help Mrs Helen observe the difficult feelings and memories of her past along with the anxieties she may have had about her future. It provided a step towards releasing the power or influence of the feelings and memories in her life.

Chaplain: It sounds like all of your thoughts and fears are preventing you from fully embracing the Sacrament of Reconciliation.

Mrs Helen: I just feel like everything would be better if I could just take it to confession and have the priest tell me what to do to get rid of my anger.

Chaplain: As we begin to work towards that goal, I know that you are aware of some types of meditation that were introduced to you during the group sessions in the MST clinic. I remember that you shared that you have not had the opportunity to experience the potential benefits of meditation.

Mrs Helen: Yes, it's not a part of my tradition, but in the group that I participated in, several women mentioned that they have tried it and it has helped them.

Chaplain: Along similar lines as meditation, are you familiar with mindfulness practices?

Mrs Helen: No, and it sounds like it may not be consistent with my faith; remember, I am Catholic.

Chaplain: I remember that your Catholic faith is very important to you, and exercising your faith is one of your core values.

Mrs Helen: Yes, it is my life.

Chaplain: Mindfulness provides the opportunity to pay attention to things that we may not regularly pay attention to, such as our thoughts and feelings. Throughout the course of a day we probably have thousands of thoughts and feelings that come and go, and although we share space with them, we often don't see them when they are with us.

Mrs Helen: That's interesting.

Chaplain: Being mindful allows us to maintain complete awareness of our thoughts, emotions, or experiences without having any judgement about them. It can be helpful to just pay attention for a few moments. They are neither good nor bad; they just are. Would it be okay if I led you in a brief mindfulness exercise?

Mrs Helen: Okay.

Chaplain: Allow your body to sit in a comfortable position, and when you are comfortable, you can feel free to close your eyes. Become aware of your body sitting on the chair and your feet in contact with the floor.

Mrs Helen: I need to open my eyes. I cannot get comfortable with my eyes closed. When that priest touched me, I was either falling asleep or waking up and my eyes were closed.

Chaplain: That would be perfectly fine. Try to focus your gaze on one particular spot on the floor. Now imagine that you are standing by the bank of a gently flowing stream, watching the water flow past you. Imagine feeling the ground beneath your feet, hearing the sounds of water flowing past, and observe how the stream looks as you watch it. Imagine that there are leaves from trees, all different shapes and sizes and colours, floating by you on the stream. You are simply watching these float on the stream; this is all you need to do for the next few moments. Now, I'd like you to notice each sensation, feeling and thought that you become aware of and imagine placing each individual one on a leaf as it floats on by. Do this regardless of whether the thoughts and feelings are positive or negative, pleasurable or painful. Whatever they are, place them on a leaf. If your thoughts stop, just watch the stream. Sooner or later your thoughts will start up again. Allow the stream to flow at its own rate. Notice any urges you may have to speed up or slow down the stream, and let these be on leaves as well. Let the stream flow how it will.

If you have thoughts or feelings about doing this exercise, place these on leaves as well. If a leaf gets stuck or won't go away, let it hang around. For a little while, all you are doing is observing this experience – there is no need to force the leaf down the stream. If you find yourself getting caught up with a thought or feeling, and the stream disappears, just notice what you got caught up with, and gently turn this into a leaf and let it float on the stream. You are just observing each experience as a leaf on the stream. It is normal and natural to lose track of this exercise, and it will keep happening. When you notice this, just bring yourself back to observing the leaves on the stream. Gently allow the image of the stream and leaves to dissolve and bring your awareness back to sitting in the chair, in my office. How was that experience for you?

Mrs Helen: Well, it was very different for me. I have never done anything like that before. It was definitely hard to stay focused. My mind kept wandering to all of the things that I need to get done today.

Chaplain: And were you able to place those thoughts on the leaves as they passed by?

Mrs Helen: I tried. What is the purpose of this exercise?

Chaplain: So often, our thoughts and feelings cause us distress. Mindfulness practices, specifically the 'Leaves on a Stream' exercise, can help you not become overwhelmed by your thoughts and emotions but to simply see them for what they are – just thoughts and emotions. Sometimes difficult memories or thoughts can greatly impact or limit the decisions that we make in our daily lives.

Mrs Helen: Yeah, I see how that may be true in my life.

Chaplain: Do you think that this is an exercise that you would use when you are alone and feeling overwhelmed by your thoughts and feelings?

Mrs Helen: I'm not sure if I will. I just pray that God will take it all away.

Session 5: Defusion

Mrs Helen was bound by the shame that had kept her secret locked in her heart along with the guilt that she carried with her for possessing feelings of anger towards her perpetrator. In ACT terms, inflexible belief in the literal meaning of one's own thoughts is termed 'cognitive fusion'. I introduced the idea of 'cognitive defusion' and invited Mrs Helen to observe her own thoughts and see them for what they were: just thoughts. We spent significant time on the thought, 'Who would believe me?' which informed her feelings of shame; and on the thought, 'God won't forgive me for my anger towards a priest', which informed her feelings of guilt that she was unable to forgive him. Here, I was inviting Mrs Helen simply to *observe* her thoughts. Despite her concentration being periodically interrupted due to the unfamiliarity of the practice, Mrs Helen found it helpful to engage the present moment. I invited her to share what she felt while observing the thoughts and what she felt about how the thoughts had informed her life.

> *Chaplain:* I want to invite you to look at your thoughts, feelings and memories, those barriers that cause you to feel stuck and prevent you from moving to the place where you want to go, to be able to confess your anger to a priest. For the purpose of this exercise, imagine that they are passengers on a bus that you are driving.

> *Mrs Helen:* Okay. Is there anyone else on the bus?

> *Chaplain:* Yes, but they are passive participants in this ride.

> *Mrs Helen:* This would have to be a pretty big, bus because I have a lot of thoughts and feelings, all of the time.

> *Chaplain:* Mrs Helen, can you name the thoughts, feelings and memories? They will be identified as passengers on the bus that you are driving.

> *Mrs Helen:* I am ashamed that I was violated by a priest. I feel guilt and shame because I can't let go of the anger. I am embarrassed that as a practising Catholic I have been unable to forgive him. I am afraid that no one would believe me. Why would anyone believe me over a priest?

> *Chaplain:* All of those thoughts and feelings are passengers on your bus and they are a very controlling and scary bunch. Picture them

as if they were a gang, working together to make you drive the bus where they want to go. What are some of the things that these passengers are saying to you?

Mrs Helen: How could you have let that happen? Who would ever believe your story? You have to keep this a secret. God will never forgive you for your unforgiving heart.

Chaplain: So as you continue to drive the bus, the gang moves from the back of the bus to the front, directly behind you, and they have got louder.

Mrs Helen: It really feels like that at times, I just feel overwhelmed by the gang of thoughts.

Chaplain: Imagine they are getting progressively louder and more intimidating. At this point you want them to get away from you, because it is overwhelming. So you decide to make a deal with them and not drive in the direction of your goal if they are willing to return to the back of the bus and sit quietly. This works only for a little while. In that moment, you may feel some relief from your thoughts and feelings, but you are still not making progress to get towards your goal. Although they may not be bothering you quite as much, the passengers have not gone away. They are still lurking at the back of the bus and can come forwards at any time.

Mrs Helen: They are always lurking and have been for 40 years.

Chaplain: What if these passengers could not hurt you or make you drive in a different direction? What if all they can do is come to the front of the bus and be scary?

Mrs Helen: Hmm.

Chaplain: If that's all they can do, then you have options in this situation. You can choose to fight with these unruly passengers, or you can choose to be willing to have them on the bus with you and continue driving in the direction that you were originally headed, moving towards your values.

Mrs Helen: I like the image, but it is so hard to ignore them. I'll try to keep that bus image in mind when I find myself feeling overwhelmed.

Chaplain: It is not an effort to ignore them or distract yourself from them but it's really about shifting your focus to what matters most to you and being able to navigate your bus in the direction that you want it to go in.

Session 6: Values clarification

Being able to identify and focus on how to live in a way that is consistent with the qualities that Mrs Helen valued was the theme of session 6. During this session, I introduced the ACT Values Sort Cards: 50 cards, each identifying a value. I instructed Mrs Helen to examine each card and place them in one of three categories: Not important, Somewhat important, or Very important. Once each value was categorised, I instructed Mrs Helen to identify her top values from the Very important category. These included: love (because Christ died for each of us); tradition (which helped to make her feel secure); and family. The core value of justice was evident in her desire to find and confront her perpetrator, as was demonstrated in her pursuit of receiving an acknowledgement and apology from the Catholic Church and the Archdiocese of the Military.

Session 8: Committed action

In ACT, committed action occurs when steps are taken that are guided and informed by values. The goal of committed action is to establish a pattern of consistently living our values or moving towards valued living, even in the midst of painful thoughts and feelings. In this session, Mrs Helen reported that she had found a parish priest to whom she could reveal the breach of her trust caused by the priest who had molested her and to confess her anger through the Sacrament of Reconciliation.

Mrs Helen: I did it! I was able to go to confession. There was a young priest, who I had never seen before. I had not planned to do it on that day but something was pulling me, not pushing me but pulling me. It was as if I had no choice, I had to do it.

Chaplain: Wow, you did it! This is what you have been working towards and you have taken the risk to confess your anger to a priest.

Mrs Helen: Yes, although it was just about a week ago, it feels surreal. I can't believe that I actually did it.

Chaplain: Tell me about that experience.

Mrs Helen: I went to another parish for confession and this parish did not have a confession booth, like my home parish does. When I entered the sanctuary, I saw a short line of people waiting to speak with the priest. I considered coming back later but then I saw the priest on the opposite side of the sanctuary, sitting on the back pew, listening to confessions and I felt compelled to wait and then felt like I was being pulled to him.

Chaplain: It sounds as if it was the right moment for you.

Mrs Helen: Yes, I could not have ever planned it.

Chaplain: I am aware that you had some concerns and anxieties about how a priest would react to your story and your anger.

Mrs Helen: No, he listened to me and was very apologetic. He was sincerely grieved by my story. At the end, he actually asked if he could give me a hug.

Chaplain: Were you comfortable with that?

Mrs Helen: Oh definitely; he was really sad about it.

Chaplain: It sounds very affirming of your pain.

Despite leaving my office with a feeling of subdued satisfaction, a piece remained missing for Mrs Helen because she had held the hopeful expectation the young priest would tell her how to release her anger. He did not. When Mrs Helen had initially sought counselling, her primary focus had been to make the confession, believing that all of her inner turmoil would be lifted if she received prescriptive instructions from a priest. So, in the absence of a quick remedy within the traditions of her faith, Mrs Helen continued engaging with the weekly pastoral counselling relationship utilising ACT with me, for about 15 additional sessions. She also continued to meet monthly with her mental health provider.

Discussion
Assessment

Mrs Helen's first encounter with MST was the result of being raped by an acquaintance a few months before she was molested by the priest. Mrs Helen had been unable to acknowledge or explore the possible significance of the acquaintance rape, because she articulated that the molestation shook her core values as defined by her theological understandings. Mrs Helen's faith tradition had taught her that men who receive Holy Orders are configured to Christ ('By the sacrament of Order, priests are configured [configurantur] to Christ' (Flannery 1975, p.885)), meaning that they fulfil their ministerial duties in the power of Christ and not by their own power. This special grace of the Holy Spirit creates a new man whose vocational calling is to serve Christ's Church faithfully.

Mrs Helen acknowledged that her anxiety would rise when she was in close proximity with a priest and that she had strategically avoided face-to-face confessional opportunities, opting for the traditional experience of engaging in confession within the safety of a confessional booth. Mrs Helen believed that through her faith in Christ, the risen Saviour, she could be made whole again. She was informed by her belief that her ability to be made whole was conditional, dependent on her willingness and ability to forgive her perpetrator. As a result of this belief, Mrs Helen condemned herself for not being able to forgive her perpetrator and believed that if others knew about her situation, they would also condemn her; therefore, her self-condemnation felt justified. Mrs Helen wrestled with feelings of betrayal by the Church while simultaneously desiring to be faithful in her relationship with God. She was fused with her theological understanding of the divine authority of the priesthood and the divinely ordered relationship between a priest and the community of faith. Mrs Helen continued to cling to her faith as a source of strength and sought answers to difficult questions about how her faith was to be lived in light of her MST and other complexities of life.

Interventions

For over 40 years, Mrs Helen had tried to avoid her thoughts and feelings regarding the trauma. Recently, she had seen articles in magazines and newspapers that described the prevalence and impact of MST, and this had unearthed the narrative that she had hidden for four decades. She sought help from the mental health providers because she felt as if she was caught in an 'undertow', which she described in this way: when she believed that she was just about to reach the surface to catch some air, then another current grabbed her and she fought with the undertow in order to survive. Mrs Helen initially believed that she had to fight and that she was expected to fight or be drowned by her painful secret. After the first few sessions with me, she began to realise that she had been expending too much energy fighting the undertow and began trying to ride with the current, trusting that she would not drown. We discussed the purpose of this consistent fighting as a means of survival and of protecting herself from experiencing unwanted emotions without sufficient support from professionals or her community. Her avoidance had been in the service of her own desire to survive in order to fulfil all of her responsibilities and obligations.

In an effort to move towards psychological flexibility, I introduced several interventions, the first of which was a brief ACT willingness activity called 'Creative Hopelessness'. This exercise, introduced during the second session, was designed to allow Mrs Helen to see the 'unworkability' of her efforts to control what was outside her control (for example, thoughts that emerged in her mind, memories, the actions of others). In ACT, the idea of acceptance does not imply that we embrace our thoughts and feelings but that we allow them to be what they are and make room for them, which releases the struggle (Harris 2009). When difficult thoughts and feelings surface, often the first reaction is to get rid of the pain but in trying to do so, the pain is often exacerbated. It creates a paradoxical experience that ACT refers to as 'experiential avoidance' (Hayes and Lillis 2012): the more we strive to avoid an inner experience, the more enmeshed we become with it. I invited Mrs Helen to share every means of experiential avoidance she had tried, and in articulating her ineffective strategies, she began to move towards the realisation that there were significant limitations in her ability to control her thoughts and feelings. Later, during that session, Mrs Helen lamented her lack of control and expressed anxiety when thinking that those uncontrollable thoughts and emotions would always be with her. From an ACT and pastoral perspective, it was important for me to stay emotionally present with her lament and anxiety and thereby model the process of simply holding this discomfort.

Much of ACT is rooted in awareness, specifically encouraging awareness of each present moment. Present-moment awareness includes paying attention to the five senses, and being aware of body and environment (Nieuwsma 2016). ACT teaches seeking present-moment awareness through the vehicle of mindfulness practices. Mindfulness is essential in the practice of ACT but, due to the external conditions of her MST experience, inviting Mrs Helen to close her eyes caused her to feel insecure and vulnerable. When we explored cognitive defusion through mindfulness during session 3, it was challenging for her to remain focused, primarily because it was unfamiliar to her and mindfulness had not been introduced within the context of her Catholic faith community. The 'Leaves on a Stream' exercise provided an introduction for Mrs Helen to begin to learn how to simply observe her thoughts and feelings, difficult ones as well as pleasant ones. She over-identified with many of her thoughts, which had led to much of her suffering.

For Mrs Helen, fusion to her thoughts was problematic because those thoughts were experienced in ways that prevented her from moving forwards and living according to her chosen values. Essentially, cognitive fusion served to keep her 'stuck' in problematic patterns of thinking that led to the familiar, inevitable consequences of emotional suffering. The difficult thoughts and feelings had been barriers to her ability to move forwards. During session 5, we explored the function of her thoughts and what end they might be serving – whether they had facilitated movement towards her values. The theme of 'Why would anyone believe me?' was consistent within Mrs Helen's narrative and questioned the validity of her story. This thought primarily informed her projected theological understandings: Mrs Helen shared that if she heard someone else share a similar story about a priest, she would question the victim's integrity. In order to encourage her observation of both internal and external experiences, I introduced an ACT metaphor called the 'Passengers on the Bus'. To begin this exercise, I needed to identify where Mrs Helen wanted to go and what would define her valued direction. She wanted to be able to confess her anger through the Sacrament of Reconciliation and begin to move towards forgiveness. To do this, she believed she must be relieved of the guilt and shame that she carried about negative feelings she had towards the priest, even though he was her perpetrator.

During session 6, I was able to facilitate the values clarification exercise with Mrs Helen. This brief activity allowed her to identify and re-engage the values that were consistent with her ability to fully live her understanding of her faith. Mrs Helen provided examples of how she had lived her values in the past, and she explored ways that she has been led to honour her values as she moved forwards. I was surprised in session 8 when Mrs Helen shared her moment of spontaneous confession due to her consistent level of cognitive fusion. Being able to acknowledge justice as a core value compelled Mrs Helen to spontaneously share her painful story with a priest whom she had not previously known.

Outcomes

The formal practice of Mrs Helen's faith was demonstrated in her commitment to attending Mass and receiving the Eucharist weekly, even when she was travelling or on vacation. She believed in the reconciliation granted as a result of the confession of sins (her anger) to a priest, who then mediates God's forgiveness through a prescribed penance and absolution. Although Mrs Helen's committed action involved making a confession to a priest, the confessional nature of our relationship allowed her to feel safe in sharing her narrative and to feel affirmed in the midst of her pain.

Mrs Helen experienced a few moments of committed action. The first demonstration of her moving from a place of being stuck and paralysed with fusion was being able to articulate her anger and embrace at least two opportunities to confess her anger to a priest during the Sacrament of Reconciliation face to face, without the traditional confessional booth. Making these steps allowed her to be vulnerable in the presence of a priest while also feeling supported. Mrs Helen has subsequently written a letter to the Pope as a cathartic effort to report the violation to the highest office within the Catholic Church, and she has taken the initiative to establish a relationship with an MST therapist to explore the significance of her response to the rape and the molestation.

Conclusion

Living her values has allowed Mrs Helen to move closer to psychological flexibility. She was no longer completely paralysed by her thoughts and feelings, even though she periodically became overwhelmed by feelings of shame. Although she continued to desire an external remedy for her internal turmoil, her desire for justice fuelled her letter writing and subsequent conversation with the Archdiocese of the Military. Her hope to experience relief from the MST was found in her search for accountability and a belief that she would be granted some emotional restitution by both the military and the Catholic Church.

As a fellow traveller with Mrs Helen for several months, I am humbled that she was able to share her secret and begin to process her understanding of her MST experience. Her willingness to receive pastoral care from a chaplain directly addressed some of her unique struggles. She experienced holding the pain of betrayal by one clergy member while taking the risk of trusting in another. The secret that she had tried to tuck away for 40 years was finally revealed, and she entered the early stages of being able to identify the impact that the molestation had had on her life. Hope, for Mrs Helen, lay in her belief in redemption and restoration.

References

Barth, S.K., Kimerling, R.E., Pavao, J., McCutcheon, S.J. *et al.* (2016). 'Military sexual trauma among recent veterans: Correlates of sexual assault and sexual harassment.' *American Journal of Preventive Medicine*, 50, 1, 77–86.

Cook, P.J., Jones, A.M., Lipari, R.N. and Lancaster, A.R. (2005). 'Service Academy 2005 Sexual Harassment and Assault Survey, DMDC Report No. 2005-018.' Arlington, VA: Defense Manpower Data Center Survey & Program Evaluation Division. Available at www.sapr.mil/public/docs/research/DMDC-Academy-2005-Survey. pdf, accessed 14 January 2018.

Flannery, A. (ed.) (1975). 'Decree on the Ministry and Life of Priests (Presbyterorum Ordinis).' In A. Flannery (ed.) *Vatican Council II: Volume I: The Conciliar and Post Conciliar Documents* (pp.863–902). Northport, NY: Costello Publishing Co; Dublin: Dominican Publications.

Frawley-O'Dea, M.G. (2004). 'The history and consequences of the sexual-abuse crisis in the Catholic Church.' *Studies in Gender and Sexuality*, 5, 1, 11–30.

Harris, R. (2009). *ACT Made Simple*. Oakland, CA: New Harbinger Press.

Hayes, S.C., and Lillis, J. (2012). *Acceptance and Commitment Therapy*. Washington, DC: American Psychological Association.

Hyun, J., Pavao, J. and Kimerling, R. (2009). 'Military sexual trauma.' *PTSD Research Quarterly*, 20, 2, 1–3. Available at www.ptsd.va.gov/professional/newsletters/ research-quarterly/V20N2.pdf, accessed 14 January 2018.

Meador, K. and Nieuwsma, J. (2016). 'ACT: Living in the Midst.' A presentation given at the Mental Health Integration for Chaplain Services, training intensive, Denver, CO, 11 May 2016.

Nieuwsma, J.A. (2016). 'Empirical Foundations for Integrating Religious and Spiritual Practices with Psychotherapy.' In J.A. Nieuwsma, R.D. Walser, and S.C. Hayes (eds) *ACT for Clergy and Pastoral Counselors: Using Acceptance and Commitment Therapy to Bridge Psychological and Spiritual Care* (pp.3–18). Oakland, CA: Context Press.

Schneider, P. (1993). 'Sacred sin: Powerful priests involved with vulnerable women.' Available at www.bishop-accountability.org/news13/1993_06_19_Schneider_ SacredSin_J_Gibbs_Clauder_2.htm, accessed 14 January 2018.

Chapter 7

Critical Response to Veterans' Case Studies

A Chaplaincy Perspective

Andrew Todd

In responding to these case studies, I do so from a different context to that of both authors and my fellow respondent. I locate myself in relation to chaplaincy within the UK, primarily as an educator and researcher in that world (although with some experience of being a practitioner). My engagement spans various kinds of chaplaincy, including significant involvement with both military and healthcare chaplains and work with them on reflective practice. The tradition of reflection in the British context differs from that in North America. In the UK, the major models are not rooted in clinical pastoral education but rather in the use of the pastoral cycle (for example, Green 2009) and the traditions that flow from it (for example, Graham, Walton and Ward 2005). Of particular significance for UK chaplains has been the question of theological reflection (including in a multifaith context). In addition, British chaplains, even in healthcare, are perhaps less likely to see themselves as clinicians than their North American counterparts, although the question of their professionalism and professionalisation is nonetheless important. What strikes me about these case studies is rooted in this setting, experience and engagement.

Intentionality and being person-centred

In relation to the practice of the chaplains in this section, central to both their approaches is acceptance and commitment therapy. As Chaplain Hanson indicates, 'ACT involves developing psychological flexibility through six core processes: acceptance, defusion, present-moment awareness, self as context, values, and committed action'; and as Chaplain Sanders indicates, 'ACT is client-centred and based on the premise that clients are whole and complete individuals who possess everything that they need to move forwards and grow. In ACT, clients set their course in the counselling relationship.' Such a person-centred approach would be familiar in the UK setting, where the much-quoted Rogerian principle of 'unconditional positive regard' has played a significant role in the development of a non-judgemental approach to chaplaincy that is responsive to the service user's espoused needs, beliefs and choices.

What I notice from both case studies, however, is a tension between the dimension of acceptance and being person-centred and the directing framework of ACT. While clearly empowering of both clients, this therapeutic approach nonetheless gives rise to *intended* outcomes in both cases. There is a 'plan' at work, which includes the offering of 'interventions' with expected 'outcomes'. This kind of intentional language is less common in the UK setting. For example, the UK Board of Healthcare Chaplaincy (UKBHC) Standards for Healthcare Chaplaincy Services uses a slightly softer register: 'Patients and their carers have their spiritual and religious needs assessed and addressed' (UKBHC 2009, p.5). Other types of UK chaplaincy, such as in the military, would use even less clinical language about their practice.

This is not to devalue the use of ACT models. For the clients in both cases, it certainly appears that 'defusion' was important for each of them; in the one case, the defusion of church attitudes to gender from God's acceptance of us as human beings; and in the other, the defusion of priestly authority from the need to recognise and be reconciled with feelings of anger at a priest abuser. Yet the ACT approach does seem to over-direct the chaplains' responses. In the case offered by Chaplain Hanson, the following ACT principles were at work in the interaction with Vicki, in just one 50-minute encounter: self-compassion, perspective-taking, defusion, and committed action based on the client's values. A particular example of where the application of these principles may have taken attention away from the client's perspective is the invitation to Vicki to consider different language for her strong feelings about identity and gender being 'like a weed'. The alternative simile of grass may well have been helpful but the ambivalence of Vicki's own simile remained to be explored.

In the case offered by Chaplain Sanders, the relationship with Mrs Helen extended over a large number of sessions. Yet even in this case, the ACT model seems to me to be somewhat over-directive in the chaplain–client relationship. Over a longer period of time, a number of specific interventions were offered, including: an activity called 'Creative Hopelessness'; present-moment awareness through the vehicle of mindfulness practices; the 'Passengers on the Bus' exercise; and the use of ACT Values Sort Cards. From the chaplain's evaluation of, and reflection on, her own practice, it is clear that she perceives and works with an overall coherence that holds and integrates these exercises. What is not clear is whether the use of so many new approaches, even over a more extended counselling relationship, allowed the client to apprehend the coherence of the experiences and integrate them into her own life and practice.

The use of mindfulness is a particular example of an approach that would require both longer exposure to the practice and a clearer commitment from a client to engage with it. A typical mindfulness course would span eight weeks (see, for example, Williams and Penman 2011). In the case of Chaplain Sanders, the intervention was offered once, and the client remained uncertain of its value. Mrs Helen's uncertainty about mindfulness remained unresolved at that point, both because of her less than positive experience of the one exercise and because it seemed to be not yet apparent to her how mindfulness might relate to her experience of prayer in the Roman Catholic tradition.

Theological reflection

For me, a further area of response concerns theological reflection. Once again, this response is rooted in the particular aim of being person-centred, including within the theological reflection that accompanies, and is integral to, a pastoral care relationship. As in relation to the use of ACT, I want to make it clear that I respect the theological reflection of the two chaplains who have offered their work as case studies. My desire is to engage in dialogue with their reflection as a way of deepening our shared learning.

One aspect of my response here has to do with working with the 'lived theology' of the client (see McGuire 2008; Todd 2017). In Chaplain Hanson's case, Vicki offered this description of a spiritual experience she had had:

> *Vicki:* I don't know if you believe this but I felt my mother come and visit me through a disabled youth who is a volunteer at my workplace. I was overshadowed with a feeling of love and acceptance through this girl who was my mother's spirit. I had a strong feeling of assurance from my mother telling me, through this disabled kid, that she loves me.

However, in her section on 'Interventions', Chaplain Hanson reframed this experience in the following way: '[Vicki's] spiritual experience – meeting her mother through a disabled youth – may be thought of as a transcendent encounter with self, spirit, or even Jesus embodied in the youth'. This rather distracts attention from what Vicki herself said, that the experience was of the presence of her mother. This might be seen as unorthodox or unusual (although my pastoral experience suggests rather that encounters with those who have died are not uncommon), but it was Vicki's lived experience and indicates a key aspect of her lived theology. This should be central to our theological reflection.

A further aspect of my response has to do with a particular challenge of these case studies for the chaplains' theological reflection: grappling with their clients' identification with the Roman Catholic Church – a continued aspect of their lived religion. A core issue in each case study is the combination of a continued desire on the part of each client to find acceptance or community within the Roman Catholic Church, with a real and entirely appropriate sense of the fallibility of that church. Mrs Helen had experienced that directly through being molested by a priest; Vicki knew this indirectly through accounts of sexual misdemeanours perpetrated by priests, which she rightly viewed as undermining the authority of the Church. Both chaplains offer us a view of their serious reflection on the issues arising from this, which complements their careful practice and support for their clients.

So, each chaplain to some extent enabled their client to create some distance from the Roman Catholic Church and its authority, especially by helping them identify and appropriate their personal values. Thus, Chaplain Hanson offered Vicki an opportunity to 'consider separating her personal faith in God from the institutional Church through *defusing* rule-based assumptions'. In the transcript of their meeting, Vicki's personal faith was identified by both chaplain and client with Jesus, and with the values he embodied and the relationships he had with the marginalised, over and against the Church. Chaplain Sanders continued to work with the fusion generated by Mrs Helen's high view and theology of the priesthood, which held her back from recognising the validity of her own narrative. Their work together also included identifying Mrs Helen's driving values.

At the same time, both chaplains also worked with their clients' desire to have a continuing sense of belonging within the Roman Catholic Church. Chaplain Hanson offered the possibility of identifying for Vicki particular Roman Catholic churches that might be more affirming and accepting of her gender identity. Chaplain Sanders accompanied Mrs Helen through her journey to being able to confess her anger towards her molester in the context of the Sacrament of Reconciliation and through her seeking restitution from different parts of the church hierarchy.

I continue to be struck by the skill exhibited by the chaplains in this. But what is perhaps not made entirely explicit, in the reflective work they do, is the risk for the clients in this process. This lies, I contend, in the difficulty of locating a newfound autonomy within the community of the Roman Catholic Church, especially given the way in which that church is constructed in the therapeutic setting. The entirely appropriate sense of a client's own authority, rooted in the identification of core personal values, may not sit happily within a community that is perceived as being primarily a rules-based institution. The possibility of cognitive dissonance is significant, not least in situations where church membership continues to be important for the client, either because, as in Vicki's case, this was an aspect of the life of her family, or because, as with Mrs Helen, being Roman Catholic remained core to her identity and sense of vocation. The risk of such a dissonance can be exacerbated by dissociating the personal and spiritual from the institutional and religious, although in these cases both chaplains mostly avoid this dichotomy.

I would suggest that there is important reflective work to be done for all of us who face this kind of challenge, in working carefully through how we construct the churches or faith communities to which clients belong. This is not about ignoring their fallibility or being unquestioning about their idealised theologies but rather about affirming that they *can* be nurturing communities supportive of personal values; and that they *can* locate those values within a positive sense of theonomy – the authority of a God that holds us, rather than subjugates us. In the case of Chaplain Sanders, this was epitomised by the priest who received Mrs Helen's confession with empathy, rather than authoritarianism, paralleling the empathy of the chaplain.

In conclusion, I am grateful to the two chaplains and to their clients for offering these thought-provoking case studies. I offer my response as part of a transatlantic dialogue about chaplaincy practice and reflection. I continue to reflect on how intentionality sits with being person-centred; and on how we reflect theologically about membership of faith communities. And I carry from the two case studies a strong sense of the distinctiveness of chaplaincy, in the way it accompanies and supports people, in their pain, in their search for identity, and in their interaction with families, healthcare, the military and faith communities.

References

Graham, E.L., Walton, H. and Ward, F. (2005). *Theological Reflection: Methods*. London: SCM Press.

Green, L. (2009). *Let's Do Theology: Resources for Contextual Theology* (2nd edn). London; New York, NY: Mowbray.

McGuire, M.B. (2008). *Lived Religion: Faith and Practice in Everyday Life*. Oxford; New York, NY: Oxford University Press.

Todd, A. (2017). 'Conclusion.' In J. Caperon, A. Todd and J. Walters *A Christian Theology of Chaplaincy* (pp.159–168). London; Philadelphia, PA: Jessica Kingsley Publishers.

UKBHC (2009). *Standards for Healthcare Chaplaincy Services 2009*. Cambridge: UK Board of Healthcare Chaplaincy. Available at www.ukbhc.org.uk/sites/default/files/standards_for_healthcare_chapalincy_services_2009.pdf, accessed 14 January 2018.

Williams, M. and Penman, D. (2011). *Mindfulness: A Practical Guide to Finding Peace in a Frantic World*. London: Piatkus.

Chapter 8

Critical Response to Veterans' Case Studies

A Psychologist's Perspective

Jason A. Nieuwsma

The cases presented in this section illustrate how chaplains addressed the needs of two different patients, both veterans, by utilising principles from the evidence-based psychotherapeutic modality of acceptance and commitment therapy.[1] As noted in the case studies, ACT contains six components, which are sometimes lumped into three overarching domains as follows: opening up (acceptance, defusion); being aware (present moment, self as context); and doing what matters (values, committed action). These practices can be highly synergistic with many practices and commitments in clinical chaplaincy, as the case studies illustrate.

Both ACT-related chaplain case studies in this section are related to sex. In considering the relationship of sex to psychosocial-spiritual functioning, it is difficult to avoid recalling Freud. While views on Freud from our vantage point in a more 'sexually liberated' society tend to attribute much of Freud's heavy emphasis on sex in psychoanalytic theory as emanating from the 'sexually repressed' culture of his time, it certainly remains the case today that sex is important. It is important for

---

1   In the spirit of full disclosure, as faculty with the Mental Health Integration for Chaplain Services (MHICS) training programme, I had opportunity to teach ACT and work with both chaplains when they went through the MHICS training.

myriad reasons. In these case studies, the reasons include the relationship between sex and issues of identify, self-worth, social acceptance, religious belief, relationship to God, interpersonal relationships, trust, values and meaning and purpose in life (to name a few). These topics are all solidly in the chaplain's domain.

Below, each case study is separately considered and critiqued. I offer the critiques in the spirit of charity and curiosity, hoping that they will contribute to creative, self-reflective thinking that can help to shape future chaplain care provision. I am fortunate to know both chaplains who provided these case studies and hold them both in high regard. As they have each already provided their own analyses of the cases, I attempt in what follows to offer some different ideas on possible directions for care.

Case study with transgender veteran

The case of Vicki allows us to consider several important issues with respect to chaplain care as well as the potential for chaplains to utilise ACT. Regardless of how often a chaplain may encounter transgender patients, this case brings up key dynamics and principles that apply broadly to a range of different patient populations.

To begin with, as Chaplain Hanson notes, it is important 'for chaplains to examine their own experience and understanding of sex and gender identity to find a place of spiritual authority (grounding) from which to meet others in their individual and unique journeys'. Such self-examination is important in being able to provide care to the broader LGBT community, and ACT allows one such avenue for personal examination – not just in the general sense but as part of being in the present moment with a patient during their journey. 'Pastoral presence' is a frequently used phrase in clinical chaplaincy and, when practised well, entails more than someone who wears the 'chaplain' label simply being physically present; it entails being intentionally, purposefully, mindfully present with patients, with their experience, and helping them to become more aware of and present to their own narratives.

In the case of Vicki, the chaplain's emotional experience in the present moment with this patient appears to be one of compassion, empathy and a desire to affirm. These are prosocial and likely therapeutic emotional reactions that simultaneously merit awareness and attentiveness on the part of the chaplain. At one point, Vicki noted that her transgender feelings would come back 'like a weed', and the chaplain responded by inviting Vicki to reframe her feelings in a way 'that might sound a bit more positive'. After all the rejection that Vicki experienced from religious institutions in her life, this was very likely a highly affirming and potentially restorative message to hear from a religious authority figure. At the same time, it is likely that the feeling or thought of her transgender experience being 'like a weed' will recur for Vicki at some point. She had had a lifetime of personal and social experience to form this thought/feeling. What happens next time this feeling comes up for Vicki? Will reminding herself of the positive reframe of 'perennial grass' be sufficient? Perhaps. And perhaps the chaplain, being present to and aware of the desire to affirm Vicki when she brought up the weed analogy, could have directed the conversation down another path.

For example, if the chaplain was aware of her desire to affirm Vicki in that moment, a decision might have been made to notice that emotional reaction and choose to go deeper with the patient in her present-moment experience. The chaplain could have instead responded, 'Like a weed... Why do you say weed?' or, 'I sense a degree of shame when you say weed' or, 'When you say weed, what comes up for you? What do you feel in your body when you say that?' It seems probable that there was a strong emotional and spiritual backstory for why Vicki had chosen the term 'weed'. It is unlikely that those who have rejected her had ever wanted to hear about the pain she associated with feeling like a weed, and while a reframe was affirming and compassionate, it did not allow Vicki to name and be present to her pain. And there could be substantial spiritual pain rooted in guilt, shame, rejection and abandonment.

From an ACT perspective, the goal would not be to leave somebody indefinitely in this pain. Rather, evidence suggests that the avoidance of psychosocial pain tends to have a paradoxical effect, often making the pain worse in the long run (perhaps the same holds for avoidance of spiritual pain). Therefore, the goal is to allow the experience to be present – to come into contact with the 'weed' – and from there to move in the direction of identified values. ACT principles of defusion and self as context could help to move from the place of being present to pain to enacting valued behaviours. There are numerous ways this could be done but, put very simply, for Vicki it could look like inviting her to notice what 'weed' felt like (defusion – there are multiple exercises that can facilitate this but exercises need not be used) and then inviting her to detect a distinction between the feeling of 'weed' and her sense of self as one who could notice such feelings (self as context).

This self also has values, some of which are hinted at in the verbatim, for example being loving to everybody. When Vicki noted this value, or this being an attribute of Jesus that she admired, it could have been another point for the chaplain to dig deeper to invite Vicki to articulate her own values. At that moment, the patient also brought up a powerful spiritual experience with her dead mother – admittedly, a comment that would be rather difficult to put on the back-burner in favour of exploring values – and the conversation then turned to the patient acknowledging that she did feel affirmed by certain people in her life. This is encouraging. From an ACT perspective, it is also terrain that requires careful navigation from a values perspective. Patients whose 'values' are contingent on the behaviour of others are likely headed for significant discouragement and disappointment. We cannot control other people. If our 'values' are to be loved, accepted or appreciated by other people, we are not in a position to choose behaviours in line with our values. We are instead dependent on others to fulfil our wishes and desires.

Values should help to guide behaviour. Vicki was in a fragile position when it came to validation, something that she had received remarkably little of and something that we all desire. The validation that she received from the chaplain was therefore precious, and may be singularly unique as an affirmation from a religious/spiritual authority. The chaplain's closing affirmation that God loved her was equally powerful and not to be underestimated. At the same time, validation alone may leave Vicki still searching for a values base to guide her. Vicki gave hints of values – admiring Jesus, wanting to find a church – but there was more to explore there. Why did she want to find a church? Was it a value for her to cultivate her spiritual life? Develop a relationship with God? Invest in meaningful social relationships? Practise loving people? If so, how could these values direct Vicki's steps? Articulating her values and putting them into action was within Vicki's control, and exercising that control could prove empowering.

Case study with survivor of military sexual trauma

The chaplain care provided in the case of Mrs Helen may not be feasible for clinical chaplains in all contexts – in particular, the ability to see patients for numerous weekly individual counselling sessions over the course of multiple months. Clearly, for chaplains who are able to devote this level of individualised attention to patients over a prolonged duration, there exists the opportunity to unpack more spiritual and emotional material, revisit key themes and help the patient work on things outside sessions. Even if chaplains are not able to spend as much time with their patients over a prolonged period, the case of Mrs Helen provides rich material for consideration and application in briefer encounters.

Mrs Helen reported two experiences of sexual victimisation, and it is notable that in comparing the two events, it is the one that on the surface appears less severe that has stuck with her over the decades. Of course, it is because of who the perpetrator was in this seemingly less severe event: a priest – a trusted confidant, an apparent friend, an embodiment of the holy, a representative of God. Given this experience, it is remarkable that Mrs Helen stayed as involved with her faith and spiritual life as she did over the years. That she should pursue 'receiving an acknowledgement and apology' is only right and just. At the same time, such a pursuit requires careful attention and discernment on the part of the chaplain. If pursued too fixedly, seeking the receipt of something from another person, as also with the case of Vicki, can risk leading someone to deviate from the path of her values.

In the case of Mrs Helen, it would be important to frame her behaviour of going to the confessional with her molestation experience as a values-based behaviour. And what is that value? Ideally, it is a value such as standing up for herself, naming and confronting wrongdoing, choosing to practise love, or any number of values that are within her power to enact. If Mrs Helen expressed her 'value' as receiving something from another, this would merit attention, first, to help articulate another value that can serve to more reliably guide behaviour (such as one of the aforementioned), and second, to attend to her desire for acknowledgement and apology as entirely reasonable and natural. This desire is not to be discounted from an ACT perspective; rather, it can be noticed and attended to – such as by inviting it to become another passenger on the bus, to build on the metaphor used by Chaplain Sanders. On a more minor note, present-moment awareness exercises need not be imaginal, especially if an individual expressed discomfort with an element of an imaginal exercise, as Mrs Helen did with closing her eyes; in such cases, patients could instead be invited to notice various things in the present moment (the feeling of the chair, the temperature of the room, their ongoing thoughts, where they feel emotions in their body, and so on).

Interestingly, even though the priest that Mrs Helen went to for confession was highly affirming and apologetic, she then found herself disappointed that the quick remedy she had hoped for did not materialise – namely, her anger persisted. This is where it becomes important to have a foundation in values as commitments that can drive behaviour even through challenging emotional experiences (such as anger). These values can absolutely include redemption and restoration, although to understand these as guiding life values, and not simply as singular temporal events, admittedly has potential theological implications for interpreting and living out these principles. For patients such as Mrs Helen, though, this territory becomes ripe for chaplain engagement.

Conclusion

Both case examples demonstrate ways these chaplains were powerful restorative forces of spiritual authority, perhaps of divine representation, for individuals who had been hurt by the Church. Both demonstrate ways that ACT principles can be effectively employed in patient care. It is to be hoped that the responses to each case provided above present additional considerations for how ACT might be used in chaplain care to address emotional and spiritual dynamics.

Part 3
The Chaplain as Ritual Leader

Chapter 9

'God is just too busy for us right now'

— Paul, a 10-year-old white male transitioning from tertiary medical centre to paediatric inpatient psychiatric hospital

Jessica Bratt Carle

Introduction

The following case features a chaplain's visit to a young boy anticipating transfer from a children's acute care hospital to a children's inpatient psychiatric hospital. As such, it serves to illustrate various considerations that arise in chaplaincy work with children and youth. Moreover, this case addresses some dynamics of spiritual care for patients admitted for psychiatric reasons. Because it is common for patients to be admitted to acute care settings until they are medically stable for transfer to more specialised psychiatric treatment settings, chaplains can benefit from greater understanding of the spiritual needs of patients and families who are anticipating that kind of transition.

Furthermore, because this case illustrates an encounter with a patient who is not only a psychiatric patient but also a paediatric patient, it invites chaplains to explore care with populations that may stretch their comfort levels. In the United States, paediatric hospital admissions for self-harm and suicidality have more than doubled since 2008 (American Academy of Pediatrics 2017), signalling an increased need for understanding and competence in spiritual care for this vulnerable population.

Background

'Paul', a 10-year-old white male, was admitted to the hospital for psychiatric reasons, specifically self-harming behaviour, two days prior to this encounter. No formal psychiatric diagnosis had been made at that time. Paul lived with his mother, who was single, and his 8-year-old brother; his father, who was divorced from Paul's mother, lived in another state. There was a known history of Paul undergoing abuse from his father.

I am a white woman and was in my late 20s at the time of this encounter. I am a Protestant Christian ordained in the Reformed Church in America. My theological training took place at Princeton Theological Seminary, where I earned my Master of Divinity degree. At the time of writing, I am pursuing a doctorate in religion, psychology and culture at Vanderbilt University. My chaplaincy training took the form of clinical pastoral education at the National Institutes of Health in Bethesda, Maryland, and at Yale New Haven Hospital in New Haven, Connecticut. Since then I have attained board certification with the Association of Professional Chaplains, and have served as a chaplain in Boston, Massachusetts; Nashville, Tennessee; Memphis, Tennessee; and Grand Rapids, Michigan.

I have chosen to refrain from identifying the facility where this encounter took place. This is because the case took place a number of years ago and, because I no longer work at that facility, I am unable to obtain permission from the patient and family, nor am I able to pursue the kind of institutional review that I would seek if I still worked at the facility. In light of these constraints, refraining from identifying the facility seems most prudent to protect all parties involved. Additionally, all the names have been changed to protect patient confidentiality.

At the time of the visit featured in this case study, I was serving both adult and paediatric populations at a 1500-bed tertiary medical centre. The encounter took place in the children's portion of the hospital, prior to the patient's anticipated transfer to the nearby affiliated paediatric inpatient psychiatric hospital. My interests in paediatric chaplaincy and child spirituality spur an eagerness to reflect on this encounter and to use it intentionally for further equipping readers with tools for providing care that is attuned to the spiritual care needs of young patients and their caregivers.

Case study

The encounter began when a nurse on the paediatric unit to which Paul had been admitted called me, around noon, explaining that his mother, Carol, was requesting that Paul be baptised before he was transferred to the inpatient paediatric psychiatric hospital later that afternoon, and that she had also said something about wanting to see a priest. From a brief reading of the patient's chart, I gathered that Paul was a bright young boy who had been having problems for some time and that these were associated with abusive treatment from his father. This current admission had resulted when Carol had brought Paul to the hospital's emergency room a few nights earlier following a phone conversation with his father, after which Paul had become so agitated that he began biting himself and saying that he wanted to bite off all of his skin. For Paul's own safety, there was a behavioural staff attendant, or 'sitter', in his room at all times – this practice is common when patients exhibit tendencies towards self-harm or harm towards others.

My plan for this visit was to explore the request for baptism and its importance for this family, and to discern what underlying need or desire might have prompted their request. Furthermore, knowing that baptism in the hospital setting is generally reserved for emergencies, I anticipated that I might have to explain such limitations to the mother and perhaps come up with another, more appropriate way to meet the spiritual needs of the situation.

When I arrived, the room was dimly lit. The staff sitter was in a rocking chair near the door. Paul appeared restless on his bed; he was sitting up, not tethered to any intravenous tubing or machines, and was playing with some stuffed animals and a blanket. A makeshift bed was on the far side of the room near the window, and Carol was lying on it with her eyes closed. The overhead TV was not on, nor was the large portable TV/ video game cart at the foot of the bed. I initiated the visit by addressing Paul, being deliberate to recognise him as a primary conversation partner. After whispering my introduction to Paul, he blurted out, 'I'm leaving in 60 minutes!' At this point his mother roused from the makeshift bed and I addressed her.

Chaplain: Hi, I'm Jessica. I'm a chaplain here at the hospital. I'm sorry if I woke you, but I did want to stop by, so I didn't miss you before you and Paul left. I heard you were hoping to speak to a chaplain before you left.

Carol: Yeah, I was hoping we could get Paul baptised before we go over to the paediatric psychiatric hospital, because he's just having a real hard time with this.

I made my way around the huge TV/video game cart and over to a chair across from the makeshift bed where Carol was still lying down, with her head propped on her hand.

Chaplain: Mind if I sit here?

Carol: No, please go ahead.

Chaplain: Yes, I had heard that you were interested in baptism, and I wanted to find out a bit more from you about what you'd like.

Carol: Yeah, I just thought it would be good if we could do it in the next hour before he gets transferred over.

Chaplain: Okay, well, typically here in the hospital we baptise in emergency situations – cases where it's a matter of life and death. In situations where the patient is healthy enough, we encourage that baptism be a part of the community of faith that the family comes from, since it is intended to be celebrated in a community that you will continue to be a part of. Of course, that's not a completely rigid rule here...but, usually, that's the guidelines for baptisms here at the hospital. So I guess I just wanted to find out a bit more about whether or not you are part of a faith community and whether baptism in that setting might be an option. Also, I just don't know if there's an urgency to this situation where it would need to be done in the next hour but I certainly want to understand what is important to you in this time of transition, and I want to support you as best as I can. So... are you part of a religious community around here?

Carol explained that they went to a nearby Roman Catholic church and that they also had tried a Methodist church briefly. They were back at the Catholic church, but the regular priest was away in France, at Lourdes. The fill-in priest was from some other country originally and didn't speak English well. Paul didn't like this priest, because he couldn't understand him, and it agitated him. In the week prior to Paul's hospitalisation, Carol had made an appointment with the parish secretary to do some preliminary things to arrange for an eventual baptism for Paul and his 8-year-old brother.

Chaplain: Oh! I see, so you had already started this process when the hospitalisation occurred.

Carol: Yes.

A woman entered the room and came and hugged Paul and sat next to him on the bed. She introduced herself to me as Paul's grandmother, Susan. I introduced myself, and she went back to talking with Paul. I returned to my conversation with Carol. Meanwhile, the sitters also changed shifts, and I greeted the new one, Cindy, as she entered. She immediately had to tell Paul to stop banging his head into the bed, as he'd been doing on and off throughout the visit.

Chaplain: Well, I think it might be worth continuing to pursue that process through your parish; perhaps they would be able to connect with you at the paediatric psychiatric hospital. I don't know for sure but they could probably work with you to make arrangements. I would be happy to call them for you if you would like. How does that sound to you?

Carol: That sounds fine, I guess. It's just that Paul is having such a hard time with everything that's happening. But I know that the Catholic church would prefer that we go through them. Plus, I guess if we do that then I could have him and his brother baptised together. I have a couple of relatives who said they are willing to be the boys' godparents, so then they could participate too.

Chaplain: Yes, I can see how that would be nice to have them baptised together and be able to have everyone there for it. I do hear you saying though how hard it is for Paul right now, and I wanted to tell you also that I would be more than happy to do something with you and Paul, some special prayers or a blessing or something to mark this transition for him. How does that sound? Would that interest you?

Carol: Yes. I think that would be really good. Anything.

Chaplain: And I'll pray for you, too, because I'm sure this experience is difficult for you as well; I can see that you're pretty tired. (*She is still lying down on the makeshift bed*)

Carol: Right now we just feel...I guess we feel like God is just too busy for us right now. (*Substantial silence*) Paul said to me that he feels like God doesn't like him, you know, because he's sick right now.

Chaplain: Mmm, that's hard. I can imagine how those feelings might come up. He's really trying to find a way to understand it all, huh?

Carol: Yeah.

Paul became really energetic again, hopping around on the bed and banging his head. His mother was distracted from our conversation and approached Paul.

Chaplain: (*Realising time and attention are both limited*) Well, shall we say some prayers and do a blessing? Are there any rituals that mean something to Paul, maybe like making the cross and laying on of hands?

Carol: Yes, both of those; whatever you want to do would be good. And just so you know, he's not acting like this just because you're here; this is just what he's been doing the whole time. So don't feel like it's because of something you're doing.

Chaplain: Thanks, that's good to know. I understand. (*Turning to Paul*) So Paul, are you ready to move to another room?

Paul: (*Pointing out the window*) I'm going, kind of over there, not far away!

Chaplain: Yeah, you don't even have to go for a long drive or anything! Paul, do you know what a chaplain is?

Paul: No.

Chaplain: Well, you know how when you go to church there's a priest or a minister there?

Paul: Yeah but I don't like him. You can't understand anything he's saying. It sounds like he says, 'The peace of the Lord be "whit chu".'

The sitter chimed in with a story about how her priest's accent makes it sound like he's telling them to 'piss the peace'. Paul laughed.

Chaplain: That's a pretty good impression of an accent you've got there, Paul. Well, a chaplain is like a priest or minister, except instead of being at the church they are at the hospital. That means that I stay here and I pray with people and bless them, and I see the other kids too who stay here on this floor where you are. Your mom and I were talking about how we could do something special for you because you are about to go to a new place. We could say some prayers and bless you, too. How does that sound? Would you like to do that?

Paul: NO! I don't wanna.

Chaplain: Oh!...that doesn't sound good?

Paul: No! Uh-uh!

Carol: Paul, you wouldn't have to say any prayers. Jessica would say the prayers for you; you could just listen.

Paul: Oh! Okay!

Chaplain: I'm sorry, Paul, I wasn't being clear! Yeah, I will say the prayers; you don't have to say them. (*Feeling as if I was rushing Paul, I sat back a moment*) Paul, who's on that blanket you keep playing with? Mickey Mouse?

Paul: Yeah!

Chaplain: Have you had that a long time? Does it go wherever you go?

Paul: I've had it since I was 6...5...4...3.

Chaplain: That's a long time! (*Pointing to the stuffed animals*) And who are these?

Paul: This is Pooh (*he throws it*) and this is Rex.

Chaplain: Rex, that's a good name for a dog. They get to go with you to your new room, huh? Do they stay in your bed with you?

Paul: Yup!

Chaplain: Well, they can be here with us for our prayers too. We'll pray that God stays right by you, just like Pooh and Rex do, wherever you go.

I invited Paul's mother and grandmother to approach the bed and asked the sitter if she'd like to join us, which she did.

Chaplain: Paul, do you think all of us here could put our hands on you, maybe on your shoulder, so that we could touch you while we say our prayer?

Paul: (*Sheepishly*) Okay...

Chaplain: That way we can make sure you know how much we care about you and how special you are.

He proceeded to lie down on his stomach with his head on the pillow, the stuffed animals tucked under his arm. He became very still and quiet. We each laid a hand on his shoulder, except the sitter held his bare foot and teased him: 'I'm going to hold your toes!'

Chaplain: Paul, you're going to be blessed all the way from the top of your head to the end of your toes! Okay, let's pray. Holy and loving God, we thank you for today and that you listen to us whenever we want to talk to you.

Paul: (*Giggling*) She's holding my big toe and it tickles!

Chaplain: (*Laughing*) God, thank you for Paul and for his laughter and his spirit. Thank you for being there for Paul and for going with him today as he changes to a new room and a new place. God, we ask that you be right by Paul's side, just like Pooh and Rex, so that he knows you are with him and that you love him. God, we ask that you help Paul to feel better and to trust the doctors, even when that means having to do things that aren't fun, so that he can get better. We ask your special blessing on Paul, and pray that he will feel the care and love of those who surround him here and elsewhere. Be with his mother and grandmother and his brother. Give them the strength and energy and patience they need to go through this time as well. God, we ask that Paul will feel safe in the new place; help him to meet new friends that he can play with while he is there. God, help Paul and all of us to know that you are there for us, that you are never too busy to hear our prayers and that you never leave us alone, even when we feel like we are alone. In the name of the Father, Son and Holy Spirit, Amen. (*We all cross ourselves, and Paul sits up and smiles*) Paul, how did that feel? Was that okay?

Paul: Yep!

Chaplain: Paul, I'm going to say a prayer for you every day while you're at the new hospital, okay? I won't see you over there but while you're there you can remember every day that I will be over here in this building saying a prayer for you. Alright?

Paul: Alright.

Carol: Thank you. Thanks so much. And now...what is the fee for your services?

Chaplain: Oh, none whatsoever! This is what I do; this is what we're here for. This is part of my job!

Carol: Oh, okay...thanks!

Chaplain: I'll be thinking of you and keeping you all in my prayers. I was wondering also if you'd like this pamphlet from our department.

It has some prayers in it that you might like. They're good for pulling out of your pocket every so often when you are feeling overwhelmed.

Carol: That sounds good. Yeah, I could use that.

Chaplain: (To Paul) Well, only a few more minutes till you go! Bye, and thanks for letting me pray with you. Bye, Pooh! Bye, Rex! *(Mother, grandmother and Paul say goodbyes)*

Discussion

Precisely because there was such a time-limited nature to this pastoral encounter, it is worth looking more closely at some of the nuances of my approach and interventions, in order to explore more fully both the limitations and the possibilities inherent in such a visit. That is, although the impact of a single visit may seem negligible in comparison with that of a spiritual care relationship that develops over time and multiple visits, in reality, many chaplain encounters are limited to single visits (Ratcliffe 2015; Bassett, in press). In these situations, I find it is all the more important to be intentional about how I might achieve the desired spiritual care outcomes within the given constraints.

My visit with Paul and his family reflects a wide swathe of chaplain interactions where patients are anticipating imminent discharge or transfer. For instance, I may be asked to see patients as they prepare to go home or to a specialised facility, such as a rehabilitation centre or psychiatric hospital, or to hospice care, whether at home or in another location. For me to dismiss such patients because they are 'on their way out', or to leave their spiritual care up to whomever they meet at their next destination, would be to neglect the needs that are often more poignant at times of transition. Moreover, doing so would neglect the real possibilities for meaningful spiritual care that exist at such thresholds. I have seen that, at their best, my visits around such times of change can comfort, equip, and empower patients and families in the face of new challenges and unknowns, inviting them to take stock of what has brought them to their current situation and what their hopes and fears may be for their next destination. For me, such visits pose particular challenges, such as initiating rapport and building on it in the same visit, but I find there can also be a sense of freedom for both me and the recipients of the visit. That is, knowing that time is very limited can sometimes prompt me to take a bolder approach, where I may feel free to skip over the kind of 'small talk' that might begin when a longer pastoral care relationship is anticipated. Likewise, for the patient or family, a visit before a major transition can invite greater self-disclosure, as the person may feel there is a singular opportunity to name and process emotional and spiritual reflections in the attentive presence of the chaplain, with whom there is not going to be an ongoing expectation of subsequent probing conversations.

Assessment

Paul came across as a child who likely knew enough about what was going on with himself that, in his 'normal' moments, he was probably very frightened by his behaviour during his self-destructive episodes. He was fearful of being transferred to a new hospital, and his mother agreed that the current hospitalisation had also been very difficult for him. He did not have a consistent routine established in the current inpatient setting, and his transition to the psychiatric hospital meant that his mother could not stay in the room with him like she did when he was here. At the pre-teen age of 10, his emerging sense of self was likely being complicated by his psychiatric difficulties, as he was trying to understand himself while riding the ups and downs of his own behaviour and the medical attention he was receiving (Collins 1984). His chart indicated that his mother was bipolar, and perhaps there was concern that this event and Paul's behaviour were signalling the beginning of another chapter in a family history of mental illness. If Paul was even slightly aware of that, it could certainly have impacted his perception of what might have been happening to him.

The family system in which Paul was situated added to the complexity of his circumstances (Friedman 2011; Lamb 2010). He was a young boy whose father was not only absent but also abusive and whose phone call had triggered a difficult episode for Paul. Instead of being a stable and significant presence in his life, his father had instead been a source of emotional and physical pain. His mother seemed to have some measure of family support, as evidenced by the grandmother's presence, but she was nonetheless dealing with this situation as a single parent and needed to find other care for Paul's sibling while she was at the hospital with Paul.

Religious faith played enough of a role in Carol's life that she turned to its rituals as a potential source of assurance, comfort or protection. Carol placed value in her identity as a Roman Catholic, and in the religious community of which she was a part, and she seemed to desire greater closeness and continuity in her relationship with the parish priest. On the part of both Paul and his mother, I saw a yearning for some meaning or sense to be made in the midst of a confusing and lonely experience, and they were both willing to seek meaning in a religious ritual. Perhaps this was both because of the weight of rituals and sacraments in their Roman Catholic tradition and also because of the power that tangible acts can have. In requesting baptism, a large part of what Paul's mother seemed to want was for something tangible and concrete to be conferred on her and her son. She was open to considering how her faith community could play a bigger role in this situation and also very open to whatever hands-on, visible actions we could carry out together in that moment.

Interventions

As with numerous other occasions where I have experienced requests for baptism that led to some other intervention, in this case Paul's mother did not get frustrated or persistent about the question of baptism. This further reflects how the request for baptism can often be a request to do something – 'Anything' – which may itself reflect a more general underlying desire for a sense of connection to others, to the divine, and to the stability of an established tradition. Baptism happens to be a ritual that comes to mind for many Christians; it is up to the chaplain to discern further, and I needed to assess whether it was the most appropriate ritual to address the spiritual needs that Paul and his family were experiencing at that time, so that I might offer the most appropriate rituals and interventions from a repertoire that may have been more expansive than what Carol had in mind. For instance, as in this case example, a blessing or prayer customised to Paul's situation proved to be deeply meaningful; but equally, creating a ritual with some tangible object, such as a comfort item (quilt or prayer shawl) or a natural object (stone or shell), might have lent symbolic weight to the intervention. Creative possibilities abound for chaplains to personalise a liturgy for transition, reconciliation, recommitment or healing. In this encounter, I chose to incorporate existing objects, namely Paul's stuffed animals, for safety reasons and because they were making the transition with him to the new setting. By highlighting their importance in his sense of safety and continuity, I sought to make associations with his family's hoped-for sense of God's presence and provision of security.

At his age and with his life experience, Paul's God-concept may have been reflective of a complicated mix of both his mother's love and care and his father's absence and abusiveness, making it difficult to find a trustworthy or stable God-concept (Rizzuto 1979). The new experiences of the emergency room and subsequent admissions to the hospital, and then psychiatric hospital, may also have put pressure on his capacity to trust, as evidenced by his mother's feeling that 'God is just too busy for us right now' and her mentioning that Paul 'feels like God doesn't like him...because he's sick right now'. It was unfortunate that the visit was interrupted at the point where those feelings were mentioned, and if there were opportunity for follow-up spiritual care, I would have made pursuing those sentiments further a key priority.

I tried to connect the image of the divine to concrete objects that were sources of consistency and comfort in Paul's life, such as his stuffed animal companions, which are illustrative of paediatric psychoanalyst Winnicott's concept of a transitional object (Winnicott 1984). In order to be intentional about honouring the child as a key figure in what can often be an adult-dominated environment of healthcare, I sought to be sensitive to Paul's preferences, asking permission for proceeding with prayer and communicating about whether touching his shoulder was agreeable to him. I also realised that I needed to clarify the euphemistic phrase 'say some prayers' and be more direct with Paul about what I meant. Furthermore, aware of Paul's experience of abuse by his father, I was also mindful not to tie a masculine parental image to God in my prayer. Likewise, sensitive to Paul's reason for being admitted, I considered that it may be challenging for a child like Paul to have a benevolent image of an ever-present loving God, not only because he has an abusive father but also because of the very real presence of someone who is literally watching over him 24 hours a day in the hospital – the sitter. Paediatric and adult patients alike can feel uncomfortable with a sitter, having the sense that they are being watched lest they do something bad at any moment and feeling that the sitter's presence reinforces the stigma that may accompany their hospital admission.

My effort to encourage Paul's mother to keep pursuing baptism for her sons in their own parish was a reflection of a broader effort to build collaboration with other faith leaders. Although I was apprehensive about coming across as restrictive when explaining the typical parameters for baptism in the hospital, my intention and hope was that Carol would recognise the benefit in grounding that sacramental ritual in a context where Paul would be known and nurtured over time by a consistent community and faith leaders. In so doing, I recognised the place of spiritual care in the hospital as something that did not supplant outside resources but should accompany them in appropriate ways, especially for patients and families who have existing relationships with spiritual communities.

Outcomes

This encounter allowed and honoured a space in which Paul's mother was free to name not only her request but also her honest feeling that God was too busy for them. My willingness to be present to her feelings, without trying to dismiss or correct them, likely provided a vital opportunity for this overwhelmed parent to be honest about the challenges she was facing and their spiritual dimensions. I deliberately aimed to be a sincere presence in that moment, while also calling to mind the possibilities of a more consistent spiritual support structure in their own parish. Moreover, I sought to foster an encounter that was more than just a transient formality, as I was mindful of the medical transition in which I found Paul and his family, and of the change in environment and caregivers they were about to experience. Though there was not a chaplain to whom I could refer Paul and his family at the psychiatric hospital, such a referral would have augmented the impact of my own visit by helping to bridge that transition. If there had been more time to continue the visit or make a subsequent visit, I would have further pursued with Carol what it meant that she felt God was 'too busy' for them. It would have been meaningful to explore with her whether this was a new feeling or one that had persisted over time and circumstance. I would have been interested to know what other aspects of a God-image accompanied her sense of God being too busy and whether there might have been other characteristics of God that Carol may have been able to identify and connect with in a positive way.

Carol's request for baptism for Paul reflects how, in situations of uncertainty and anxiety, patients and families often look for something concrete to help them experience and mark a sense of divine care in their lives. My visit also underscores how tangibly powerful the experience of prayer can be, and how it can facilitate immediate effects of physical connection, calming and centring. Such tangible outcomes are all the more meaningful in a situation like Paul's, where the intangibles of mental illness contrast so sharply with some of the more tangible physical problems that can be addressed in the hospital. Helping Paul and his family identify the tangible resources and practices in their spiritual lives likely gave them a sense of grounding as they pursued further psychiatric care for Paul.

Conclusion

This case illustrates the possibility that spiritual care can be delivered even in encounters that are brief. Such brief spiritual care encounters may not be fully satisfactory, and it is certainly possible to find aspects of the care that could be developed further, but nonetheless, the care in this case was responsive to the needs of the moment. In particular, this case demonstrates the importance of being attentive to the developmental needs of children and the spiritual needs of families who are facing mental health challenges. While many chaplains may feel particularly stretched by situations that involve young children, and particularly children hospitalised for psychiatric reasons, this case shows there is value in offering our sincere presence and care as we convey that, even when they and their families may be in the midst of the distressing feeling that 'God is too busy' for them, we are not 'too busy'.

References

American Academy of Pediatrics (2017). 'Children's hospitals admissions for suicidal thoughts, actions double during past decade.' *American Academy of Pediatrics News*, 4 May 2017. Available at www.aappublications.org/news/2017/05/04/PASSuicide050417, accessed 14 January 2018.

Bassett, L. (In press). 'Space, time and shared humanity: A case study demonstrating a chaplain's role in end-of-life care.' *Health and Social Care Chaplaincy*, 5, 2.

Collins, W.A. (ed.) (1984). *Development During Middle Childhood: The Years from Six to Twelve*. Washington, DC: National Academies Press.

Friedman, E.H. (2011). *Generation to generation: family process in church and synagogue*. New York: Gulliford Press.

Lamb, M.E. (2010). 'How *do* Fathers Influence Children's Development? Let Me Count the Ways.' In M.E. Lamb (ed.) *The Role of the Father in Child Development* (pp.1–26). Hoboken, NJ: John Wiley & Sons.

Ratcliffe, R. (2015). '"I am frightened to close my eyes at night in case the witch comes to me in my sleep" – Yesuto, an African man in his early thirties troubled by his belief in witchcraft.' In G. Fitchett and S. Nolan (eds) *Spiritual Care in Practice: Case Studies in Healthcare Chaplaincy* (pp.113–132). London: Jessica Kingsley Publishers.

Rizzuto, A.-M. (1979). *The Birth of the Living God: A Psychoanalytic Study*. Chicago, IL: University of Chicago Press.

Winnicott, D.W. (1984). 'Transitional Objects and Transitional Phenomena.' In D.W. Winnicott *Through Paediatrics to Psychoanalysis: Collected Papers* (pp.229–242). London: Karnac.

Chapter 10

Connecting family members through ritual

– Jakob, Hulda and their family in palliative care

– *Guðlaug Helga Ásgeirsdóttir*

Introduction

The approach of palliative care is to provide care and treatment to people with life-threatening diseases and to support the patient's family members. In palliative care, the emphasis is on assessing and treating pain and other symptoms across four domains: physical, psychological, social and spiritual. As one of the main domains, spirituality is considered to be important to the same extent as the other dimensions (Saunders 2006; World Health Organization).

Within palliative care, the family is recognised as having a spiritual value and the importance of family work is stressed, with the family viewed as the unit of care (Saunders 2006; World Health Organization). In caring for the families, longer awareness of the impending death of a loved one is crucial in that it offers family members the opportunity to prepare for the death by, for example, having conversations about death and making practical arrangements (Hauksdóttir *et al.* 2010).

Background

The family involved in this case study included a dying husband, whom I have decided to call Jakob, and his wife, Hulda, also a disguised name, both in middle age; their adult children and their families; and the extended family, consisting of Jakob's sister and her family. The case shows how the chaplain, as a member of the interdisciplinary team, was able to establish a connection with the family members and earn their trust. Using interventions that were both religious and non-religious in character, the case not only underlines the complexity of the chaplain's work but also illustrates how the chaplain is in a unique position to address special and complex situations.

Jakob was well educated, with an advanced university degree. He had worked both in Iceland and abroad, ultimately as a consultant on building projects, and had established his own business. He began work early in life participating in building bridges of various kinds; when he was older he designed buildings that served numerous purposes. Hulda had a university degree and had specialist knowledge in social and legal aspects of the Icelandic community; she had a strong sense of fairness and social justice. The couple had always been very close; they were best friends and had much in common. They had two adult sons, Steinn and Helgi. The family came across as a strong and united unit, as well as their extended family, which included Jakob's younger sister. Jakob had been diagnosed with advanced cancer a few months before admission to the Palliative Care Unit (PCU) at The National University Hospital of Iceland (Landspitali). For various reasons, the diagnostic process had been hard and prolonged, and the following weeks had been very difficult and painful. Over a short period, Jakob had repeatedly been admitted to the emergency unit of the hospital.

I have been working for around 20 years as a hospital chaplain at Landspitali, with special emphasis on palliative care. Before working as a hospital chaplain, I worked as a pastor at the Gerontology Department of the capital Reykjavik's Social Services. I was ordained as a pastor in 1991 in the National Church of Iceland (NCI), which is the officially established Christian Church in Iceland. The NCI is an Evangelical Lutheran Church and is a member of the Porvoo Communion. My professional work has always been in the NCI's special service section, where the emphasis is on meeting people and their needs within a specific specialised context. I am also educated as a family therapist and have a doctoral degree in theology. The holistic view in palliative care, with emphasis on the spiritual along with the physical, psychological and social dimensions, is the approach that I advocate in all my work and fits in completely with my Christian theological beliefs. Palliative care has, to some extent, influenced both my private and professional life. After I started my position as a hospital chaplain at Landspitali, my mother, who had been diagnosed with her second cancer, came into the service of the Palliative Home Care Team from the Icelandic Cancer Society. As the chaplain at the PCU, I have been able to participate in the development of the Unit and have laid the foundations for the pastoral and spiritual care.

Landspitali is the largest hospital in Iceland and provides services nationwide. The hospital offers various clinical services such as outpatient clinics, day patient units, inpatient wards, clinical laboratories and other divisions. At the same time, the hospital is a university hospital with major teaching and research interests. All medical and nursing students in Iceland receive their clinical education at this university hospital. About 100,000 individuals receive hospital care at Landspitali annually and the number of employees is approximately 5000 (Landspitali 2016). In 2016, the number of deaths in Iceland was some 2300, with about 730 deaths in Landspitali (32%) (Statistics Iceland). In 2015, about 70 per cent of the families who lost a loved one at the PCU at Landspitali accepted a service at the deathbed with a chaplain (information gathered at the PCU). The Palliative Care Services at Landspitali comprise the PCU, which is the first specialised palliative care unit in Iceland (established in 1999), a specialised Palliative Home Care Service (PHCS) and a Palliative Care Hospital Based Consulting Team (PCHBCT). All three entities work in close collaboration with each other. The service of the PCU has evolved and developed over the years and today consists of a 12-bed, seven-day inpatient ward, a three-bed, five-day inpatient ward and a day-care and outpatient service. The PHCS provides specialised treatment to palliative care patients living at home in Reykjavik and its surroundings. The PCU and the PHCS are situated in a beautiful natural environment at the same site. The PCHBCT is a specialised palliative care consulting service applicable for all the units at Landspitali and also offers assistance to other hospital and healthcare institutions in Iceland.

As of January 2017, the population of Iceland was 338,349 inhabitants. The Christian faith has been the predominant religion in

Iceland, and in 2016, 71.55 per cent of the inhabitants were registered in the NCI. In the same year, Siðmennt, the Icelandic Ethical Humanist Association, had a membership of 0.44 per cent of the population and the membership in the Roman Catholic Church Diocese was 3.73 per cent of the population (Statistics Iceland).

Cases where the death of a sick family member has occurred require careful discernment (McCurdy and Fitchett 2011). In this case study, written consent on the behalf of the family members has been obtained from a family representative. Efforts have been made to disguise the case such that the identity of those included in the study is anonymous and demographic information is minimised as much as possible. In the process of documenting the case, the family representative was given the opportunity to read the text.

Case study

Before being admitted to the PCU, the family had been at the intensive care unit at the hospital where Jakob had been placed on a respirator. When the family came to the PCU, Jakob was in a critical condition, having breathing difficulties that resulted in anxiety attacks. The family was heavily burdened by the sickness process. Moreover, the family was cautious and expressed little trust for the healthcare professionals. This was revealed in how the family approached the staff at the PCU: they had strong opinions about the treatment Jakob had received and some of them openly commented on the hospital's service, how they had experienced it as unsatisfactory and difficult. Furthermore, they indicated that Jakob's and their own needs had not been met by the healthcare professionals, and that the treatment he had received had not been effective or sufficient. The interdisciplinary palliative care team had a dual role: to care for Jakob and to help the family, which included building an open and trusting relationship between the professionals, patient and family. When Jakob was admitted to the PCU, an immediate referral was made to the chaplain because the case was assessed as needing instant attention.

First ritual: A christening

In the first contact with the family, I introduced myself to Jakob, who was in a critical condition, and the family members who were present at the time. Jakob was mentally alert and able to understand but he had difficulties in expressing himself verbally because of his severe condition. Jakob, Hulda and their family welcomed me and soon asked about the possibility of having a christening at the PCU. It was Jakob's wish that his grandchild would be baptised and his son, Steinn, wanted to fulfil that request before the death of his father. Steinn approached me with his concerns, expressing his willingness to christen his child as he knew it would mean a lot to his father but also that the christening as such was not an issue for him. I discussed the essence of the christening with him and his wife and planned with them how, when and where we would try to let the christening take place. Steinn made it clear that he didn't share the Lutheran Christian beliefs on a christening but in my discussion with him I suggested that perhaps he could interpret the act as something good for the family in this situation, which he agreed to and accepted. He discerned that, in the christening event, the family members would be sharing a meaningful moment, surrounded with good thoughts and prayers, united and embracing the new life that had been given to them. In this context, it is also worth mentioning that the family did not present itself as religious or as practising a faith in any sense.

The christening took place just one day after Jakob's admission to the PCU. In the planning, we agreed on having the christening at the bedside, because Jakob was too weak to go to the Unit's chapel. It was also decided that Jakob would be one of the child's godparents along with two other family members. The family was united in preparing the christening; they all wanted to realise it and make it happen before Jakob's death. The staff and I, together with the family, created an appropriate environment for the service. The grandchild was put in a christening gown from its mother's family and the extended family prepared a christening feast with a cake bearing the grandchild's name. The christening followed the rituals from the NCI. At the beginning of the service Jakob presented with severe breathing difficulties and needed support from Hulda, other family members, and me. I had to pause the service to attend to his needs;

I took his hand and spoke quietly to him, explaining that we would take a break until he was feeling better. We all tried to help him by creating a secure and calm atmosphere, assuring him that we were by his side and that we would take care of him and his needs. Jakob's condition stabilised rather quickly, so we were able to continue the ritual from where we started.

During the christening, I held Jakob's hand to make him feel more secure and to give him some comfort as the event was very emotional for him. Jakob participated actively in the christening by placing his hand on his grandchild's head, and all who were present prayed together the Lord's Prayer. The name of the grandchild had not been revealed until the christening (the child was named after Jakob). I participated in the celebration that took place after the christening, which was held in one of the PCU's meeting rooms. The atmosphere was warm and intimate, and I perceived a sense of gratitude from the family members. They felt that the service had been meaningful and satisfying, despite the grief and the difficult circumstances. By sharing this moment with them, I had begun to build a relationship with individual family members and the family as a whole. I discerned their appreciation and that they were satisfied with the service I had provided.

Over the next few days, I attended to the family, had conversations with family members and tried to show them that they were cared for and that their wellbeing was central to the professionals at the Unit. I felt that, by sharing with them the act of christening, they realised that I was trustworthy and willing to do my best to meet their needs and share this intimate and painful time with them. I had not been intrusive in any way (by telling them how to do things or trying to convince some of them about my beliefs concerning the act of christening). I was just willing to give them my service on their own presumptions at this critical moment in their lives. I was supportive and agreed with them that the christening was important at this moment, and I did everything in my power to make them feel that I was putting all my professional skills, care and energy into making the christening come to a reality and to give it meaningful content. I responded instantly to their needs, which meant that Jakob was able to participate in this important family event. I had many encounters with individual family members; I stayed with them, had conversations, guided, delivered relevant information, and I was at Jakob's bedside. He was not able to communicate verbally but he could show his appreciation of me coming to see him by squeezing my hand or nodding his head.

Second ritual: At the time of death

When Jakob died, a nurse at the PCU informed me about his death and said that my service was requested. When I came to the Unit I expressed my sympathy to the family members and offered Hulda a special service at the deathbed, at which time the family had an opportunity to say goodbye to their loved one. The family members gathered together and I explained to them how their farewell could take place. I stayed with them, embraced them, and talked to them about the sickness and dying process. Among other things, I asked them about the moment of death and how they had experienced it. They shared their memories and feelings, and they had the opportunity and time to be together or alone at the deathbed, just as each one of them felt they needed.

The hospital's working guidelines assume the importance of offering the respective family a chaplain or other religious or non-religious leader to meet with them and have a service at the deathbed. The purpose of this procedure is to give the family the opportunity to say farewell through a formal channel and to have a moment to themselves to reflect on the situation. In general, and in this case, the service was tailored to the family's needs. I addressed the family members, read a psalm from the NCI's psalm book and recited passages from the Bible. In addition, the family members and I participated in praying known Icelandic prayer verses, as well as the Lord's Prayer. I performed a special blessing over the deceased and a blessing directed to the family members. Afterwards, the family members had some private and personal time. They then gathered together with me and we had a conversation in which the family members were able to share their memories, talk about the illness process, and ask questions if needed. I gave the family practical information concerning the next steps following the death, their departure from the hospital, and the Unit's follow-up programme. After staying with the family for a long while, I bid farewell to the family members, emphasising that they were welcome to contact me or the staff at the PCU if they felt they needed further assistance from the Unit.

Third ritual: After death

Hulda came a few days after her husband's death to collect the death certificate. Coincidentally, I met her when she arrived at the Unit. A short conversation ensued in which I asked her about the family's situation and we discussed practical arrangements. Thereafter, she asked me if I was able to take care of her husband's funeral, which I agreed to do. I proposed a plan concerning the preparation and arranged a meeting. Following this, I had a number of meetings, conversations, phone calls and emails to prepare the family service and funeral. In all these contacts, my main concern was to support and assist the family members both in arranging the services ahead and in their grieving process.

In Iceland, the tradition is to have a special family service for the nearest family and friends where the coffin is open and where people have the opportunity to see the body of the deceased loved one for the last time. The family service can take place on the same day as the funeral but it can also be scheduled some days before. In this case, the family service and the funeral took place on the same day, approximately ten days after Jakob's death. The family service is very personal and intimate, and people have the opportunity to put a sign of love and affection into the coffin, for example a farewell letter or a little gift. Sometimes the family members help to close the coffin and prepare it for the funeral.

Before the family service began, I went, as I always do, into the chapel where the service was to be held to check everything was as it should be. I looked at how Jakob had been laid into the coffin to know if I was satisfied with his appearance. When the family and their nearest ones came, I welcomed them and talked to the individuals who were contributing to the service, to give them my support and encourage them. The family service consists of prayers, music, some reading of texts from the Bible, a special blessing over the deceased person, and a blessing for the attendees. The family service lasted approximately 30 minutes, then the funeral began. Funerals in Iceland are usually a public event that is typically announced in the media and therefore has a social meaning and effect. Jakob's body was to be cremated so the coffin was carried outside the church where the church attendees could pay their respects and condolences. I walked out of the church with the family after the coffin and waited there with them until everyone had paid their respects and the family had accepted their condolences.

The funeral was well attended and the family had a gathering afterwards where they could meet the church attendees who comprised relatives, friends, co-workers and fellow citizens. I was also present at the gathering afterwards, where I talked to various family members and others who had attended the funeral. I think it is important to be visible and present and not to leave the grieving family once the funeral service is over. When I said goodbye to the family members, I especially told them that I was there for them and that they could be in touch whenever they needed. I thanked them for the time we had had together and said that it had been a privilege for me to be with them at this time of their life. When I said goodbye to Hulda, I told her I would be in touch just to see how she and other family members were coping and that I considered it my role and responsibility to be with them at the ash burial, which we would schedule later on.

Fourth ritual: Ash burial

The ash burial took place some days after the funeral. I met the family at the cemetery for the ash burial, accompanied by a funeral home worker who came with the urns. The grave site had been arranged by the funeral home but on arrival at the grave site, Hulda and the other family members were not content with the site chosen. They considered it inappropriate and openly expressed their discontent. A potential crisis was about to occur that required an immediate and careful response. I discussed this matter with Hulda and told her that Jakob's remains would not be buried in a place she did not approve of. The family stood to one side, and a discussion took place between the funeral home worker and me. After a brief time, a solution was reached in which a new grave would be arranged, and the family accepted this.

In the service, the family was addressed, a prayer was read, and a blessing was performed over the site and Jakob's remains. The family members then participated in shovelling earth over the grave and a cross was put on the grave along with a beautiful flower arrangement that the family had brought with them. Afterwards, Hulda invited me to their home to have some refreshment, which had been prepared before attending the ash burial. After the ash burial, I again urged them to be in touch if there was anything they felt I could help them with, and I also told them that I would contact them for a follow-up.

Several contacts were made through telephone and interviews with Hulda after the funeral and ash burial. During this time, she gradually expressed her and the family's feelings and thoughts about the diagnosis and the illness process. She described how the family members had experienced the event as extremely difficult and painful. In addition, she felt that the healthcare professionals had not met the needs of either Jakob or the family. She was angry, frustrated, discontented and disappointed. She felt that the healthcare professionals had not been listening to her and the family members, and that Jakob had not been given adequate treatment and care. She felt that they had been met with disrespect and that correct decisions concerning the treatment had not been made in the illness process. She especially criticised the time before admission to the PCU. She felt that she was denied the bereavement process because her thoughts and emotions centred on the experience the family had had in the previous stages at the hospital.

Discussion

Assessment

The spiritual assessment conducted on behalf of the members of the interdisciplinary team at the PCU takes place from a clinical standpoint in compliance with standard working guidelines at the Unit for pastoral and spiritual care. These working guidelines underscore the importance of assessing the need for referring cases to different professionals in the team. Furthermore, a bereavement risk assessment checklist is used to evaluate factors that identify families who could be at risk in their process of grief and bereavement. Several factors are assessed, including:

- whether there are children younger than 25 years of age in the family

- whether there are visible conflicts or communication difficulties

- the family's perception of the patient's suffering

- awareness of impending death

- other events that can cause stress, for example previous losses, divorce, financial difficulties etc.

- extremes in disease progression.

The assessment aims to recognise families that are in need of additional support in their bereavement and prepare them in the best possible way for the death of their loved one (Halfdanardottir *et al.* 2013). This assessment is discussed at the interdisciplinary team meetings, where the team members' views on risk factors are taken into consideration. In addition, the team members decide which next steps might need to be taken. Needs are evaluated from several perspectives, such as who is suffering most in the family, how the family members evaluate their support system and coping strategies (for example, their inner resources and strength), and how their beliefs and value systems are manifested. The trinity model presented by Wright (2005, 2017) is of value in this regard. The model is intended for use in clinical practice and underlines that spirituality, beliefs and suffering are composed of interrelated and interconnected components. According to the model, it is necessary to explore, examine and enquire about these concepts when caring for people and families that are experiencing difficult times, such as serious illness and the loss of a loved one.

I made my specific spiritual assessment both personally and in collaboration with other team members. I discerned that the family members needed someone who could be there for them, who was able to approach them and listen to their concerns, as well as how they had been and were experiencing the present situation. The family needed someone who was able to stay with them, respond to their inner thoughts and suffering, and acknowledge that all they wanted was the best for their sick family member. They needed understanding, care and love, support, encouragement and also some transcendental awareness and strength from a higher power, for which I, as a chaplain, was a representative. The rituals that I participated in with them were a powerful tool that helped to put some framework in the process; they helped me in approaching them and they provided some stability and security at times when the family members were experiencing frustration and changes in their lives.

Interventions

The first intervention that took place was the referral from the members of the interdisciplinary team. The arguments for the referral were that the service of the chaplain was considered important and that the family needed support during these trying and sensitive circumstances. The spiritual approach was considered particularly relevant because the family was in a deep state of psychological crisis and mourning. This intervention played an important role as it marked the beginning of my accompaniment with the family. The other interventions consisted of being with the family, numerous conversations with the family group and with individual family members, and contact via phone, emails and rituals. I will give special attention to the rituals as they proved to be a fundamental intervention in the work with the family and were like milestones in the whole process.

RITUALS

During the time with the family, several meaningful rituals were performed. The request for the use of rituals came from the family members, which I interpreted as being their way of asking for support, guidance and accompaniment in their difficult circumstances. The rituals helped the family to focus on the important tasks they shared and had to deal with together as a family unit. The rituals had both spiritual and religious implications. They connected the family members together in a profound way, in the sense that they came in touch with their inner emotions and feelings and could actively contribute by putting their own values and perspectives into the situation to create meaningful moments that they shared. The religious implications reached out to something beyond themselves by using the Christian heritage to connect the family members with real strength.

The newborn baby played an important role because the infant was the driving force that connected the family with my service. Jakob, by wanting his grandchild to be baptised, now built a new bridge, one that connected his family and the service of the PCU. Jakob's wish for the christening of the grandchild revealed the family's spiritual aspects and how the spiritual dimension was important during this difficult time in their lives. The christening was something he had been brought up with in accordance with the Lutheran Christian heritage in Iceland and it was something he still valued. He gave his family this gift and by so doing he emphasised what was important for him, namely gathering the family together in a supportive, sustaining relationship in which a new member was welcomed into the family while another was saying goodbye.

Regarding the funeral, I guided, informed and gave the family options and suggestions on the family service and the funeral, for example concerning the musical performances and other practical matters. It was my aim to let them feel that I wanted the family service and funeral to be as meaningful as possible, and that I was also doing my best to achieve what they wished for. I prepared the sermon with them, the eulogy, where I sat with them, asked them about Jakob's life, his upbringing and childhood and his character, and listened to them reveal their memories and feelings about him and what he had meant to them. In my preparation, I tried to capture both what they had shared about Jakob, how I had perceived him and his personality these last days, and how I had felt his character through them and their family home, which I had been invited to in the preparation process. I told them that the sermon would also contain some words that I wanted to give them and the other funeral attendees at this time, because I firmly believe that my role is to talk about people's circumstances and to use my Christian faith, beliefs and life values to give something that can strengthen, comfort and be of support in times of death, distress and sorrow.

The family members used their efforts and energy to prepare most of the rituals and to actively participate in an earnest and sincere way throughout the illness and bereavement process. I was able to approach the family and get to know individual family members through the rituals that I participated in and prepared in collaboration with them. Thus, the rituals were a decisive element in my work with the family members, and they gave me the opportunity to be with them throughout the different stages: from Jakob's admittance to the PCU, through the time of his death and in the process after death.

The significance of rituals is underlined in the palliative care approach and is considered to offer meaning to people at this point in their life. Spiritual practices, both religious and non-religious, have been experienced by those who receive palliative care as a sense of connectedness with something higher than themselves and as an inner resource for hope and strength when facing the ultimate frontier in the life cycle – death (Ásgeirsdóttir *et al.* 2013). Rituals are meaning making and, within the family context, serve as links between the past, present and future, creating continuity and functioning as connective threads from generation to generation (Romanoff and Thompson 2006).

CONVERSATIONS, PHONE CALLS AND EMAILS

There were numerous conversations, phone calls and emails during the illness and bereavement process. In the conversations, the focus was on meeting the entire family as well as each individual family member. The emphasis was on accompanying the family, being with them, meeting individual needs, providing support and walking along with them in their difficult times. The conversations were on the family members' terms within a certain professional frame, where the emphasis was on being with the other person in the midst of suffering, adapting reflective or active listening to others, guiding, sharing and delivering information. The phone calls also had a pastoral and spiritual content, and both the calls and the emails were used to clarify, discuss and aid in making decisions on practical matters.

Outcomes

This case reveals the importance of the chaplain's availability and the notion that the chaplain is considered as being outside the healthcare system, in that the chaplain is in the spiritual and religious realm and represents certain life values and beliefs. The pastoral and spiritual approach in the case changed the family's position within the healthcare system – a position that evolved from being somewhat unhelpful, not giving the family members the voice and weight they needed. The family was in a difficult situation, struggling to be heard as their main concern was that Jakob was cared for in an adequate way and that he received all the best treatment that the healthcare system could provide.

When I came to work with the family, a new focus evolved, which resulted in growing inner strength, security and some structure around the family's life. The work with the family was complex and had many angles. It underlined the importance of being with the family members and helping them to be able to endure and to emphasise what they thought was most important for their wellbeing and that of Jakob in the circumstances. The family members began to experience that they were heard, seen and listened to and that their contributions were appreciated. This established a sense of security and a structure, which gave some stability in the ever-changing circumstances in which they were situated. The healthcare professionals had better access to Jakob and his family, which resulted in better symptom care and influenced the mental status of the family members in a positive way. This was primarily achieved through the rituals and my functioning as a spokesperson for the family. With regard to the rituals, these proved to be exactly what the family needed. Wright (2017) discusses the phrase of 'softening suffering'. She emphasises that suffering cannot be diminished or alleviated for people experiencing illness and loss; however, she argues that the intensity of suffering can be lessened through various means. The rituals helped to soften the family members' anguish and despair by strengthening their inner resources and network.

Conclusion

This case demonstrates how the chaplain is able to earn the trust of a family with a terminally ill family member, and how rituals can be of relevance at such crucial points in life. In this case, trust was earned by being with the family and by using a variety of rituals that helped them to focus on what really mattered to them in the sickness and bereavement process. Because of the reciprocal relationship and trust that had been built between the family and me, the family was able to accept the service at the Unit, which resulted in Jakob receiving better symptom control and in turn made the family feel more comfortable and at ease. The rituals served as interventions at decisive times and created a sense of security and support that had both spiritual and religious implications; the rituals provided a framework and connected family members with each other, with themselves, and with the transcendental realm of human existence.

In addition, the family members' request for rituals could be interpreted as their inner need for something that could give them meaning and substance and be of value for them at this time in their lives. As such, they were supported in addressing their spiritual and existential concerns. The family members embraced the rituals as their way of saying goodbye to their loved one; they made the rituals their own and in doing so gave them content and value. Furthermore, a change in time occurred, where previous experience was set aside for a while and the preparation for the imminent death began. The focus shifted to the present moment, to the situation as the family was living and experiencing it, to the 'here and now', and I managed to help the family to concentrate on the present situation and the imminence of death.

References

Ásgeirsdóttir, G.H., Sigurbjörnsson, E., Traustadottir, R., Sigurdardottir, V., Gunnarsdottir, S. and Kelly, E. (2013). 'To cherish each day as it comes: A qualitative study of spirituality among persons receiving palliative care.' *Supportive Care in Cancer*, 21, 5, 1445–1451.

Halfdanardottir, S.I., Ásgeirsdóttir, G.H., Hreidarsdottir, I., Ingvarsdottir, A., Petursdottir, E. and Thorbergsdottir, K.J. (2013). 'Use of a bereavement risk assessment checklist in an Icelandic hospital.' *European Journal of Palliative Care*, 20, 4, 192–195.

Hauksdóttir, A., Valdimarsdóttir, U., Fürst, C.J., Onelöv, E. and Steineck, G. (2010). 'Health care-related predictors of husbands' preparedness for the death of a wife to cancer: A population-based follow-up.' *Annals of Oncology*, 21, 2, 354–361.

Landspitali (2016). Hospital Statistics. Available at www.landspitali.is/um-landspitala/languages/english/hospital-statistics, accessed 14 January 2018.

McCurdy, D.B. and Fitchett, G. (2011). 'Ethical issues in case study publication: "Making our case(s) ethically".' *Journal of Health Care Chaplaincy*, 17, 1–2, 55–74.

Romanoff, B.D. and Thompson, B.E. (2006). 'Meaning construction in palliative care: The use of narrative, ritual, and the expressive arts.' *American Journal of Hospice and Palliative Medicine*, 23, 4, 309–316.

Saunders, C. (2006). *Cicely Saunders: Selected Writings 1958–2004*. New York, NY: Oxford University Press.

Statistics Iceland. Available at www.statice.is, accessed 14 January 2018.

World Health Organization (2018). 'WHO Definition of Palliative Care.' Available at www.who.int/cancer/palliative/definition/en, accessed 14 January 2018.

Wright, L.M. (2005). *Spirituality, Suffering and Illness: Ideas for Healing*. Philadelphia, PA: F.A. Davis Company.

Wright, L.M. (2017). *Suffering and Spirituality: The Path to Illness Healing*. Calgary, Canada: 4th Floor Press Inc.

Chapter 11

'I do want to get this funeral planned'

– Daisy, a former colleague in hospice care

Patricia Roberts

Introduction

At the centre of this case study is care for 'Daisy' (all names are pseudonyms), a nurse in her mid-60s who was dying of an aggressive form of cancer. I was new to the hospital and was in the process of learning the different groups and subgroups of employees and patients within the hospital when I became aware of Daisy's needs. As I cared for Daisy, her family and co-workers, I attempted to both respect the traditional Christian practices that characterised chaplaincy, as it had been practised at the hospital, and create an atmosphere that welcomed greater diversity. Additionally, recognising that the Christian religious rites of my background might be limiting when working with those who have no religious belief or alternative belief systems, I sought to meet the needs before me, rather than attempt to mould those in need into my spiritual stance.

Background

Daisy was a well-loved nurse at a medium-sized hospital in the southern USA. She had worked in this hospital for over 30 years. She started as a staff nurse and gradually worked her way up into senior management. Known for her optimism and generosity, she sponsored many student nurses, encouraged the secretaries in the department, and was generally well-known throughout the hospital for her ready smile and spirit of helpfulness. Daisy grew up in a small town near the coast in an area of great historical significance during the American Civil War. She had two sisters and an elderly mother, all of whom still lived in the town where Daisy grew up. Daisy was of European decent, and her siblings were members of the Daughters of the American Revolution,[1] although she never joined. Daisy was married with adult children.

I am Euro-American in my mid-50s with a Master of Divinity degree. I am ordained by the Christian Church, Disciples of Christ, a rather liberal Protestant denomination. At the time I met Daisy, I was a new Director of Chaplaincy and the first female chaplain hired at this hospital. Daisy and I both reported to the same supervisor, and it was from our mutual supervisor that I learned that Daisy was ill. As our visits progressed, I asked Daisy for her permission to share her story as I felt that our work might be a learning opportunity for future chaplaincy students. She readily agreed.

Case study

As I began working at the hospital, Daisy had returned to work, in remission after being hospitalised at another hospital for several weeks. I took the opportunity to introduce myself when we happened to attend the same meeting. I suspected that she could benefit from some spiritual and emotional support, and I wanted her to know that I was available should she feel the need.

A week later, I approached her in the hallway outside her office and made some general observations about the weather. Daisy immediately confessed that she was always cold, due to the cancer. Her face was

---

1 The Daughters of the American Revolution is a lineage-based organisation for women descended directly from someone who had been involved in the USA's struggle for independence. The organisation promotes historic preservation, education and patriotism.

drawn but I could see she had been quite pretty before the cancer took its toll. She smiled, yet her eyes were sad. She bemoaned how her clothing now hung on her. She stated flatly that she was not going to spend any money on new clothing, that there was 'no use'. It seemed that she had dropped her pretences, not knowing me personally but responding to my chaplain role.

I started my ministry with Daisy as 'the aesthetic witness', a term coined by James E. Dittes which describes how 'The pastoral counselor witnesses – steadfastly, undistracted, relentlessly – the life experience of the counselee, the harried pilgrimage of a soul that has too often scurried in shadow. Lucid listener, the counselor beholds what has been averted, attests to what has been dismissed, hopes and shames alike' (Dittes 2005, p.137). I was determined to make a space for Daisy to grieve her loss.

Listening to the finality in her voice regarding how her clothing fitted her, I suspected – rightly, it turned out – that she was not in remission and that she was not going to live very long. Even though my ministry with her began in a busy hospital hallway, I was able to listen closely as she talked. Much of what she said was about her feelings of frustration and anger at the cancer. She seemed to be sorting out her priorities and her life. At first, she did not share much about her family or personal relationships beyond that she adored her dog, Jumbo, loved to golf and hoped to retire to her lake house. Later, I found myself wishing that I had asked her more questions about her background. However, at that point in time I had no idea in what direction this relationship might progress.

Daisy and I continued to have 'hallway' talks for the next month. She shared that she had grown up in the Methodist Church but had felt disconnected from that faith and simply considered herself spiritual. I sensed that there was a story behind her feelings, although I never had a chance to discover why she felt as she did. Meanwhile, I continued to field enquiries from Daisy's co-workers who appeared to feel a real stake in her recovery. I also observed that, because of their needs, Daisy found herself in the position of fighting an aggressive cancer and holding up the brave front for everyone around her while she was at work. I sensed that she had started her fight against the cancer aggressively but as time passed she had become more resigned to the fact that the cancer was not abating. During our conversations, she alluded to feeling a sense of guilt regarding her own feelings of resignation when her children were so determined that she would recover. From a pastoral care stance, it became all the more imperative that I deliberately carve out the space for Daisy to talk about her feelings of anger, fear and helplessness, without having to 'be strong' for the chaplain. On more than one occasion, Daisy expressed her weariness of 'pretending' to be strong. However, she was resolute to continue in her role and resisted any suggestions that she share her feelings with her family or co-workers. It seemed to me that she was intent on continuing to play her expected part within her family system.

Daisy did not attempt to placate her co-workers on the topic of religion. At times, it seemed that she enjoyed their discomfort with her spiritual views. It seemed that the entire clerical staff in that department felt that Daisy needed to 'get right with the Lord'. They would bring tracts and booklets to leave with her. This group of people also openly and aggressively prayed for her recovery. Two women in the office expressed their concern about Daisy's relationship with a certain doctor who worked in their department. I knew this doctor from previous conversations. Although he did openly state that he professed atheism, he was always ready for a conversation on religion and faith. He had worked with Daisy for many years. He came from a Sikh background and he shared his Sikh beliefs with Daisy, offering a different perspective on the afterlife, in which she took great solace.

Knowing the pressure that she was feeling from her co-workers, I felt it was important that, as the 'religious' person, I offer support without pressure. I would 'pop in' from time to time, although most of those visits were merely times Daisy shared medical updates.

Three months later, I took two weeks off from work for surgery. Christmas was approaching and while I was out, Daisy made the decision she would retire at the end of the year. When I returned to work, Daisy had retired and 'disappeared' from my life. From time to time, I wondered how she was doing but I did not reach out to her.

Just before Easter, Daisy returned, working for another agency housed within the hospital. This was no surprise to me, since it had seemed that work was one major way that Daisy distracted herself from her declining health. She was even thinner now, walking with a cane. Due to my own surgery, I was using a knee scooter to make my way throughout the hospital. I would see her from time to time and we would share pleasantries but nothing of substance. She always seemed to be accompanied by her new co-workers.

Easter was early that year, and shortly thereafter a nurse manager named Sharon asked that I preside at her wedding. It was a large wedding, catered and hosted in a historic building in the countryside at the edge of town. There were many employees in attendance. Although it was spring, it was unexpectedly cool and wet, with the actual wedding held in a decorated stable. The chill made me thankful for my white clergy robe and stole. I had removed my foot brace for the actual service. When I looked out into the congregation, I noticed Daisy in the crowd, our eyes met and we exchanged smiles. After the ceremony, I looked for her at the reception but she had already left.

First visit

Three weeks later, Sharon, in tears, gave me Daisy's number and said that Daisy had requested that I call. She informed me that Daisy's condition had worsened and the hospice had taken over. The entire nursing department took this news very hard, but Daisy's former department had thought she was in remission, so they took the news especially hard. They were in shock.

I placed the call but only got the answering machine. I left my number. Eventually, I received a call from Daisy's adult daughter, Ashley. She said that her mother was in the hospice and had requested that I officiate at the funeral. She gave me directions to her mother's home and we set up a time to meet.

From that point, the experience was disorienting for me. I was still navigating the world on a knee scooter because of my surgery, transported from place to place by my youngest daughter. It is not my practice to offer any spiritual support outside the confines of the hospital to employees or patients, yet somehow this felt important and my supervisor agreed.

Daisy's condition seemed to have a wide ripple effect throughout the hospital and I speculated that I would be encountering further spiritual care challenges resulting from Daisy's death. Needing to find my place within this hospital system, the care of Daisy outweighed my previous practice of confining pastoral care to working hours.

My first meeting with Daisy and her family took place in Daisy's home. Daisy was sitting in a large chair. She looked smaller than I remembered and pale. She was wearing a new wig and she had lipstick on. Her smile was still as contagious as ever, though, and she seemed genuinely glad to see me. Daisy introduced me to her sister Barbara; the resemblance was certain and she seemed to be an older version of Daisy. Barbara shared a few details about their family, then excused herself and allowed Daisy and me to have some privacy.

Daisy began to share some broad ideas of what she wanted in her funeral. She seemed stumped when thinking about musical choices. It did not take me long to realise that Daisy had a strong need to project her vision on to me and to control her funeral since she had so little control of anything else. The more she spoke, the more obvious it was that she had other things on her mind. So, I enquired:

Chaplain: Daisy, you seem agitated.

Daisy: (*With a sigh*) My husband just doesn't 'get it'. He thinks that I should just let things go and relax. How can I do that? I'm dying! We have been fighting a lot, and I have been in so much pain I can't sleep, and neither can he.

Chaplain: I am sure this must be painful for him to see you like this, especially since he can't fix it.

Daisy: (*Again with a sigh*) I am sure that is what it is. We are both so tired, and he must work. He said he has to work or we won't have health insurance. At least he gets to get out and away. I am just so mad. We have not been married long enough. You know, we haven't been married all that long, just seven years.

After this visit, I felt a bit frustrated because our conversation never returned to the funeral. I felt that attending to Daisy by providing a sounding board for her feelings was sufficient, yet inside I began to doubt I would have enough information to plan the funeral service. I struggled to retain my stance as the aesthetic witness and found myself wanting to move the conversation in the direction I needed.

Second visit

A week later I met with Daisy again. Her health seemed to be rapidly declining and her eyes seemed to be losing their sparkle. However, she was neatly dressed in her robe and a new blonde wig. This visit was more focused on the funeral. Her plans were more specific and it sounded more as if she was planning a wedding than a funeral. Daisy requested prayer during this visit, which was new.

Daisy's daughter Ashley established a blog about her mother that she kept updated daily. This was to discourage phone calls and to allow Daisy's friends and co-workers to keep abreast of her condition. I decided not to read the blog; instead, I decided to assess Daisy personally.

According to one of the nurses at the hospital, one of the blog posts reported that Daisy was spending more time in her bed and her family was moving her bed to the sunroom where she could look outside. A group of secretaries and clerks from work read that post and solicited money to bring numerous plants to Daisy's house, 'so that when she looked out her window, she could see the beautiful flowers on her deck'. Several co-workers went to Daisy's home and 'surprised' her with their gift of 20 or so azaleas, bougainvillea, geraniums and so on.

Third visit

A week later, I called to make sure that Daisy was feeling well enough for a visit. This was my third visit to her home. This time it was Daisy's sister, Lois, attending to her. Daisy was waiting, bundled up with a blanket over her robe. I expected to see her in her hospital bed but she was sitting in the same chair. She no longer bothered to wear a wig, instead covering her head with a grey scarf wrapped securely around her head.

Chaplain: I hear that the ladies at work brought you some plants.

Daisy: I really love those girls, and I really appreciate the thought.

Lois: There is a note on the door, and we've asked that only close family visit. If anyone asks, would you please tell them that sending cards is enough?

At this point, Daisy was rapidly weakening. As a caregiver her entire life, she no longer had the energy to provide the care to her visitors that she wanted to bestow and they wanted to receive. Her face looked more drawn this day and she appeared to be in pain. I could not help but notice a huge bouquet of roses in the living room.

Lois: Dr Singh came for dinner last night, and he brought those flowers for Daisy. He said they have special significance. (*Motioning me over to the flowers*) The red rose in the middle is Daisy. It signifies her precious life. The ring of yellow roses represents hope and external existence of the soul in this world and the beyond. The outside ring of white roses represents peace and God that surrounds and gives life to everything represented in the inner circles. He said that these are a tradition in India.

Daisy: I think the flowers are beautiful. Dr Singh and I have been talking about life after death. He says life is a continual rebirth. I find that so comforting.

I sat down across from Daisy as she commented that her 'diet' was not going well. She smiled faintly, a shadow of humour left.

Daisy: The nausea is almost unbearable. I am trying to avoid the morphine. I do want to have the most quality time that I can before it's too late.

I opened the conversation directly.

Chaplain: Speaking of souls and afterlife, how is it with your soul?

Daisy: (*Sighing deeply*) It brings me comfort when I think that the soul itself is not subject to death. A part of me will remain. Still, my pain is so distracting. I can't sleep at night and the nausea is so awful. I don't know if I even believe in God any more.

Her sister quickly interjected, 'Daisy, you know that's just not true.' This elicited another sigh. I joined Daisy by simply stating, 'Dying is hard work.' To which Daisy nodded in agreement.

Daisy: I do want to get this funeral planned, so I don't have to think about it. Ashley was here last night, and we spent the evening writing my obituary. Lonnie [*her son*] wouldn't come over. His wife said that he can't stand to see me this way.

Chaplain: That must hurt.

Daisy: (*Nodding affirmatively*) I want the funeral to be at our home place on the beach. I want everyone to come there. It is so beautiful, and I have so many wonderful memories there. I used to swim every day. I miss that.

Chaplain: Earlier you said that you find comfort in the idea of a part of you living on, or returning. What do you need to finish?

Daisy: I have thought about that. There is so much I wanted to do with my life. You know, I have everything a person could want but I still want to stay and enjoy it. I was looking forward to retirement; Perry and I were going to spend our time on the golf course. We were going to take our grandkids out on the boat. There is so much I will miss.

We sat in silence, Daisy asked for a prayer. This was only the second time that she requested a religious ritual. I asked her what she wanted to me to pray.

Daisy: I want God to give me the strength to die and I want God to take me quickly. This is so hard on my family.

I lifted her wishes to God. I looked and observed the tears in Daisy's eyes.

As I was leaving, I thought to enquire what Daisy would like for the memorial at the hospital. She quickly replied.

> *Daisy:* I don't want any memorial at the hospital. I want everyone to come to the funeral. I have already hired a caterer. (*I guess my surprise was evident*) I don't want anyone to have to do any work at all.

The next day at work, I sought out Dr Singh. He explained that, although he had worked with Daisy, they were not particularly close until she became quite ill and sought his support religiously. He shared that he felt honoured to help her and that he really liked her family. He told me the details regarding the type of cancer Daisy had and how deadly it was.

It seemed that Dr Singh's religious support was somewhat like my own approach: supportively listening and only addressing explicit religious questions when asked directly. He and I worked out a system of support for Daisy and her family. We exchanged phone numbers and promises to keep the other informed.

Fourth visit

As Daisy's health began to decline my visits became more frequent. A few days later I returned, and we discussed the final music choices for her funeral. Daisy had picked two currently popular songs, both of which I had never heard before.

> *Daisy:* I know that isn't a funeral song, but Joshua loves this song, and we dance to it all the time.

Daisy's face was serene as she thought of dancing with her grandson.

> *Daisy:* I don't really have anything in common with the other grandchildren. Just Joshua. He is special.

> *Chaplain:* Special?

> *Daisy:* Yes, you will see. Joshua has some handicaps. My son is a recovering addict. I don't know if that caused it. I know that after Joshua was born things were very difficult and my son ended up

divorced. His new wife has some children but they don't stay with her too often. I have spent lots of time with Joshua.

This other song is for my husband. He is a good man, and this has been difficult. I know it will be hard on him.

We sat quietly as Daisy seemed to retreat into her own thoughts. After a few moments, I engaged her.

Chaplain: I am glad you were able to choose some music, but I was thinking about your mother and your older relatives. I know that your mother is elderly and very active in her church. Do you think we should have a hymn as well? She might find that comforting.

Daisy: Oh yes, that would be great; I hadn't really thought of that. What do you suggest?

Lois: I can get Ed and his band to play it.

Daisy: (*Emphatically*) No bluegrass. I hate bluegrass.

A glimpse of the old Daisy had appeared, if only for a moment. Lois seemed taken aback but quickly recovered as I returned to the subject.

Chaplain: I have a list of common songs that are often sung at funerals.

Daisy: Oh no, if we are going to use hymns, I want number 11 and 53.

Daisy had hidden the fact that she was indeed quite familiar with her childhood religion, even knowing the page numbers of the hymns. This made me wonder the more about her faith, and I made a mental note to explore that with her when we were alone.

Fifth visit

It was four days before I visited again. This time I met Daisy's daughter, Ashley, for the first time. She answered the door, introduced herself and quickly showed me into the room, then excused herself. Daisy was much weaker at this point. She would doze off and then quickly wake to talk.

She talked about her career and the time she spent in California earning her degree. She talked about how lonely she was away from her family.

Daisy: It's like that now; I am lonely. Everyone is here but I feel alone. (*We sat a while in silence*) Where is God? Why won't God let me die now?

Chaplain: That is a big question and I am not sure that any of us have answers.

Daisy: Why did this happen to me? I don't think I was a bad person.

Chaplain: Do you really feel that God is punishing you? I know that personally I do not see God that way. (*Daisy sighed and cried*) We all must face death; that is for sure. It is a natural process but it does seem unfair the way it happens sometimes. (*She nodded*) Daisy, God knows your heart. I am sure that you are not being punished for anything you have done. You are frail and ill because you are human. You have done your best in life and that is all any of us can hope to do.

Daisy: (*Softly*) Chaplain, thank you. Do you think that it is time that I allow them to give me morphine so that I can rest?

Chaplain: (*Taking her hand*) Daisy, have you made your peace with those important to you?

She nodded yes. I just squeezed her hand, and she held tight. Her nurse returned, and I excused myself.

Daisy's death

I kept in touch with Daisy's family daily via phone. A week later, just after midnight, I received a call from Perry, Daisy's husband. He said that the hospice nurse had said that Daisy wouldn't last much longer. 'Could you come here and pray?'

When I arrived, Perry and Ashley were sitting on a sofa near Daisy's bed, settled in for the wait. Jumbo was in the bed, sleeping at Daisy's feet. Daisy looked ashen and her eyes were more sunken. She slept quietly except for the occasional gasps and rattles. Perry looked weary and sad. Ashley, too, looked exhausted. They discussed how the two of them would share Jumbo. They talked about all the small talk things that people do to fill up the vacuum of expectation. It became obvious that Daisy was on her own schedule, as usual. Perry requested prayer, so we gathered around the bed and prayed for Daisy to have a smooth transition and that all the loved ones would have strength in their grief. She died shortly after I had excused myself. I called Dr Singh as soon as I received word.

Daisy's funeral

Hundreds of people arrived for the funeral, although I only saw three of Daisy's co-workers. The sky filled with black clouds and the wind was fierce. The sound was tricky in the wind but the musician and I managed. Daisy's mother and aunts stayed on the porch, sitting in rockers to listen. The remainder of the family sat directly in front of our makeshift altar in the yard. The spirit of the service was upbeat and sad in the same moment. My eulogy was heartfelt. I began the meditation with a quote from Anna Quindlen (1997), 'The living are defined by whom they have lost', and I utilised Quindlen's theme of death as the ultimate taboo in our language, tying it to the loss everyone was feeling with Daisy's death.

> *Chaplain:* Daisy was much more worried about her loved ones she was leaving behind than she ever was worried about herself. Although she was frustrated at the end that God did not follow her orders and take her up on her command, she was ready to move on, let go her cup of suffering. I told her that God was no better at listening to instructions than she was! She laughed at that. She had made her peace with God.

Daisy's family and friends laughed at that, knowing that was exactly who Daisy was. The service was not overtly religious but addressed the needs of the Christians who attended, particularly her mother. Family members received the message well and stated that the service was 'just how Daisy wanted'. Afterwards, Dr Singh sought me out to tell me how well my message resonated with the attendees.

Discussion

Assessment

My first indication of Daisy's needs came from a conversation with my supervisor who was weighing the ethical and legal issues of visiting and caring for someone who directly reported to her. The fact that my boss mentioned Daisy to me at all alerted me to the importance of the matter.

I met Daisy at a critical juncture of her disease process. When we first began talking, it was dawning on her that she might lose the battle against cancer. As the pastoral relationship deepened, Daisy began to let down her guard and share her intimate fears and sorrow about dying. As a caregiver, Daisy had cared for others and provided strength to others, yet she had not learned how to give that same grace to herself. Daisy had not attended church in years and did not have spiritual support, although her family was very supportive of her. However, her family needed to attend to Daisy physically and to their own grief, so I felt it was important to provide the pastoral care to Daisy.

The choice to provide care for Daisy was an exception to my own past practice of keeping work relationships separate from other relationships. I normally focus on caring for patients and not current or former employees. However, something about Daisy's case intrigued me, and I felt that Daisy needed a religious 'guide' for her journey as well as a religious 'authority' to stand by her when she was pressured to conform to the religious norms of her co-workers.

Interventions

I felt that my stance with Daisy, as 'the aesthetic witness', as someone bearing witness to her story, was an appropriate one. I was reassuring when needed but ultimately it was Daisy who did the work. As a chaplain, my goal is not to give the patient hope or faith; rather, my job is to facilitate the process in which the patient finds their own resources and strength. Daisy's death was one I would classify as a 'good death' because, although it was untimely, it was on her own terms.

During my first visit, I listened as Daisy seemed to be sorting out her situation, acknowledging that she was angry but in an undefined way. Although she named her anger, her voice seemed to betray her fear. I wondered if she was angry about her death, the fact that her husband seemed distant or that she hadn't had enough time together with her husband. I declined to enquire, because I was not sure that Daisy had sorted her feelings; nor was I sure that such sorting and identifying was even necessary. I connected her frustration to a frustration with God; but, on reflection, I suspect that that was my own connection rather than Daisy's. I wondered if the realisation of the reality of her impending death was sinking in because I could clearly see that she was frightened about the prospects of dying.

On my second visit, I began to discover that a sense of parallel process was happening. Since I feel safest when I am in control, I could recognise this in Daisy. My 'intellectual self' was craving the safety of having information and trying to understand the business of funeral planning that involved renting tents and having a caterer, while my 'pastoral self' was challenged to attend to the process of Daisy's work planning her own funeral. However, I felt she was beginning to trust that I, as her minister, would provide support without the pressure to conform to a frame of religious expression, with which she wasn't comfortable. Becoming acquainted with, and trying to be sensitive to, the needs of so many new people – Daisy, her family, her co-workers – was disorienting for me, and it was a challenge be present with all of them.

At my fourth visit, Daisy and I discussed the final music choices for her funeral. Daisy had picked two currently popular songs, neither of which I had heard before. When I looked them up, later that night, I was surprised. Not at the church music, which was typical, but one of the popular songs she had chosen to play for her grandson had a great dance beat, and it also had sexually explicit language. I did not know how I felt about playing that song but I decided to rest with it.

Daisy had given me very specific instructions that she did not want a memorial service at work: she had wanted a celebration, not a sad memorial, and she had wanted everyone to attend her funeral. So, following the funeral, I faced a dilemma when hospital employees desired a memorial service. I had to weigh the needs of the living people, whom I work with and see daily, against the wishes of Daisy. I felt that there had to be a way in which to honour both needs and desires, so instead of the traditional memorial service that Chaplain Service provides when employees die, I created a new ritual that would give closure and help Daisy's co-workers and friends begin the healing process. The memorial for Daisy was not a religious ceremony. The staff brought Daisy's favourite foods and mingled, taking turns sharing memories. Many physicians, fellow nurses, and administrators stopped by. A colleague had created a display of silly pictures taken at departmental functions through the years that showed the silly side of Daisy and how much she loved her co-workers.

Outcomes

Daisy had what I consider to be a good death. My pastoral stance as a supportive listener allowed Daisy the space to formulate, articulate and eventually receive what she needed to face death with some sense of agency. I also provided comfort to Daisy's family. As I was the spiritual person, they were able to turn over those duties to me and attend to Daisy in the ways that they knew best. Since the family assumed that Daisy and I were close as co-workers, they trusted that I would know what Daisy wanted and therefore did not feel the need to impress their own wishes.

Daisy's co-workers had specific ideas regarding my role as a chaplain. They also seemed to have expectations for Daisy's behaviour as their dying friend. The co-workers' recognition that I was the religious 'authority' allowed these caring friends to trust that Daisy's religious needs were being met. Eventually, what had been a cautious relationship, between me, as the new chaplain, and these employees, became a trusted relationship. One of the outcomes of this case was that I earned acceptance within my new employment and people began to approach me for their own ministry needs. This was particularly aided by the memorial service. After this, the staff seemed no longer focused on their anger and inability to control Daisy's disease but moved towards acceptance and mourning. By directly involving those closest to Daisy in the creation of the memorial, the service provided a much-needed focus for the grief and energy of those participating that addressed their feelings of helplessness.

Conclusion

I believe the words I preached from Anna Quindlin, 'The living are defined by whom they have lost' (Quindlen 1997). Daisy had a wide sphere of influence within the hospital, her community of friends and her family. As a new chaplain in the hospital, I was not yet familiar with the people and the issues associated with the institution but I knew that chaplains are more than just the corporate ritual leader. Employees often spend more time with each other than they do with their own families, and that creates tight bonds. The chaplain has an opportunity to provide care to employees, which, in turn, improves the care that those employees provide to patients. Unlike the pastor of a church, who has a single prayer book or a set of rituals, chaplains are called to be many things to many people of diverse beliefs. Chaplains have an opportunity to be creative in their provision of care and comfort to those who are hurting. My boss, feeling unable to help her own employee, handed her care over to me, the chaplain. This demonstrates that even senior leadership reaches a wall that only a chaplain can cross. The chaplain's role is to meet people where they are in life and then create meaningful rituals of comfort or rites of passage. In this case, I used my role to create space for differences in belief and non-belief among those involved. In addition, as a result of my care for Daisy, I created many new relationships and earned trust within the new community.

References

Dittes, J.E. (2005). 'The Ascetic Witness.' In R.C. Dykstra (ed.) *Images of Pastoral Care: Classic Readings* (pp.137–149). St Louis, MO: Chalice Press.

Quindlen, A. (1997). 'The Living Are Defined by Whom They Have Lost.' In P. Theroux (ed.) *The Book of Eulogies: A Collection of Memorial Tributes, Poetry, Essays, and Letters of Condolence* (pp.338–340). New York, NY: Scribner.

Chapter 12

'For myself and for your people with whom I pray'

– Mrs Pearlman, an 82-year-old woman with a terminal diagnosis of advanced Alzheimer's disease

Amy E. Goodman and Joel Baron

Introduction

The High Holy Days, also known as the Days of Awe, are the spiritual, religious and liturgical culmination of the Jewish year. Tradition informs us that on Rosh Hashanah the names of the righteous are inscribed in the Book of Life, guaranteeing another year of life; it is this same book in which God 'seals' our judgement on Yom Kippur. Our acts of repentance can compensate for the rest of the year when the final ruling is levied on Yom Kippur. Communal worship, communal confession of sins, and communal rejoicing are central to the traditional practice of these most awesome days.

The themes of the High Holy Days – of renewal and rebirth; of life and death; of repentance and forgiveness; of memory, meaning and legacy; of love and gratitude – are frequently in the bodies, minds, hearts and souls of our hospice patients. Our patients are unlikely to live to witness another New Year. They may be reciting *Yizkor* (memorial) prayers this year knowing that others will be mentioning *their* names when reciting *Yizkor* next year. Our patients may be praying *Yizkor* in memory of those whose names may never again be mentioned by any living soul. The resonance of these liturgical and spiritual messages will undoubtedly impact the religious practice and spiritual lives of their families as well.

During the Rosh Hashanah *musaf* (additional) service, the *shaliach tzibbur* (prayer leader) offers *Hin'ni* ('Here I Am') on behalf of the *tzibbur* (congregation), a prayer practice that began in the Middle Ages, when most of the individuals in a congregation did not hold their own *machzorim* (prayer books). In a community-based hospice programme, the chaplain serves as *shaliach tzibbur* for a patient and perhaps for a family. The chaplain sits with the patient in the patient's home, room or at their bedside. Realising this, and understanding the limits of endurance for many hospice patients, our hospice spiritual care team created a small booklet of some of the most recognisable pieces of the High Holy Day liturgy. With this 'liturgy' in hand, chaplains might share one, several or, less likely, all of the liturgical elements with a patient. These prayers are available for chaplains themselves as meditation pieces, helping to create an appropriate internal *kavanah* (intention) as they prepare to enter the patient's home.

Our patients may not be able to participate in communal worship because of advancing and terminal illness, physical and cognitive decline, an inability to ambulate or travel, pain and symptom distress or any number of limitations. Yet their spiritual lives endure; they have spiritual and religious needs during this sacred season. The fixed language and centuries-old ritual of our tradition is flexible enough to offer the spiritual opportunities to our hospice patients and 'the re-examination of our varied relationships with God on the annual judgment day' (Kaunfer 2010, p.101) and throughout this holy season. A spiritual caregiver's ability to offer prayer alongside or on behalf of our patients, with a nuanced understanding of themselves as service leaders, can in fact become a meaningful personal spiritual experience that deepens the spiritual caregivers' own prayer lives during the Days of Awe.

Therefore, spiritual caregivers must understand their own theology of spiritual care concerning those suffering from advanced and terminal illness. Spiritual care of the dying 'is a dynamic and demanding process, in which each expression of pastoral ministry is unique but not *ad hoc*, grounded in established resources but capable of flexible translation according to the needs of the moment' (Beuken 2002, p.39).

Our spiritual care team assembled the 'liturgy' knowing that, in building an appropriate and contextualised High Holy Day experience for Jewish hospice patients, individuals can connect to traditional prayers, familiar melodies and resonant messages of life and death. A skilful spiritual caregiver can support patients, their families, friends and caregivers in revealing new meaning and understanding within the fixed liturgy that spotlight the special nature of this sacred time. As chaplains, we also have the opportunity to uncover new meaning and discover novel understandings in our own prayer lives as a result of providing this sensitive, compassionate spiritual care to our patients.

As mentioned, our liturgy was intended to facilitate a contextualised High Holy Day experience for our Jewish hospice patients. Translating these prayers required, in some cases, our borrowing from more than one translation and inserting our own commentary in order to reflect the need of the liturgical moment. In reciting a sacred text in pastoral relationship with another person, convention tends to employ the 'jussive' case (for example, '*May* the Lord...'). Additionally, our convention in the liturgy was to translate Lord as 'the Eternal' or 'Adonai' interchangeably. These translations deemphasise the gendered elements of the Hebrew text and reflect the internal meaning of יהוה/YHWH ('to be perpetually/eternally'). For example, in citing a sacred text, 'The Lord bless you and protect you!' becomes 'May the Eternal bless you and protect you!'

Our spiritual care team borrowed heavily from the Jewish Publication Society's translation for biblical texts, while also reflecting what happens 'in practice' and what makes sense in the given pastoral relationship. Similarly, for some of the High Holy Day liturgical pieces, we blended translations from several *machzorim* (prayer books) that worked best for our context. All along, our spiritual care team strove to honour the core themes and messages of the Days of Awe, though we needed to clarify, soften or nuance translations to be appropriate for the hospice patient.

Background

Our hospice agency is part of a large not-for-profit elder-care organisation that manages both health services and supportive housing for people in a full range of settings, from independent living to long-term care. Hospice is one of the community-based services offered by our organisation, one whose health services care for people at home, wherever home may be – a skilled nursing facility, an assisted living facility, or perhaps the very home in which the patient was born and has lived their entire life. 'Mrs Pearlman' lived in a skilled nursing facility, 'Windmill Terrace', that provides routine nursing care for individuals with advancing serious and chronic illnesses. This facility, located in a suburb of a city in the north-eastern United States, houses approximately 50 patients, most of whom share their rooms with another patient. Approximately 30 per cent of the residents are Jewish, 50 per cent Roman Catholic, and 20 per cent primarily Protestant Christian denominations. The overwhelming majority of the facility's residents are white, and receive government benefits in order to finance their room and board at the facility. In addition to the skilled nursing care offered by the staff to the residents of this facility, some patients with end-stage or terminal illness receive hospice care from an outside agency. These hospice agencies provide additional support for people who are within the final weeks and months of their lives, including additional care from the agency's home health aides, chaplaincy and social work support, and nursing expertise around pain and symptom management related to care at the end of life. The hospice staff can be considered an interdisciplinary team of consultants for those residents of the skilled nursing facility who are nearing the end of their lives.

Mrs Pearlman was an 82-year-old woman with a terminal diagnosis of advanced Alzheimer's disease. She had co-morbid conditions of coronary artery disease and diabetes mellitus. Her clinical decline was evidenced by anorexia with decreased meal portion consumption, weight loss, concern for aspiration of oral secretions, decreased ability to engage and increased daytime sleepiness, and there were newly onset indications of poorly controlled pain; she was fully dependent on others for ambulation, transfer, dressing, bathing, toileting and feeding.

Mrs Pearlman had a history of psychological manifestations of her Alzheimer's disease. These manifestations included a history of behavioural disturbances and hallucinations. Symptoms had been generally managed with medication since she had been enrolled on hospice services.

Mrs Pearlman was part of a cohesive family system with several primary family members visiting regularly. She had an affable personality, and throughout her life had demonstrated resilience and strong coping skills. Mrs Pearlman often spoke about religion and this persisted as she continued to decline cognitively. She shared that she was raised Orthodox Jewish and that her grandfather had been a rabbi. She conveyed that she was more 'interested' in the spirituality of Judaism than the strictures of Orthodoxy, though lighting *Shabbes* (Sabbath) candles, singing Jewish songs and exchanging holiday blessings strongly resonated with her. When asked about prayer, Mrs Pearlman rarely declined an offer of blessing. She expressed openness to be present during prayer services that were Jewish as well as 'Catholic' or 'Christian', as she shared with the chaplain that 'prayers offered from the heart are all heard by God'.

'Rabbi Jacobs' is a 73-year-old man who came to his rabbinate later in life, having spent his 'first career' primarily as a business executive. Rabbi Jacobs was raised in a Conservative Jewish home in the midwestern United States. He belonged to a Reform Synagogue in the eastern United States during his married life, though he and his wife recently changed their affiliation to a classical Conservative *shul* (synagogue) in the same community, where he and his wife feel much more 'at home'. Rabbi Jacobs first became acquainted with Mrs Pearlman nearly a year before she became a hospice patient, as it was her habit to sit in her wheelchair across from the main nurses' station for her unit and greet people as they walked by. Some nodded to her, some would ignore her, and some would stop and chat. Rabbi Jacobs was in the latter group and often looked forward to their brief conversations as he was in the facility visiting his own hospice patients. Despite Mrs Pearlman's obvious cognitive decline, she would always greet Rabbi Jacobs with 'Hello Rabbi', which Rabbi Jacobs took as a sign that the fact that he was a rabbi was important to Mrs Pearlman. They would chat every week or two as there were a number of hospice patients whom Rabbi Jacobs would visit at this facility, so by the time Mrs Pearlman herself became a hospice patient they had already discussed a number of Jewish holidays and wished each other a 'Good *Shabbes*' many times, and it had become their custom that Rabbi Jacobs would always greet her with a kiss, either on her forehead or cheek.

The following case study involves the spiritual relationship between a hospice patient and her primary hospice chaplain (Fitchett 2011, pp.12–14). Both individuals and the skilled nursing facility are identified by pseudonyms in order to protect the identity of Mrs Pearlman, whose personal information is legally protected by Medicare hospice guidelines and the Health Insurance Portability and Accountability Act of 1996 (HIPAA),[1] legislation in the United States aimed at protecting data privacy and safeguarding medical information. Rabbi Jacobs's identity has, therefore, also been anonymised, primarily to protect Mrs Pearlman's identity. Also, hospice work is often collaborative in nature and, over her time receiving hospice services, Mrs Pearlman received spiritual care from more than one chaplain. Anonymising Rabbi Jacobs's identity also serves to simplify the narrative flow of the spiritual care offered by two hospice chaplains. Because the hospice chaplain who provided the majority of Mrs Pearlman's spiritual care is an older, white male, Rabbi Jacobs's identity has been gendered male.

Case study

Early in her spiritual relationship with Rabbi Jacobs, as a hospice patient, Mrs Pearlman had presented tearfully and expressed that her tears were because she was 'being called home'. With chaplain support, Mrs Pearlman shared that 'home' was a 'beautiful place', where 'God saw all people as beautiful inside and out'. She also expressed that family and friends were welcoming her 'home'.

---

1   https://aspe.hhs.gov/report/health-insurance-portability-and-accountability-act-1996.

Rabbi Jacobs began his High Holy Day visit as soon as he arrived at the facility. Having parked his car, he turned off his music, rolled down his car window and opened the excerpts from the High Holy Day liturgy assembled by the hospice spiritual care team. Rabbi Jacobs read the words of the *Hin'ni* prayer to himself, humming a High Holy Day melody, beginning with an excerpt from the traditional *Hin'ni*:

> Chaplain: (*Reciting in Hebrew*) Here I am. So poor in deeds, I tremble in fear, overwhelmed and apprehensive before You who hears the prayers of the people Israel. Although unworthy for the task, I pray and seek favour for Your people Israel, for they have entrusted me with this task. Therefore, God of our ancestors – of Abraham and Sarah, Isaac and Rebecca, Jacob and Leah and Rachel – O Gracious, Compassionate and Awesome God, I pray for mercy for myself and for Your people with whom I pray. (After Goldberg *et al.* 2015, p.17 and Feld 2010, p.312)

Rabbi Jacobs will occasionally employ personal prayer as a vehicle for self-care. When a patient may be in extreme distress, Rabbi Jacobs's personal prayers strengthen his spirit as he prepares to observe such suffering. For the High Holy season, Rabbi Jacobs has come to 'utilise' the *Hin'ni* prayer on a consistent basis, both to engage the spiritual and theological importance of these holidays and to humble himself with the awareness that this may be the patient's last High Holy Day season. Using this prayer regularly supports Rabbi Jacobs in creating a *kavanah* (intention) for himself, the essence of which he shares with his patients.

Rabbi Jacobs concluded his *kavanah* for this High Holy Day spiritual visit and went to meet Mrs Pearlman in a communal space in the facility, called the 'Namaste Room'. This room is a calm day room where patients, who in most cases are not verbally communicative, spend their days listening to soothing music as they sit in reclining chairs. The goal of this space is to provide a calming, minimally stimulating environment for patients with Alzheimer's disease, Parkinson's dementia and other dementias. 'Namaste' means 'I bow to you' and, when recited with hands placed together at the centre of the chest, respectfully acknowledges the soul before you and increases the flow of energy from the heart chakra.

It is unclear whether this meaning was known to the staff and patients; however, Rabbi Jacobs found the space conducive to chaplain visits with soft conversations, and staff indicated this was not contraindicated for other patients who rested in the 'Namaste Room'. During this visit, approximately eight residents, including Mrs Pearlman, were resting in reclining chairs about 18 inches (half a metre) apart. As is typical in this space, the lights were low and calming music was played to promote a relaxation response while residents were well attended by two or three aides. As on other days, the calming music was primarily a mixture of what has come to be called 'spa music' and gentle instrumental settings of tunes from the 1930s and 1940s, most of which would be culturally familiar to the age and background of the patients present.

Rabbi Jacobs pulled a chair close to Mrs Pearlman's side and spoke directly into her ear. This approach had proved effective in previous visits between Rabbi Jacobs and Mrs Pearlman.

Chaplain: Hi, Mrs Pearlman. It's Rabbi Jacobs.

Mrs Pearlman: (With her eyes closed) Hello Rabbi.

Chaplain: (Taking Mrs Pearlman's hand) Shall we light *Shabbes* candles?

The imagined lighting of *Shabbes* candles, a Friday night tradition, had become a shared ritual between Rabbi Jacobs and Mrs Pearlman, regardless of the day of the week of the visit.

Mrs Pearlman: Yes.

Rabbi Jacobs led their reciting of the blessing together in Hebrew. He then put his hands on Mrs Pearlman's head and recited *Birkat Kohanim*, the Deuteronomic Priestly Blessing. Rabbi Jacobs then kissed Mrs Pearlman on the forehead.

Chaplain: (Reciting in Hebrew and English) May the Eternal bless you and protect you! May the Eternal deal kindly and graciously with you! May the Eternal bestow His favour upon you and grant you peace! (Numbers 6:24–26, after Lieber 2001, p.804)

(Directly to Mrs Pearlman) Good *Shabbes*, Mrs Pearlman.

Mrs Pearlman: (Still with her eyes closed) Good *Shabbes* to you.

Chaplain: The High Holy Days are coming very soon.

Mrs Pearlman: Yes. My daughter is doing a lot of cooking right now!

Chaplain: (A smile in his voice) I'm sure. There's just so much preparation for the holidays. What's your favourite dish to eat during the holidays?

Mrs Pearlman: It's always *kugel* (noodle pudding).

Chaplain: Mmmm. I'm sure you make a good one.

Mrs Pearlman: I used to, but now it's my daughter who does.

Chaplain: Does she make it with your recipe?

Mrs Pearlman: (Smiles but no answer)

Mrs Pearlman was getting a little tired, so Rabbi Jacobs decided to take a break from the talking.

Chaplain: Would you like me to sing a little bit or recite some liturgy from the Holy Day?

Mrs Pearlman assented to Rabbi Jacobs's question, consistent with communicating her consent to previous offerings around ritual and recitation of Sabbath blessings.

Rabbi Jacobs offered a brief High Holy Day ritual of approximately 20 minutes. He shared liturgical melodies, prayers and poems from Mrs Pearlman's Eastern European tradition and Orthodox background. Using a conversational style as opposed to a prayer book style, he drew out themes within the liturgy of God's kingship, of judgement and forgiveness, of the sheltering presence of the Eternal that welcomes all Jews 'home' in life, death and peace.

Chaplain: (Singing in Hebrew) Hear, O Israel, Adonai is our God. Adonai is One. You shall love Adonai, your God, with all your heart, with all your soul, and with all that is yours. Take to your heart these words, with which I command you this day. Teach them again and again to your children. Recite them when you are in your home and when you are away, when you lie down and when you arise... Thus you will remember and fulfil all My commandments and be holy before your God. I am Adonai, your God, who brought you out of the land of Egypt to be your God: I am Adonai your God. (After Feld 2010, p.209 and Goldberg *et al.* 2015, p.30)

Mrs Pearlman sang some of the opening line with Rabbi Jacobs but became silent and smiling during the remainder.

Rabbi Jacobs sang very quietly, aware of the others who were resting in the room. He sang close to Mrs Pearlman's ear, which not only helped breach Mrs Pearlman's hearing deficit but also created an intimacy between them, almost as if Rabbi Jacobs was telling Mrs Pearlman a secret. The sense of intimacy was both ways.

Chaplain: (*Singing Kol Nidrei in Hebrew*) [From] all vows...we now request release: Let their burden be dissolved, and lifted off, and cancelled, and made null and void, bearing no force and no reality. Those vows shall not be binding vows, those prohibitions shall not be binding prohibitions, those oaths shall not be binding oaths. (After Teutsch 1999, p.693)

Both sat silently, with Rabbi Jacobs holding Mrs Pearlman's hands. After a while, Rabbi Jacobs spoke.

Chaplain: I don't think I will ever tire of that melody. It just sets me up for the day of fasting to come. Makes me feel such gratitude for being a Jew and for what God has given me.

Mrs Pearlman: Yes.

They sat in silence together a bit longer.

Chaplain: (*Singing in Hebrew*) Avinu Malkeinu, hear our voice; be kind and sympathise with us. Avinu Malkeinu, have mercy on us, answer us, for our deeds are insufficient; deal with us charitably and lovingly, and redeem us. (After Feld 2010, pp.243–244)

(*Responding to Mrs Pearlman's tears*) So beautiful that God gives us an opportunity to be forgiven for what we've done intentionally and by mistake – and we get to do this every year! So, do I sound as good as Barbra Streisand?!

Mrs Pearlman: (*Smiling*) Absolutely.

Chaplain: We have a woman *Chazan* (Cantor) at the *shul* (synagogue) we attend, and she brings such heart to these songs.

Mrs Pearlman continued smiling.

Chaplain: Why don't we sing the last verse of *Adon Olam*?

Rabbi Jacobs selected a lively version of this song, a version that would be most familiar to a woman of Mrs Pearlman's generation.

Chaplain: (*Singing in Hebrew*) My soul, entrusted to Your care; Both when I sleep and when I wake. My body, too, will rest in You. Adonai, is with me, I have no fear. (After Feld 2010, p.249 and Goldberg et al. 2015, p.94)

Mrs Pearlman smiled and hummed along while Rabbi Jacobs sang the final verse.

Chaplain: Do you have any fears now?

Mrs Pearlman: No. I feel good. I've had a good life.

At the conclusion of this ritual, Rabbi Jacobs placed his hands on Mrs Pearlman's head, offered the *Birkat Kohanim* (Priestly Blessing) again and, as had become their custom, offered a kiss of blessing on Mrs Pearlman's forehead.

Chaplain: (*Reciting in Hebrew and English*) May the Eternal bless you and protect you! May the Eternal deal kindly and graciously with you! May the Eternal bestow His favour upon you and grant you peace! (Numbers 6.24–26, after Lieber 2001, p.804)

Mrs Pearlman: Thank you, Rabbi.

Chaplain: Shana tovah u'metukah [A happy and sweet new year], Mrs Pearlman.

Mrs Pearlman: Shana Tovah [Happy New Year].

Discussion

There are very particular challenges in providing spiritual care for patients with Alzheimer's disease, dementia or other advanced cognitive deficits. Our patients may respond inappropriately, their responses may have little connection to what the rabbi is saying, or they may not respond at all. Early in his chaplaincy career, Rabbi Jacobs received advice from a colleague whose entire work was with cognitively challenged patients. The advice was to 'walk through the looking glass with the patient, inhabit the space with her, and don't worry about "looking crazy" to the outside world!' Rabbi Jacobs evolved, in his own practice, to begin with the recitation of *Asher Yatzar*, a prayer from the morning liturgy that raises up the creation of the human body and reminds the praying person that this body is God's Creation, its existence is a miracle and that this particular body was created whole, despite its evident decline at this stage. Rabbi Jacobs's practice continues with the recitation of *Elohai Neshama*, the ensuing prayer in the liturgy, which gives testament to the existence of a soul within each body, a soul that was created by God, that belongs to God, and that will live with God for eternity. Marrying this mindset with these prayers and offering a non-anxious presence for the patient has proven particularly impactful when offered to patients with advanced cognitive deficits.

Assessment

Over the course of their relationship, Rabbi Jacobs identified several care goals for Mrs Pearlman's spiritual care. As Mrs Pearlman would often use the word 'love' in her conversations with Rabbi Jacobs, and as she only conversed about those closest to her – her deceased husband, her daughter, and her grandchildren – Rabbi Jacobs came to understand that Mrs Pearlman's primary spiritual goal was *love*, certainly love of family. But he also came to understand that it was also about love of God, love of faith. Among Mrs Pearlman's needs at the end of her life were the needs to receive and offer love, to explore connection to family and friends, to remember the Sabbath and the lighting of candles, and to express her connection to God and her departed loved ones.

The next spiritual care goal was *gratitude*. Mrs Pearlman consistently sought opportunities to express her thankfulness in appreciation of the blessings in life. However, her gratitude, while very much tied into her love of family, was about more than that; it was for life itself and for what a wonderful life she had had. There was no visit at which she didn't express this. Rabbi Jacobs continued to offer the opportunity for her to give voice to her gratitude, and to speak the words aloud for her when she was no longer able.

Rabbi Jacobs's third spiritual care goal was rooted in *identity*. His work nurtured Mrs Pearlman in continuing to live true to her own unique identity – to her *neshama* (spirit or soul) – both in this world and in the world to come, for all the moments of her life. Mrs Pearlman had a strong sense of self and of her place in relation to family, staff, God, and even to Rabbi Jacobs.

And finally, Mrs Pearlman's spiritual care was grounded in *hope*. Rabbi Jacobs had dedicated his work to nurturing hopefulness in Mrs Pearlman's life, amid the realities of her terminal diagnosis. Although she would not live all that much longer, Rabbi Jacobs wanted her to see that *Shabbat* and lighting candles still came every week; that her daughter visited once or twice every week; that there were people with her who would always love her; and that hospice staff would make sure that her days were lived without pain. Although Mrs Pearlman's own hope was that she would one day be able to return home, Rabbi Jacobs assured her that while she was living where she was, home would always come to her.

HIGH HOLY DAY PLAN OF CARE

Given his enduring pastoral relationship with Mrs Pearlman, Rabbi Jacobs outlined a spiritual plan of care for the High Holy Days. Rabbi Jacobs's care plan prioritised offering Mrs Pearlman an appropriate and timely religious experience, one that contextualised to the High Holy Day season. Rabbi Jacobs intended to provide spiritual care that was consistent with Mrs Pearlman's physical, cognitive and emotional needs, and that was sensitive to her ability to endure and her cognitive capacity to participate. Rabbi Jacobs planned to include Mrs Pearlman in offering gratitude in whatever way she was able to and to incorporate her expressions of hopefulness of 'returning home'. Rabbi Jacobs planned to emphasise the safety, support and belonging as part of the Jewish community in all moments and stages of Mrs Pearlman's life.

Interventions

Rabbi Jacobs's spiritual care interventions had included encouraging Mrs Pearlman to verbalise her feelings in addition to affirming her internal and external strengths. Rabbi Jacobs provided active listening and consistently offered prayers, blessings and Jewish rituals. His fidelity as a pastoral caregiver affirmed the presence of the Divine and encouraged Mrs Pearlman's value as a person.

- For the spiritual care goal of *love*, Rabbi Jacobs recited *Sh'ma* and *V'ahavta* (Deuteronomy 6, Deuteronomy 11, Numbers 15), connecting the love we are commanded to offer the Eternal, giving all our hearts, body, soul and strength, with the Oneness the Holy One offers in welcoming all into God's eternal kingdom. Mrs Pearlman joined Rabbi Jacobs with the opening verse and continued smiling throughout his recitation. This central prayer of our faith tradition joined Mrs Pearlman to the Eternal One, whom we are remembering in this prayer, while uniting previous generations to future generations: 'I am *Adonai*, your God.'

- For the spiritual care goal of *gratitude*, Rabbi Jacobs sang the haunting melody of *Kol Nidrei* (All of Our Vows), one of the liturgical focuses of the *Erev Yom Kippur* service. The central message communicates: 'We are grateful that we have lived another year and praying that our vows may be forgiven.

We are grateful that when our time comes, we will be offered forgiveness and released from our unfulfilled obligations.' The familiar melody of *Kol Nidrei* offered a calm that was further communicated in the way Rabbi Jacobs held Mrs Pearlman's hand throughout his singing and embraced the contemplative silence that followed.

- For the spiritual care goal of *identity*, Rabbi Jacobs sang another piece of musical liturgy, *Avinu Malkeinu* (Our Father, Our King), from Mrs Pearlman's Ashkenazi tradition. Hearing this familiar melody brought tears to Mrs Pearlman's eyes. This recitation connected Mrs Pearlman to her past, her present and her future. This prayer honoured Mrs Pearlman's *neshama* (spirit or soul) through all the moments of her life. Rabbi Jacobs acknowledged Mrs Pearlman's tears by taking her hand, holding it gently and reciting another refrain of *Avinu Malkeinu*.

- For the spiritual care goal of *hope*, Rabbi Jacobs shared from *Adon Olam* (Lord of the World), drawing the focus toward Mrs Pearlman's journey from this world into the world to come and nurturing the hopefulness Mrs Pearlman expressed in anticipating her return 'home'. Mrs Pearlman hummed along with this tune while Rabbi Jacobs sang the final verse. Rabbi Jacobs provided Mrs Pearlman with an opportunity to reflect aloud: 'I feel good. I've had a good life.' Amid the realities of her cognitive decline, Rabbi Jacobs offered a prayer of safety, comfort and peace as she continued to find meaning in her life through ritual and meaningful moments with family.

Specific professional activities included nurturing Mrs Pearlman's life review, which provided the opportunity 'to reflect on and integrate spiritual experiences and to preserve them for others' (Piderman *et al.* 2015, p.2). In previous spiritual encounters, Rabbi Jacobs recalled Mrs Pearlman's Orthodox Jewish upbringing and followed the train of conversation which led to changes she observed over her lifetime and associations she made between Rabbi Jacobs and the sweet memories of her grandfather. These memories were honoured in the liturgical melodies Rabbi Jacobs heralded in this High Holy Day encounter. Rabbi Jacobs provided supportive education around Mrs Pearlman's expressions of anticipatory grief, normalising her tearfulness and sorrow, and supporting the appropriate 'encounter with vulnerability and ultimate mortality' (Piderman *et al.* 2015, p.2) that one expects from someone reflecting on their serious illness and engaging in the navigation through their own dying process.

Outcomes

Throughout the visit, Mrs Pearlman was deeply engaged and extremely emotionally expressive, though predominantly non-verbal. She smiled when Rabbi Jacobs greeted her and kissed her forehead, a greeting that had become their standard. Mrs Pearlman continued to indicate a positive response to this visit by moving her head and hands, keeping time with the melody. She occasionally repeated a word or two from the High Holy Day liturgy. Frequently, Mrs Pearlman sang or hummed parts of the familiar refrains of these prayers. She stopped smiling when Rabbi Jacobs sang the evocative *Kol Nidrei*, the prayer that signals the beginning of the Yom Kippur liturgy and a shift in the emotional tenor of these Days of Awe. She became tearful during Rabbi Jacobs's singing of *Avinu Malkeinu*, an emotional setting of the prayer popularised by Barbra Streisand in the late 1990s. Tears remained in Mrs Pearlman's eyes when Rabbi Jacobs recited *Birkat Kohanim* (the Priestly Blessing), the way they concluded most of their visits. As was her typical response, Mrs Pearlman said, 'Thank you'. When Rabbi Jacobs departed, he shared the traditional holiday greeting, '*Shana Tovah*' (Happy New Year), to which Mrs Pearlman responded in kind.

Conclusion

In the Hasidic world view, death is the time of 'ultimate unification with the Holy One, and thus a time for celebration rather than tears and sadness' (Baron and Paasche-Orlow 2016, p.102). This mystical Jewish tradition, which has its origins in the 18th-century Eastern

European teachings of the *tzaddik* (a righteous one), the Ba'al Shem Tov, suggests that the inevitability of death is necessary to the soul's journey into eternity and its reward in the world to come (Baron and Paasche-Orlow 2016, p.xv). In the context of hospice care, even more than in our yearly recitation of the High Holy Day liturgy, 'life experience and common sense tell us that "to annul" the terrible decree of our death is not possible' (Kushner 2010, p.111). By directing our own intention as spiritual caregivers toward the sacredness of the season, the realities of our patients' mortality, and, by extension, our own vulnerability, 'we can be liberated from our terror' (Kushner 2010, p.111). As we say humbly in *Adon Olam* year-round during our worship services, *b'yado afkid ruchi*, 'into God's hands I commit my soul' (Kushner 2010, p.111).

Just as the *shaliach tzibbur* offers *Hin'ni* on behalf of the congregation, Rabbi Jacobs saw himself functioning as the prayer leader for his 'congregation'. He reframed what is historically a communal practice into an individualised, spiritual experience for Mrs Pearlman. Rabbi Jacobs connected the tradition with a particular attention and sacred intent to this moment in Mrs Pearlman's journey through her life. In summoning the core of this communal tradition in his spiritual care for Mrs Pearlman, Rabbi Jacobs welcomed her spirit into the community's High Holy Day experience, of which it would not otherwise have been a part. This sacred collaboration is what God modelled for us in his compassionate care for Abraham; it is what we spiritual caregivers and *shelichei tzibbur* (prayer leaders) model for our 'congregations'; and it is what Abraham and our patients model for us in welcoming us as their guests with 'radical hospitality' (Wolfson 2006, p.45).

Rabbi Jacobs directed his *kavanot* (intentions) toward Mrs Pearlman's spiritual experience within this sacred time and, in doing so, he opened his own heart; his personal and communal prayer experience was transformed by his pastoral and prayer experience with Mrs Pearlman. Rabbi Jacobs, in effect, transported himself into the role of *shaliach* (emissary) for Mrs Pearlman, for himself and for his community. The rabbi/chaplain's High Holy Day experience was transformed in having participated in a collaborative effort to create the space wherein the Eternal may dwell.

References

Baron, J.H. and Paasche-Orlow, S. (2016). *Deathbed Wisdom of the Hasidic Masters*. Woodstock, VT: Jewish Lights Publishing.

Beuken, G. (2002). 'Sacrament of anointing and pastoral care of the sick.' *Scottish Journal of Healthcare Chaplaincy*, 5, 1, 36–40.

Feld, E. (ed.) (2010). *Mahzor Lev Shalem*. New York, NY: The Rabbinical Assembly.

Fitchett, G. (2011). 'Making our case(s).' *Journal of Health Care Chaplaincy*, 17, 1–2, 3–18.

Goldberg, E., Marder, J., Marder, S. and Morris, L. (eds) (2015). *Mishkan Hanefesh: Machzor for the Days of Awe. Vol. 1: Rosh Hashanah*. New York, NY: CCAR Press.

Kaunfer, E. (2010). 'Passing before God: The Literary Theme of Un'taneh Tokef.' In L. Hoffman (ed.) *Who by Fire, Who by Water – Un'taneh Tokef* (pp.98–102). Woodstock, VT: Jewish Lights Publishing.

Kushner, L. (2010). 'Death Without Dying.' In L. Hoffman (ed.) *Who by Fire, Who by Water – Un'taneh Tokef* (pp.109–112). Woodstock, VT: Jewish Lights Publishing.

Lieber, D. (ed.) (2001). *Etz Hayim: Torah and Commentary*. New York, NY: The Rabbinical Assembly.

Piderman, K.M., Radecki Breitkopf, C., Jenkins, S.M., Euerle, T.T. *et al.* (2015). 'A chaplain-led spiritual life review pilot study for patients with brain cancers and other degenerative neurologic diseases.' *Rambam Maimonides Medical Journal*, 6, 2, 1–8.

Teutsch, D. (ed.) (1999). *Kol Haneshamah: Prayerbook for the Days of Awe*. Elkins Park, PA: The Reconstructionist Press.

Wolfson, R. (2006). *The Spirituality of Welcoming*. Woodstock, VT: Jewish Lights Publishing.

Chapter 13

Critical Response to the Use of Ritual Case Studies

A Pastoral Theologian's Perspective

Herbert Anderson

Introduction

A ritual is a patterned activity with symbolic meaning. Rituals are particularly beneficial in healthcare facilities because they make a habitable and hospitable space in an alien world. Authentic rituals also provide the occasion, the language and the gestures for us to encounter realities and truth that, left to ourselves, most of us would choose to avoid. Rituals build a fence around our fear and provide a container for pain and grief. Along the way, rituals may deepen our anguish and make it possible to endure or transcend pain by sharing it with others. Rituals may 'soften suffering', as Chaplain Ásgeirsdóttir suggests, but that is not the only ritual aim. Honest grieving heals when we are able to live in a narrative that is larger than the suffering we experience (Ramshaw 1987).

The role of ritual in spiritual care is the constant in these four cases – two around the beginning of life and two around the end of a life. In each, the chaplain makes a strategic choice based on the perceived needs of the family and/or patient, religious traditions and hospital policy. Smith has argued that rituals are beneficial in times of suffering and through times of transition but that they need to be 'the right rite, an ethical rite, the spiritually appropriate rite' (Smith 2012, p.19). Because developing an appropriate rite often requires the capacity to improvise in the moment, having in mind principles of ritual formation is a necessary reflective tool for chaplains.

Responding to the request for baptism

A request for baptism in two situations was answered differently following two distinct methods of reflection. Jakob's request that his newly born grandson and namesake be baptised before his death was honoured instantly by Chaplain Ásgeirsdóttir even though the family did not present itself as religious and the infant's father expressed disbelief about Lutheran teachings on baptism. The chaplain's willingness 'to give them my service on their own presumptions at this critical moment in their lives' determined her response. The case refers to christening, which can be regarded as simply a naming ceremony or, as in this case, an English equivalent to baptism. Although the chaplain was attentive to the family's desire to honour Jakob's deathbed request, there is insufficient critical reflection on the juxtaposition of two ritual moments with different focuses. Christening/baptism is more than is needed. It would have been an appropriate rite for Jakob to bless his infant namesake from his deathbed while his dying remained the family's primary focus. Later, after Jakob's death, the family might choose to have young Jakob christened as a ritual of welcoming and celebrating new life. Because of her role in the hospital, the chaplain's ministry inevitably focused on Jakob's dying and rituals at his death. We hear no more about the infant Jakob. The interaction of birth and death sometimes means that the child is overlooked because the grieving is so intense or the grief may be buried in order to focus on welcoming the child. The concurrence of death with the birth of a child, as Walsh and McGoldrick (2004) have observed, may also a) interfere with parenting because the grief is overwhelming, and b) be the impetus for high achievement or dysfunction later in life because the child was overlooked in favour of grief.

The mother of 10-year-old Paul requested that he be baptised before his transfer 'in the next hour' to a paediatric psychiatric hospital. The hospital policy, to baptise only in case of an emergency, clarified the limits in which Chaplain Bratt Carle could exercise creativity about prayers and blessings appropriate for the moment. The chaplain identified the need to provide a moment of calming assurance for Paul, who was already an agitated child prone to self-harm and now doubly anxious in this transition. The chaplain determined a spiritually (and ritually) appropriate rite for the situation that was even more expansive and inclusive than the mother had in mind when she requested baptism. When the 'sitter' (assigned to watch for patient self-harm) chose to hold his toes while the chaplain, his mother and grandmother touched his head, the chaplain began the short ritual with these thoughtful words of assurance: 'Paul, you're going to be blessed all the way from the top of your head to the end of your toes!'

End-of-life rituals

The intimate encounter between Rabbi Jacobs and Mrs Pearlman during Jewish High Holy Days in an Alzheimer's unit demonstrates the comforting and orienting power of ritual and song for both the patient and the chaplain. Although Rabbi Jacobs attended carefully to the needs of the patient, his interventions were shaped by traditional rites. Nonetheless, the Rabbi reframed what is historically a communal practice into an individualised, spiritual experience for Mrs Pearlman, which in turn connected the tradition to her own journey with sacred intent. Through prayers and song, Rabbi Jacobs welcomed her spirit into the community's High Holy Days, which would not otherwise have been possible for her. In the process, his own personal and communal prayer was transformed by his pastoral and prayer experience with Mrs Pearlman. The Rabbi's experience reminds us of the reciprocal, sustaining power of a shared ritual moment. The chaplains reporting the case observe that Rabbi Jacobs's vision of radical hospitality for each patient, when linked with his non-anxious presence, has been particularly impactful for patients with advanced cognitive deficits.

Chaplain Roberts's relationship with Daisy, a well-beloved hospital nurse, began as 'hallway' talks and ended with presiding at her memorial service. In between those moments, she cared for Daisy both in the hospital and in her home. Because she was new and needing to find her place in the hospital, Chaplain Roberts determined that the care of Daisy outweighed her previous practice of confining spiritual care to working hours in hospital. Her interpretation that Daisy's condition seemed to have a ripple effect throughout the hospital and that there would be further spiritual care challenges resulting from her death was used to justify Chaplain Roberts's extensive involvement in Daisy's dying. Providing spiritual care for Daisy beyond the hospital walls set a precedent that will be difficult not to repeat. The absence of any reference to the content of the rituals with Daisy seems to reflect the chaplain's intent 'to meet people where they are in life and then create meaningful rituals of comfort or rites of passage'.

Creating new rituals

Rituals, like stories, give form to human existence. In each case, the chaplain was challenged to listen carefully to the patient's stories, discern the need, draw from traditional ritual practice or imagine and improvise a new ritual response appropriate to the new situation, and then implement the ritual while continuing to listen. This work of ritualising occurs today in a more 'liquid' or flexible context increasingly open to ritual transfer and invention. While there are few ironclad rules for creating new rituals appropriate to the situation, Anderson and Foley (1998, p.130) have identified some useful principles to be kept in mind when improvising a new ritual:

- *Respect the chronological priority of the human story in shaping the ritual.* Let the whole story of a crisis or transition be told honestly without rushing to resolution.

- *Use non-verbal symbols or significant objects in ritualising.* In Paul's transition, it was particularly sensitive for the chaplain to bless Paul's transitional objects Pooh and Rex.

- *Resist the impulse to explain the action.* Part of the purpose of a ritual in hospitals is to create a safe container for the baffling array of feelings and thoughts that patients experience.

- *Attend to the particularity of the moment.* The christening of infant Jakob by the side of grandfather Jakob's deathbed is a complex moment requiring pastoral and ritual sensitivity.

- *Avoid overcomplicating the ritual.* Less is more. A single act of blessing or handing over a gift or telling a story is enough, as Rabbi Jacobs achieved in modifying an extensive ritual of Jewish High Holy Days with song.

Further observations

In addition to use of ritual in spiritual care, these cases contain several issues common to chaplaincy.

Making the most of a single visit

As Chaplain Bratt Carle observes wisely, knowing in advance that her meeting with Paul would be a single visit prompted a bolder approach to care because she was initiating rapport and acting on it simultaneously. She also needed to *listen carefully* to layers of vulnerability, *focus* on what might be possible given the limits of the situation, and trust that she had greater freedom to act *creatively* because of the time limits. 'I find', she observes, 'it is all the more important to be intentional about how I might achieve the desired spiritual care outcomes within the given constraints.' Envisioning every patient visit as the only opportunity for care might add *gravitas* to a chaplain's ministry.

Expanding the hospital chaplaincy

The decision to extend care beyond the hospital walls to Daisy in her dying and to Jakob's family after his death raises new questions about the limits of chaplaincy. These questions are likely to increase as fewer and fewer patients are identified with religious communities to which they might return. Chaplain Roberts's care for Daisy outside the hospital had the supervisor's blessing but it is unclear whether these caring activities were conducted on the chaplain's personal time.

Ritual intimacy and the spiritual power of music

The use of song as part of Rabbi Jacob's spiritual care for Mrs Pearlman is a reminder of the power of music for those who are dying. Music and sound, it has been said, 'weave a magic carpet for the soul's journey home' (Sciberras 2012, p.42). When music is improvised or modified, as the Rabbi did, it has the potential to touch the soul of the one dying.

Transitions are a common theme in spiritual care

Transitions are by their nature liminal. So are rituals. Leaving the security of a hospital for home or for another healthcare facility may be an unfamiliar adventure generating fear and apprehension. In any event, transitions are a time of anxiety and ambiguity for which rituals provide a safe passage.

Chaplaincy as public relations

From the perspective of a healthcare institution, a significant part of a chaplain's work is public relations – in the best sense of that word. Chaplains meet with family members or interact with patients' religious leaders, often in the role of interpreting hospital practices for patients and their families. From the beginning to the end of Jakob's dying, the family let Chaplain Ásgeirsdóttir know how unhappy they were with the hospital's services. The chaplain's willingness to fulfil uncritically Jakob's deathbed request may illustrate how easily spiritual care can be influenced by an expectation that public relations is part of the work of chaplaincy.

Finally

Because direct feedback loops are limited in medical contexts, patient and family care is enhanced through dependable self-criticism. In my judgement, there was insufficient critical self-reflection by the chaplains in these interventions. In order to report positive outcomes, all the interventions were well received and had positive results. The chaplains tended to interpret the response of patient families positively. The need to demonstrate the usefulness of spiritual care in the hospital setting is understandable but cannot cancel out critical self-reflection without diminishing the effectiveness of spiritual care. Chaplains cannot predict or orchestrate the results of spiritual care but they can and must determine their own behavioural goals and reflect critically on their own effectiveness in achieving those goals.

References

Anderson, H. and Foley, E. (1998). *Mighty Stories, Dangerous Rituals: Weaving Together the Human and the Divine.* San Francisco, CA: Jossey-Bass Publishers.

Ramshaw, E. (1987). *Ritual and Pastoral Care.* Philadelphia, PA: Fortress Press.

Sciberras, A.M. (2012). *Death the Door, Music a Key: A Girl, a Harp at the Bedside of the Dying.* Houston, TX: Strategic Book Publishing.

Smith, S.M. (2012). *Caring Liturgies: The Pastoral Power of Christian Ritual.* Minneapolis, MN: Fortress Press.

Walsh, F. and McGoldrick, M. (eds) (2004). *Living Beyond Loss: Death in the Family* (2nd edn). New York, NY: W.W. Norton & Company.

Chapter 14

Critical Response to the Use of Ritual Case Studies

A Chaplain's Perspective

Mark Cobb

Introduction

Healthcare chaplains practise care at the interface of religion, spirituality and health, and this inevitably means dealing with constraints that are all too evident in the four cases under consideration. The obvious constraints of time, place and circumstance are overlaid with the limitations derived from an ethical caregiving relationship, the pastoral imagination and theological accountability and the professional requirements of practice, to name but a few. These are daily realities for chaplains who must navigate personal, professional and social boundaries to be available to others, find common ground and turn constraints into creative possibilities of meaning and hope. In three of these cases the chaplains help others to face the ultimate boundary of death, and in the fourth the chaplain enters briefly into a complex situation of distress and transition. All four cases involve some form of ritual as an intervention and, before we look at the cases, it is therefore worth briefly considering the nature and form of ritual.

Rituals are ubiquitous to human social life to the extent that ritual is considered by some to be 'the social act basic to humanity' (Rappaport 1999, p.31). Religions make extensive use of rituals, and the formal prescribed behaviours of ritual are also pervasive in healthcare practices (Elks 1996; Davies 2012). Chaplains are therefore well placed and resourced to understand and make use of ritual as an effective intervention. In this context, rituals are typically performed, first, to support the existing practices of patients and their carers, and second, to address significant pastoral needs present, for example, in times of suffering and transitional states. Rituals exist in performance and they provide chaplains and those who participate in them with the means to address the sacred aspects of life, enact profound meaning, confront suffering, and relate the temporal to the eternal. I will now attend to each case in turn, including the use of ritual, and then highlight some general themes for further discussion and debate.

Case study 1: Paul

The entry point for this case was a request for baptism which immediately set up an expectation and a constraint, the former from the family and the latter from the chaplain. This tension framed the initial approach by the chaplain, who set out to explore the request, what may have motivated it and whether there may have been other ways of meeting the spiritual need. However, before any dialogue could be established, the case study situated the encounter and provided a sense of the space occupied by the people, the equipment and the stuffed animals. It is that almost blink-of-an-eye moment when you arrive on the scene and form an instant impression of what is happening. Awareness of the surroundings and a sensitivity to place helped ensure the chaplain's entrance was respectful; it may help orientate the chaplain to the immediate scenario and it may suggest contextual factors that could impact on chaplaincy care.

The chaplain in this case carefully explained that baptism was usually only provided in the hospital in emergency situations and used skilful communication to both clarify the position and remain open to spiritual need: 'I certainly want to understand what is important to you in this time of transition, and I want to support you as best as I can.' This set a clear positive aim to the purpose of the chaplain's visit, and the rapport established in a very short time enabled Paul's mother, Carol, to explain that, 'I guess we feel like God is just too busy for us right now... Paul said to me that he feels like God doesn't like him, you know, because he's sick right now.' Paul then became agitated and Carol broke from the conversation with the chaplain to attend to him.

This was a critical point in an encounter known to be a one-off visit, and with limited time and the attention of those present, the chaplain decided not to try and explore the experience of God expressed by Carol any further but instead offered ritual, possibly as some sort of alternative (rather than substitute) for the baptism originally requested. This was a tactical move not without risk but the chaplain remained attuned to the situation, built further rapport with Paul and resolved an initially negative response. The encounter moved on to the ritual of prayer, with Paul's timid consent to have hands laid on him and all present invited to participate. The image we are then presented with is of a 10-year-old boy who had self-harmed and experienced abuse by his father, passively lying on his stomach, his head on a pillow and with hands laid on his shoulders and his bare foot by two strangers along with his mother and grandmother. This image presents some concerns which are absent from the chaplain's rationale and reflection, and includes issues of power, the ethics of physical contact, and, in particular, what Paul's subjective experience of his body might have been, how he might have related to his harmed body, and how he might have perceived the nature of touch.

Touch is a feature of many religious rituals but in this situation, it may have been a potentially ambiguous or threatening action despite attempts to make it safe by incorporating objects of comfort known to Paul, namely his stuffed toys. The chaplain in this case study is evidently a skilled and sensitive practitioner and it may be that consideration was given to the issues outlined. Clearly the overriding constraint of time prevented a deeper exploration of spiritual needs but there is a possibility in situations of this nature that the option to do something, and to be seen as being useful, is a more compelling motivation than staying with the discomfort and distress.

Case study 2: Jakob

Baptism also provides the presenting reason for contact with a chaplain in this case study, although it was the patient's grandson for whom the family wished to have a christening service, and the constraint was the limited time available to Jakob, the grandfather, whose advanced disease signalled his closeness to death. The urgency of the situation provided a basis to conduct the baptism in the Palliative Care Unit, and the chaplain found sufficient common ground with Steinn, Jakob's son and father of the child to be baptised, to frame the baptism not in explicitly religious terms but as a supportive and meaningful family event. Such negotiations and accommodations are common in the work of chaplains who seek to act in the best interests of patients and clients while maintaining an integrity to their sponsoring faith community or belief group.

The ritual of baptism in this case was performed in the context of Jakob's worsening condition and last days of his life. In other words, it took place at a point of transition for Jakob, the dying grandfather, but also for his newborn grandson, who was to be welcomed into his family and the Church, the eternal family of God. The departing and the arriving came together with their family through ritual that was deeply caring and named death and new life in its liturgical acts and utterances. For the chaplain, it can be assumed that this was a ritual of hope and an expression of God's grace even through death. For the family, dealing with contrary emotions and major transitions, the ritual offered a safe space to hold immediate concerns and struggles and reminded them of a larger sense of meaning and belonging beyond the individuals gathered.

The chaplain, in performing ritual, occupied a unique role in relation to the family and other members of the multidisciplinary team, and it is obvious from this case that this position then enabled a continuing pastoral relationship of care and support when Jakob died. Although this case does not include any verbatim transcript, what we do gain is an appreciation of the arc of pastoral care that extends from the first encounter through to the final contact following a series of rites of transition. Throughout this, the chaplain demonstrated detailed attentiveness to the needs of the family and a strong professional duty to ensure their interests were foremost. However, there is one aspect that emerges in this case which remains without further reflection and that is the discontent and anger, expressed in particular by Hulda, about Jakob's care and treatment prior to his admission to the Palliative Care Unit. This disclosure is indicative of the level of trust that the family had developed in this skilled chaplain, and it may also suggest their perspective on the place a chaplain occupies in relation to the clinical team and healthcare system. What is not explored are questions about whether the chaplain has an advocacy role for the family and how outstanding issues following the death of a family member can be resolved.

Case study 3: Daisy

Chaplaincy care for work colleagues is often a routine aspect of the chaplain's role and is typically in response to major life transitions and the various existential and vocational dilemmas that face people. In this case, the care of a former employee was an exception, and emerged from an established but passing pastoral relationship with the chaplain while Daisy was still working in a senior nursing role and based largely on 'hallway' conversations. The entry point for the case study was triggered by the progression of Daisy's condition to the stage that required hospice care and specifically Daisy's need to plan her funeral. What followed was a series of domiciliary visits in which the presenting need was addressed episodically, and the verbatim transcripts illustrate an evolving sequence of conversations, deepening trust, disclosure and spiritual care.

The arc of care in this case is evident through the unfolding dialogue between Daisy and the chaplain, which began at a necessary distance and carefully moved towards a respectful nearness that fostered authentic exchange and support. The shift was paralleled in the content of the conversation as it moved from practicalities to reflections on finitude and talk about God. Throughout this, the chaplain bore witness to Daisy's hopes and fears and was finely attuned to the interpersonal space that Daisy required to maintain her own integrity, control and safety, as she faced her own mortality. What is particularly evident is the way the chaplain was able to catch glimpses of Daisy's vulnerabilities and struggles, and sensitively use these insights to intimate and point towards how she might navigate the final stage of her life's journey and narrate her closing chapter.

It is notable how sensitive the chaplain was to the impact of Daisy's dying on the wider nursing and hospital community. Chaplains can occupy representative roles for organisations and provide vicarious care on behalf of a wider community. In this case, as Daisy was a highly respected senior member of the community, there was the challenge and privilege of accepting this role, negotiating appropriate boundaries and remaining an authentic self. The chaplain here was also something of a go-between, honouring the wishes of Daisy while enabling the needs of the wider community to be met; this required skilled diplomacy, a clear sense of the primary interests that needed honouring, and the courage to chart what was considered to be the right course. Rituals also feature in this case study at both an interpersonal level, in the form of prayers of petition and intercession, including the marking of Daisy's 'smooth transition' as she was dying, and at the group level, enabling participation of the family and the wider work community in the funeral and memorial events. The approach taken is highly relational but it is not clear from the presentation of this case the extent to which the chaplain drew on her particular theological tradition and practices. Chaplains vary in their capability to work outside a tradition's orthopraxis, in part because of the constraints their own theological formation can impose; but they should not shy from the practice of theologically informed spiritual care and ritual, providing it remains open to the lived experience of those they serve.

Case study 4: Mrs Pearlman

This highly evocative case study is deeply grounded in a Jewish sensibility, a lived appreciation of the power of ritual's form and language, and a well-developed pastoral imagination for Jewish patients living in a skilled nursing facility including those with advanced Alzheimer's disease. This case study presents a window into an existing pastoral relationship of over 12 months between the resident, Mrs Pearlman, and the chaplain, Rabbi Jacobs, during the High Holy Days. What is immediately notable in this case is how the chaplain prepared his heart and mind for the pastoral duties he was to undertake. This intentional orientation and focus set the spiritual and theological context for the Rabbi's chaplain visit and made him open to the pastoral needs of others.

The entry point for this pastoral encounter was through the lighting of *Shabbat* candles, which follows the *halacha* (Jewish law) for this in an imaginary form but with the blessing spoken. This pragmatic and well-established practice with Mrs Pearlman established a familiar rapport with the chaplain and initiated a ritual sequence that was sensitive to her cognitive limitations and maintained fidelity to her tradition, which included the custom of singing prayers and chanting psalms. This apparently customary intervention was significant, not least because there is evidence that musical memory is distinct from semantic memory and is typically preserved for many people with Alzheimer's disease. Music may, therefore, provide a means by which social and communication functions can be stimulated and enhanced (Cuddy, Sikka and Vanstone 2015), and consequently a person's quality of life enriched. In this case, the chaplain's singing connected Mrs Pearlman to her lived spiritual tradition, which evoked some musical participation and related memories and thoughts. The chaplain was also careful to balance musical stimulation with silence and the opportunity for Mrs Pearlman to respond and be listened to.

The quality of attentiveness and skilled communication is evident in this case, in which the chaplain pursued a highly contextual and relational approach guided by a set of spiritual care goals based on his understanding of Mrs Pearlman developed over time. The approach is highly referenced to specific theology, ritual and music with a strong theme of fidelity to both pastoral caregiving and to Mrs Pearlman's Ashkenazi Jewish tradition. In taking this approach, the chaplain honoured Mrs Pearlman's life, maintained her spiritual identity, affirmed her personhood and promoted her sense of belonging to her faith community. Pastoral care of people with dementia and other forms of memory loss presents particular challenges to faithful chaplaincy practice, and this case illustrates some ways in which effective care can be offered. What stands out is the chaplain's capacity to be 'in the moment' with Mrs Pearlman and how he had learned to relate to her, to stay with her in the moment, and to share with her in God's created time (Swinton 2012).

General themes

Standing back from these cases, there are at least four more general themes that warrant further consideration and which I lay out briefly. First, rituals can be a significant resource in the chaplain's practical toolkit when used wisely and with due regard to context. Rituals create order out of the chaotic and disparate; they enact and express transcendent truths in the midst of disorder and incomprehension; they confront suffering through dealing with hopes and fears; they deal with human limits by marking transitions and crossings; and they place the temporal within an eternal horizon of the Holy (Tweed 2006).

Second, there is a tactile nature to pastoral care, from the informally supportive to the ritual form, which requires ethical consideration with particular regard to issues of power imbalance and ambiguity of the intention from the perspective of the other person's perception of the situation (Liegeois 2016). Professional codes of conduct provide minimal guidance on such matters but chaplains should discuss this responsibility and practice more openly.

Third, if theology is to remain a qualifying discipline for chaplains, then theological reflexivity should be a lively feature of chaplaincy case studies, both in terms of expounding a chaplain's working theology and generating new theological insights.

Fourth, and finally, the use of case studies remains work in progress for chaplains. They are not without their problems, not least in the way they are retrospectively constructed from a particular perspective; but at their best they can be compelling narratives of the encounters chaplains have with people at profound moments in their lives, they can make visible what is often unseen at the time, and they can provide the wider chaplaincy community with a rich source of learning and wisdom.

References

Cuddy, L.L., Sikka, R. and Vanstone, A. (2015). 'Preservation of musical memory and engagement in healthy aging and Alzheimer's disease.' *Annals of the New York Academy of Sciences*, 1337, 223–231.

Davies, D.J. (2012). 'Ritual.' In M. Cobb, C. Puchalski and B. Rumbold (eds) *Oxford Textbook of Spirituality in Healthcare* (pp.163–168). Oxford: Oxford University Press.

Elks, M.L. (1996). 'Rituals and roles in medical practice.' *Perspectives in Biology and Medicine*, 39, 601–609.

Liegeois, A. (2016). 'Physical Touch in Pastoral Counselling. A Practical Theological Approach.' In R. Bieringer, D. Baert and K. Demasure (eds) *Noli Me Tangere in Interdisciplinary Perspective: Textual, Iconographic and Contemporary Interpretations* (pp.431–447). Leuven; Bristol: Peeters.

Rappaport, R.A. (1999). *Ritual and Religion in the Making of Humanity*. Cambridge: Cambridge University Press.

Swinton, J. (2012). *Dementia: Living in the Memories of God*. Grand Rapids, MI: William B. Eerdmans Publishing Company; London: SCM Press.

Tweed, T.A. (2006). *Crossing and Dwelling: A Theory of Religion*. Cambridge, MA; London: Harvard University Press.

Part 4
The Chaplain as Self-Reflexive Practitioner

Chapter 15

'I'd like you to get to know about me'

– Kristof, a 50-year-old atheist academic admitted to a hospice for palliative symptom control

Steve Nolan

Introduction

To date, case studies published by chaplain–researchers describe work in which the author appears more or less confident that there was a positive patient outcome. These cases provide real value both educationally – in that they demonstrate good practice for chaplains new to the profession and offer material for the continuing professional development of experienced chaplains – and in research – in that they provide data that may prompt further research questions or fill out (or challenge) existing theory (Fitchett 2011). But equally, it should be possible to find educational and research value in case studies that report work where the outcomes are less than obvious. This case study reports work about which I am somewhat ambivalent. In part, this is because the work was frustrated by a number of factors that were beyond my control; but in part also, it is because I over-identified with my patient, 'Kristof'. This is not to say that my work with Kristof was without any good effect – there are aspects of the work that I believe were helpful to him. However, I think my work in this case would have been more effective if I had maintained my normal level of objectivity in relating with Kristof. This case, then, is an attempt to expand the case study literature with a case where I, as the chaplain–researcher, have questions about my work.

Background

I began working as a hospice chaplain in June 2004. My spiritual
formation began within Roman Catholicism but, after exploring
the possibility of the priesthood and engaging with the Charismatic
Renewal, I left Catholicism to join an independent evangelical church,
whose style was Pentecostal. In my early 20s, I spent two years in an
evangelical Bible college and then worked in churches in Kent and
the Midlands. My theological understanding began to change and,
following a short break working in advertising, I trained for Baptist
ministry in a theologically liberal college in my home city of Manchester,
where I undertook bachelor and master's degrees in theology and
religious studies. Following ordination, I served seven years in a small
church in northwest London, where I undertook doctoral studies (in
religion and contemporary continental philosophy) and began to
engage in interfaith work. I describe my theology as liberal/radical,
and my spiritual exploration has led me to explore different branches
of Christian spirituality and to find help in eastern perspectives,
particularly Buddhism. I am dual qualified: I have a master's degree in
therapeutic counselling (an integrative approach), and accreditation
with the British Association for Counselling and Psychotherapy as a
counsellor and psychotherapist. This dual qualification informs my
perspective as chaplain and will inform this case study (Nolan 2017).
Nevertheless, I am clear in my own mind and with the people in my care
that I serve as a chaplain. At the time of my work with Kristof, I was 57.

'Kristof' (not his real name), a man in his early 50s, was admitted to
hospice care for symptom control of pain associated with a cancer, the
nature of which meant that his diction was extremely poor and that it
was always difficult to discern his speech. His notes indicated that he had
been suicidal, which was associated with endogenous depression, and
that he had attempted to take his own life – he had stated that he wanted
to choose how and when he would die. His most recent psychological
assessment, which concluded that he was not currently depressed, did
little to mitigate his care team's concern, not least because, while he
had said he didn't fear death, Kristof remained anxious about the dying
process. Kristof viewed his admission as a pivotal point in deciding

whether he would be able to gain some hope of quality of life. His notes recorded: 'No religious faith but would welcome chaplaincy support.'

I work at the Princess Alice Hospice, Esher, an independent, 28-bed inpatient hospice, in the south of England. As an independent charity, the hospice provides palliative care, free at the point of need, to adults with cancer and other life-limiting illnesses; it supports families and carers during the illness and provides free bereavement care afterwards. The hospice care area covers a ten-mile radius and takes in over one million people across a large part of Surrey, southwest London, and Middlesex.

Formal permission from an ethics committee is not necessary for a case study; however, the case has been submitted to, and approved for publication by, the Princess Alice Hospice Research Committee, on condition that identities and identifying details, including names, are disguised. All the verbatim accounts were written up within 24 hours of the intervention.

Case study
First meeting: Friday, mid-afternoon

Kristof was seated out of sight of the doorway. I knocked and in his muffled voice he invited me in. I introduced myself as the chaplain and immediately Kristof got up, shook my hand, and moved to sit with his back against the wall and his shoed feet on the bed, leaving his chair for me. Without hesitation, Kristof began explaining that his big issue was pain; that he was never out of pain, and that he had come to the hospice to try to get on top of it. I asked if he was in pain at the moment, and when he said he was, I asked if he was alright with me being with him.

> Kristof: (In a muffled and at times indistinct voice) Yes. I'm not going to turn down any offer of help. But I have to say that I'm not religious, although I respect other people's religion and I believe in a higher power. I'm not arrogant enough to think (here, what he said was unclear). I see you being here as an offer of help and I'm not going to

turn away anyone who could help me. I'm dying. I've had this thing for about a year. I've had chemo and radiotherapy, and I've probably got a few months left now.

I usually feel uncertain in negotiating the opening moments with a new person. I'm very aware that I am initiating the meeting and that I may be wrongly perceived as having a 'religious agenda'. This makes me slightly anxious that I will be rejected before I've had chance to establish a working relationship (what counsellors/therapists term a 'working alliance'). In introducing myself to Kristof, I wanted to connect with him in a way that would allow me to be of some use to him.

> *Chaplain:* My role is to support people in their religious needs, if they have any, either directly or by liaising with others; but, if a person isn't religious, my role is to support them in whatever way I can.

> *Kristof:* I'm here because I took an overdose of diamorphine.

I had been briefed about Kristof's failed suicide, but at this point he wasn't naming his action as deliberate. Nonetheless, the directness with which he spoke about his overdose suggested he wanted to make it a significant part of our conversation. Because of this, I felt it was important to allow Kristof himself to tell me about his intentions.

> *Chaplain:* Did you intend to take an overdose or did you do that by accident?

> *Kristof:* I meant to do it. I was in so much pain. The killer dose is 4gms but I took a slow release formulation and it just put me out for 27 hours. First time I was out of pain in a year. That was good. I suppose that's technically a sin. But maybe Christianity is less harsh these days. Is it less harsh?

Suicide divides contemporary Christian opinion, some harsh and judgemental. I didn't want to leave Kristof with any sense that I would be judging him, so I tried to make my position explicit.

> *Chaplain:* I think the people who make the rules about suicide do that when they are quite well, and when you're well, you don't want to

kill yourself. But when you're in so much pain, you might think, 'I'll do whatever it takes to get out of pain.' I don't think that's a sin. I don't think that, if there is a God, he would see that as a sin.

Kristof: What I'd like help with is in trying to understand who I've been, and to do that in relation to Christianity; what my life has meant. I'd like to look over my life and see what I've been, who I've become. I think a lot about myself, especially in the night. It would be good to talk to someone about all this. I'd like you to get to know about me.

Our conversation was interrupted by two doctors. I was concerned that they might intrude on my time with Kristof but, when they saw we were in conversation, they apologised, said what they needed to say, and left. Picking up Kristof's invitation to 'get to know about me', I held in my mind what he had said about wanting help to understand who he had been in his life, so I enquired about his research work. Kristof explained his research interests, where they had led him as a researcher, and where his work had taken him in the world. He spoke about his wife, from whom he was now amicably separated, and her career, and about his school-age children. In particular, he reflected on the maturity of one of his children who didn't want to talk with Kristof about his dying.

I was struck by Kristof's directness in speaking about dying, and also the degree to which he had been preparing for his death. I thought that, by acknowledging his openness, I might encourage Kristof to speak more personally about his dying. (In counselling/therapeutic terms, I 'reflected' it back to him.)

Chaplain: There's a saying about it not being possible to look the sun or death full in the face; that it's too painful.[1] But I'm struck by how you seem to be doing that, looking directly at dying.

Kristof: I don't want to do it all the time. But I've had a tremendous gift getting this. I've had time to get everything sorted out. I've got

---

1   The quote is from the 17th-century French nobleman and author François de la Rochefoucauld: 'You cannot stare straight into the face of the sun, or death' (Yalom 2008, title page).

my finances in order, made my will, done the kid's memory boxes, bought them jewellery that will last them for the rest of their lives. I've bought my wife a bloody expensive present to remember me by. Now it's time for me. Up to now, it's been about others but now it's time for me.

This seemed the moment to return to what Kristof had said earlier about understanding the meaning of his life.

Chaplain: You said that you'd like to try and understand who you've been, and to do that in relation to Christianity.

Kristof: Yes.

Chaplain: I'd like to try to help you with that, if I can; if you think you'd be able to talk with me.

Kristof: I'd like that too. I'd look forward to it. I think we'll get on well.

Kristof needed to be elsewhere. I said I'd be back after the weekend and would call again then.

Second meeting: Thursday, late morning

It was almost a week before I was able to see Kristof again. There were various reasons for this, not the least of which was a difficult outpatient appointment he had had at a London hospital. I caught up with Kristof the day after his appointment. He seemed relaxed and wanting to talk, and he welcomed me into his room. Again, Kristof's voice was muffled and far from clear but he explained some of his recent history. Kristof had been diagnosed about a year ago. He had been considered suitable for surgery but having initially agreed to undergo the painful procedure, Kristof contracted a virus and the operation had to be postponed. On recovering, he reflected on his prospects, which he described as a lot of pain, followed by a long period of pain, with a 5–10 per cent chance of survival, or not much pain, and a certain outcome. With the support of his family, he decided against surgery.

Kristof: (*His voice muffled*) I've always wanted to be in control of things, and this was a part of my life that I could control. I'm not a betting man – well, I am a betting man – but I wouldn't bet on 5–10 per cent odds!

His desire to control his life seemed congruent with his desire to end his life in a hotel room. In the context of reviewing his life, it felt important to offer him the opportunity to talk about his desire to take his own life.

Chaplain: And you still retain the right to take your own life? Is that still an option for you?

Kristof: (*Nods*) What do you think?

I wanted to reiterate my unconditional acceptance of him, so I repeated what I had said previously about suicide.

Kristof: You think that but the Church thinks differently. I was brought up with fire and brimstone sermons. Welsh Baptist! Not at home, this was school – an overly enthusiastic Christian teacher scared everyone to death! I rejected that as soon as possible. I've not really thought very much about religion since. I still think religion is important. I'm not so arrogant as to say it's not true; at its best, it's done a lot of good. I think there is a lot of fact in the Bible. It's basically a collection of moral stories about how to live but it's based on fact. Jesus existed. Whether he was the son of God, I don't know, but he definitely existed.

It seemed to me that Kristof had, in fact, thought a good deal about religion. I voiced my observation.

Chaplain: Well, you say you've not thought very much about religion but it sounds as though you've thought quite a lot about it. I have some sympathy with what you say. If there is a God, then God is mystery, and the stories are attempts to speak about what it is impossible to know.

Our conversation continued in this vein for a few minutes. Then Kristof said:

Kristof: I'm getting tired talking now but I would like to talk some more. I've enjoyed it. If you're around tomorrow, you could come again. What I really want to talk about is something more personal. It's about how I face my own death. I think we've hit it off – we seem to see things in the same way. I'd like to talk about how I face my own death.

Chaplain: That's fine. I'll come back tomorrow.

Third meeting: Monday, late afternoon

In fact, Kristof was unavailable the next day, and it wasn't until after the weekend that I next got to see him. Kristof had had another outpatient appointment at the London hospital and said that he was too wearied to talk. Nonetheless, he did tell me about his visit and about the proposed treatment, which would target fast-growing cells – cancer cells but also all fast-growing cells, such as blood cells and hair. His speech had become more difficult to understand, and I struggled to grasp everything he said, but he reiterated that he wanted to do some work on himself.

Kristof: I've always been very logical about thinking about my death. It's going to happen; there's nothing I can do about it. But I've (*here, his speech was unclear*). But I want to understand more about me before I die. It's a poisoned chalice and I think you're going to get it!

Chaplain: Well, maybe we'll drink it together.

The next couple of days would be taken up with appointments for chemotherapy, and we left it that I would look out for him on those days but aim to see him again on Thursday.

Fourth meeting: Thursday, early afternoon

I expected Kristof to be tired from his hospital trips and the chemotherapy but when I entered his room he welcomed me in. I enquired how things had gone at the hospital, and he explained his new treatment regime. Kristof was ready to talk but for the first time he was using a pen and notebook. His diction was very poor and he struggled to articulate his first few words, so he wrote, 'My logical side has always been stronger than my emotional side.' He followed it immediately with, 'How true is that sentence?'

> *Kristof:* That's what I want to talk about. As an academic, I've always been logical. So I've never been afraid of death; you live, you die. It's going to happen but I don't want to die. I'm on chemo. I know it won't cure me but I want to get my speech back. I've never believed in God. *(Pausing, and thoughtfully considering his words)* I've never believed but I've never denied other people's beliefs. But now I'm starting to think about it. *(Pausing)* I'm not sure any of this is making sense.

Without wanting to direct him, I did want Kristof to keep talking, so I spoke in an attempt to encourage him.

> *Chaplain:* I don't think it's surprising that you're thinking in this way. I guess when you're told you have a life-limiting illness…I guess you think about *everything* in a different way.

> *Kristof:* Mmm. I don't think I'm thinking about it.

Kristof struggled to enunciate the word he was trying to say. On his notebook he wrote, 'cynical'.

> *Kristof:* *(Smiling)* I feel like I'm on holiday in Albania!

I was unclear what Kristof meant. Possibly it was another reference to the poisoned chalice but he was struggling to articulate, and I felt it would be burdensome to ask him to repeat. Nonetheless, it seemed that I had caught Kristof at a point where he was open to doing the thinking he had previously said he wanted to do about his life and beliefs, and I wanted to encourage him in doing that.

> *Chaplain:* I think it's understandable that you might think about these things. Most of us go through life knowing that we're going to die but we don't think about it; it's just something 'over there' *(gesturing into the distance)* that's not really going to affect me.

Kristof: Mmm.

Chaplain: But for you, it's very real. It's no wonder that you might now think about God. It's understandable that you might go through life without ever thinking about whether God exists. But then, when you get ill, you begin to think about all sorts of things and have all sorts of emotions that perhaps you never had before. I don't think it's surprising that you're thinking like this, thinking about the meaning of life, of your life.

Kristof: The meaning of *my* life. Mmm. I've made an inventory – you know, like how many cups and saucers – the things I've done. I think about my achievements. I've been a small cog. I've had some significant failures; but I've also had some limited successes. I used to think I hadn't done very much – that used to get at me. But then I thought, 'Sod it!' I've managed to achieve some things.

Chaplain: I think it's about expectations.

Kristof: I'm no worse than a lot of people; I'm better than some. I've not done too bad with what I had.

Chaplain: I think that's a really important shift to make, to realise that we all start from different places.

Again, I wanted to encourage Kristof in thinking about his life, so I decided to disclose a little of how I felt about my own achievements: coming from a working-class family, with little active educational support, underachieving at school. This prompted Kristof to reflect on his own working-class family background: 'I'm working class.' He spoke about his mother, resentful of being made to leave school and start work at 14 and who, in later life, completed an Open University degree; his father, a manual labourer, whose own father had had mental health issues. He spoke about his wife and her career success.

Kristof: She made a lot of money. I made quite a lot but not as much as she did.

He started to speak about the properties they owned, then he interrupted himself.

Kristof: I'm waffling. Give me some direction.

I tried to gather some of the threads of what Kristof had said that was relevant to his desire to think about facing his death.

Chaplain: You seemed to be talking about your legacy.

Kristof: My legacy. I sorted all that out. There's insurance policies, so there will be enough money to take care of things.

Kristof had misunderstood my use of 'legacy'. I tried to clarify my meaning.

Chaplain: But your legacy in your impact on other people.

Kristof: My philosophy has been simple: do good to people; don't do harm to anyone. There's only been one person I've harmed.

Again, his diction was unclear, making it impossible to hear the details of this 'confession', and he moved quickly on.

Kristof: I don't know how long I'm going to be here.

Mindful that suicide was still part of his thinking, I wanted Kristof to clarify what he meant.

Chaplain: What do you mean when you say that?

Kristof: Well, I know that I'm very ill. I'm aware that I'm dying, but I'm not dying very quickly. I'm here to sort out my pain but I'm looking after myself, I'm moving around, going out. I'm on this chemo for a week, then I go back to the hospital to see how that's going. Where do I go from here?

I said that I knew the social worker had been trying to see him and that that may be something to talk to her about. Kristof was looking tired and explained he wanted to rest before his mother came to visit later in the afternoon. But he suggested I came back the following afternoon, after his wife's visit in the morning, which he expected would be 'heavy'.

Fifth meeting: Thursday, late afternoon

With the best of intentions, it can be difficult to follow up on planned visits and, although I encountered Kristof around the hospice, it was another week before I got to speak properly with him. He was alone, watching TV when I arrived at his room. He invited me to join him and I sat in a chair next to his; it was set at a right angle to him. Kristof turned the sound down but left the picture on – a 1950s British war movie, which would have claimed my attention but which, thankfully, was out of my line of vision. Without pause, Kristof began to tell me where things were up to with regard to his treatment: his pain control was improved; chemo was still an option; if things got better, he would be moving out of the hospice; *if* things improved, he might expect to have between two and eight weeks to live – 'In fact, zero to eight weeks, because they told me that two weeks ago'! He also said that he would likely be moving to a nursing home soon.

The matter-of-factness with which Kristof spoke was striking, and I considered highlighting this to him; but equally I was struck by the fact that he didn't once look at me as he spoke. Instead, facing the TV, Kristof looked at notepapers he had on his bed, at the TV, at things around in the room, all the while crossing and uncrossing his legs, now picking up this notepaper, now that, now opening and closing a pocket multi-tool he had with him. I found his speech clearer this visit and he once again spoke about suicide.

Chaplain: Is that something that you still have in mind?

Kristof: Definitely. No one here sees it as suicide. They understand that it's a way of ending the pain.

I asked if he had thought about how he would kill himself and he explained his plan to overdose on morphine and be 'dead within two hours'. He contrasted his experience of suffering with his terminal illness with that of a person suffering with depression.

Kristof: With depression, suicide is a permanent solution to a temporary problem. But this isn't temporary. This will kill me – and it will hurt me.

He went on to say that he was at peace with his dying, 'Now that I know how I'm going to die, what will happen to me.'

Again, he reviewed his life, rehearsing things he'd told me about his provision for his children; about not needing to ask forgiveness from anyone; about his wife's successes and their relationship. At that point, the dietician interrupted to have a conversation about a RIG (radiology inserted gastrostomy) tube. After she left, Kristof explained that, while he had previously refused a RIG, because his pain was now better controlled, he felt there would be benefit from having proper nutrition.

Continuing, Kristof spoke about faith. He rehearsed what he had said about not believing but also not challenging the beliefs of others. Then he caricatured those who hold conservative – 'with a small "c"' – religious beliefs as always being right, not being open to question new ideas or think for themselves

Kristof: But there's basically analytic Christianity or there's 'You-have-to-believe-what-you're-told.' I prefer analytic Christianity.

Chaplain: What do you mean by analytic Christianity?

Kristof: Christianity that you discuss and question and ask, 'Do I believe that?'

Chaplain: Thinking Christianity.

Kristof: Thinking Christianity! I think there comes a point where you have to say, 'I'm sorry but there are some things that you absolutely have to believe.'

Given what Kristof had said previously about rejecting religion when he had been at school and now not seeing himself as religious but believing in a higher power (spiritual but not religious?) and accepting that Jesus existed but being uncertain about his divine status, his last comment caught me unawares and I didn't anticipate what followed.

Chaplain: Do you?

Kristof: Yes, I think so. And I think the one thing you have to admit, the one thing you have to believe in, is the Resurrection.

Chaplain: Do you?

Kristof: Yes, I think so.

Chaplain: Do you believe in the Resurrection?

Kristof: Yes, which means I believe he was the son of God.

Chaplain: Really?

Kristof: But do I believe he was the son of God? I don't know. (*Without irony*) I'll find out in eight weeks.

We had been talking for over an hour and, although Kristof was clearly engaged and enjoying our conversation, he was looking tired. As I left to let him rest, he thanked me for coming.

Kristof: That was an interesting discussion. You picked a good moment today.

Sixth meeting: Tuesday, early morning

Since my last meeting with Kristof, plans had been made for his discharge. On the morning he was due to move out I called to see him. My time was limited, but I wanted to say goodbye. When I arrived, his things were packed and lined up with several bags of drugs and dietary supplements. Kristof was opening the packets of his new drugs to check what he would need to take and when. We exchanged a few words about his hospital visit the previous day; he mentioned that he was 'edgy' about moving on. Unexpectedly, he reintroduced the subject of the Resurrection; something he had never understood. I told him about Oscar Romero, an Archbishop of San Salvador, who had received death threats for defending poor El Salvadorians against a corrupt government. In 1980, Romero was shot dead while saying Mass but before the shooting he had said, 'If they kill me, I shall arise in the Salvadoran people'.[2] I suggested that I found it helpful to think of resurrection in the sense of inspiring others.

---

2   www.westminster-abbey.org/our-history/people/oscar-romero

Kristof: There's nothing inspiring about my life. My life has no significance.

Kristof may have been thinking about his own 'resurrection'. If so, I failed to hear that and chose instead to try to rescue him.

Chaplain: I think that depends on how you measure it. If you measure it against the 'great order of things', then none of our lives are significant; but if you measure it in terms of the lives of the people around you, I think our lives have great significance.

Kristof: I've got no time for the great mass of humanity. Individual humans...I'll do what I can to help individuals. But taken *en masse*, humanity has been quite disastrous. It's different with individuals. I met this guy who didn't have money to get to Eastbourne. I gave him a tenner and all the cigarettes I had and he said, 'You're a very kind man.' But I'm not. I just went around the corner and bought some more.

Chaplain: I think it's a question of perspective.

Kristof: Mmm, I don't have any perspective.

My time was up. I needed to attend the weekly ward round, so I began to say goodbye. Kristof commented on his time in the hospice and quality of care he had received.

Kristof: When I've settled in, perhaps you'll come and see me; in fact, I'd actively welcome you to come and see me. I'll be more focused; I'm a bit distracted today. I'd like to talk more about Christianity. I don't know much about it.

I said I would like to visit him. As I left he said, 'It's been quite nice to chat.'

Over the next three weeks, I saw Kristof four more times: twice at his new place of care. My hope on each occasion was to give him the time and space to do the work on himself that he had said he wanted to do. However, due to his distracted state of mind, this didn't happen. Kristof was once again admitted to hospital. When I telephoned to arrange to visit, I was shocked to learn that he had died from a sudden bleed.

Assessments, interventions and outcomes

Assessments

Notwithstanding the lack of clarity in his speech, Kristof was very clear about what he thought he wanted from our working together. He saw me as 'an offer of help' that he was not going to turn away, despite the fact that he had long ago rejected religion and saw himself now as 'not religious'. At the conclusion of our first meeting, my assessment was that Kristof wanted help to think about his life and who he had become, and to make sense of his life in relation to the Christianity that he had until now rejected. This request, made at our first meeting, seemed perplexing and it is possible that Kristof himself did not fully understand his meaning; but, in retrospect, I now see that, over the duration of our relationship, he did drop several clues that further explicated his likely meaning.

When we met for the third time, Kristof said that he had 'always been very logical about thinking about [his] death'. Then, at our next meeting, he drew a distinction between two sides of his personality, identifying with his 'logical side', which had 'always been stronger than [his] emotional side'. At our fifth meeting, having previously wondered openly about the divinity of Jesus Christ, Kristof affirmed a belief in the Resurrection, and drew what he saw as the only logical conclusion, that 'I believe [Jesus] was the son of God'. This unanticipated affirmation of faith caught me off-guard. I now think that Kristof was struggling to find some accommodation between the competing needs of the logical and emotional sides of his personality. Logically, he could not believe in God, the divinity of Christ or the Resurrection – his logical side demanded his atheism; but as a young man, dying prematurely with a sense that he had underachieved, the idea of resurrection had powerful emotional and existential appeal, and his emotional side longed, if not for faith, then for reassurance that there might be more. My reinterpretation, which cast resurrection in humanistic terms of inspiring others, drew a bitter response: 'There's nothing inspiring about my life. My life has no significance.'

With the benefit of hindsight, I think Kristof wanted or needed somehow to locate himself emotionally within the Christian narrative of death and resurrection. My failure, at this point, was to meet him (largely) on his logical side, and I think the main reason I failed effectively to assess Kristof's actual – rather than his presenting – spiritual needs is that I 'over-identified' with him. Over-identification is a term used to name the way a counsellor/therapist may identify, to an unhelpful degree, with the person they are working with to the detriment of the counsellor/therapist's objectivity. As someone who has aspired to an academic career, I allowed myself to over-identify with Kristof's career in academia, and I think that this seduced me into losing my objectivity and to forgetting that ours was a chaplain-to-patient relationship, not an academic-to-academic one. Something in me wanted him to acknowledge me as a fellow academic – which probably accounts for why I eventually disclosed some of my personal details to him, something I almost never do and only ever with great caution! As a consequence, I failed to ask myself the obvious and very basic question: why would an atheist academic see a chaplain as a potential source of help to die well?

With the wisdom of hindsight, I would now assess Kristof's overwhelming spiritual needs as twofold: first, a need to reconcile the competing sides of his personality – logical and emotional – in a way that maintained the integrity of both; and second, a need to find a sense of assurance that, in some counter-intuitive way, his death would not be his end.

Interventions

I think my interventions with Kristof can be generalised under two headings: reassurance and life review.

From experience, I have found that reassurance, in the form of well-intended encouragement, is usually unproductive. If a person is feeling guilty or anxious, my comforting words, however wise I may think them, will not form the bridge they need to cross from their guilt or anxiety to peace of mind. The person needs to build their own bridge and I see my job as helping them construct it. At our first meeting, Kristof asked me a direct question about how the Church might view his attempt to take his own life. There were several ways I could have responded but I chose to try to reassure him that, even if the Church (or a part of it) judged his action as sinful, I wasn't going to judge him. My motivation was directed towards developing a working relationship with Kristof, which, in my usual practice, depends on my unconditional positive regard. I wanted Kristof to know from the beginning that I would accept him, no matter what he said or did.

However, in responding in this way, I broke two basic rules: first, it is *more effective to show rather than tell* – in other words, there was no gain in trying to force-feed my acceptance, it would have (and I think did) become evident in the way I respected him and behaved towards him; second, it is important to *be led by the person's needs* – in other words, I failed to respond to the question Kristof actually posed and instead addressed the one I would have liked him to have asked! In retrospect, I would have perhaps responded more wisely if I had simply enquired as to why it might be important that the Church had become less harsh. At least, that would have stayed with Kristof's agenda and given him the chance to explore the question for himself. (I observe a similar dynamic during our fourth meeting. During our conversation, Kristof said, 'I've never believed but I've never denied other people's beliefs. But now I'm starting to think about it.' I responded with reassurance where it would have perhaps been more helpful to him had I tried to help him explore his new thoughts.)

More positively, some of my other interventions – in my view, the majority of them – were responding to Kristof's explicit desire to engage in an extended life review: 'What I'd like help with is in trying to understand who I've been, and to do that in relation to Christianity; what my life has meant. I'd like to look over my life and see what I've been, who I've become'. To that end, I tried to pick up on Kristof's invitation to 'get to know about me', with the aim that, in the process of him telling me about himself, Kristof would also review his life and come to understand more clearly what his life had meant.

This work began during our first meeting. Picking up on Kristof's invitation to get to know him, I enquired about his research work. As with my response to his question about the Church and suicide, there were other ways I could have encouraged Kristof to talk about himself:

simply asking him to tell me about his life would have been effective and would have left the initiative with him, which would likely have revealed something of what was to the fore of his mind at that moment. (In retrospect, enquiring about his research work fed my curiosity about his academic background; however, notwithstanding this, Kristof took the conversation to his main concerns: his wife and his children, his preparations for dying and a particular concern about his children.)

Life review continued to be a feature of at least part of most of our meetings, most powerfully during our fifth meeting. Kristof had been speaking poignantly about his relationship with his wife and his continuing love for her and then abruptly counterpoised this, in a way that caught me off-guard, with his thoughts about Christianity and the possibility of belief that surprised even him – that he was open to believing that Jesus was the son of God. How far Kristof took that possibility and whether it ever became personal faith, I cannot know. But it interests me to see that he got to this position of belief himself by following the logic of his premise. The rapidity of his move left me a credulous spectator but it is an instance of a frequently observed phenomenon, which is that the chaplain (or counsellor/therapist) often acts as the catalyst for the person to do the work they need to do but would not, or could not, do alone.

Outcomes

For Kristof, the outcomes of our meetings were mixed. I'm clear that I failed adequately to both assess and respond to his spiritual needs. Crucially, it seems that, during our sixth meeting, Kristof had been thinking about resurrection, not with his logical side, treating it as a detached theological concept but emotionally, engaged with a real and pressing existential concern. Regrettably, I failed to hear that concern and, in so doing, failed to help him in the task he wanted me to help him with: to explore who he had been and what his life had meant, and to do that 'in relation to Christianity'. I'm equally clear that this was largely due to the fact that I over-identified with him. Kristof and I shared similarities in our working-class backgrounds and academic aspirations, which made over-identification all too easy; I also connected with his religious questions more than he knew.

But this is not to say that my work with Kristof was without any good effect – there are aspects of the work that I believe were helpful to him. Suicide remained Kristof's pain relief of last resort – 'No one here [in the hospice] sees it as suicide. They understand that it's a way of ending the pain.' At our first meeting, he had tested me about his overdose – 'I suppose that's technically a sin.' And although he didn't respond directly to my honest answer, he did open the door to our working together. When the subject came up again, he affirmed that he found value in our relationship: 'I think we've hit it off – we seem to see things in the same way. I'd like to talk about how I face my own death.' Clearly, my ability to not be defensive in talking about suicide and, again, my willingness to be open to his questioning of religion, eschewing any presumed 'authorised' response in favour of honest discussion, had been important to Kristof and established a basis of trust between us. It is to the credit of my role as chaplain, despite on this occasion my ineptitude in that role, that Kristof was able to have the kinds of conversation he had with me, which he would have been unlikely to have had with any other healthcare professional.

Discussion

For me, there is, both educationally and in terms of raising questions for further research, a good deal to learn from a case about which I remain uncertain as to how it benefited the patient.

Counsellors/therapists are very familiar with the concept of the 'use of self' (Rowan and Jacobs 2002). Psychodynamic therapists may call this 'countertransference', while those who work within the person-centred or humanist approaches will prefer to talk about empathy or presence. Either way, what they are talking about touches on the counsellor/therapist's ability to be self-reflexive. It is important to be clear about what is meant by 'self-reflexive'. Self-reflexivity is not the same thing as reflecting on practice, which in the UK is recognised as an essential capability for all chaplains (UKBHC 2015). Self-reflexivity is the ability to reflect on oneself and the way in which one is being influenced and shaped by an experience; to reflect on one's experience of the experience. Counsellors/therapists need the ability to be self-reflexive *in the moment*; to be able not only to be with the person they are listening to as fully as they can be, engaging with them and understanding their experience but also *at the same time* to monitor how the experience of being with this person is affecting them. This key skill takes time (perhaps years) to develop and demands a great deal of honest, personal work; it is intended to build self-knowledge in order to make possible the intentional use of self and, for this reason, it is a core element in counsellor/therapist training. In my experience in the UK, developing the ability to be self-reflexive is less obviously part of chaplain training. Yet, as this case study demonstrates, the chaplain's intentional use of self is crucial to the quality of the work. I understand this. As a trained and accredited counsellor/therapist, I have done – and continue to do – that work on my self, and I've even written about it. Elsewhere I've argued that 'spiritual care depends on a high degree of presence, such that I would conclude *presence is the mode of spiritual care*' (Nolan 2012, p.129, emphasis added). But, again, as this case study demonstrates, it is work that is never finished! There is always more a chaplain can learn about themselves.

In terms of research, the turn from 'process' to 'outcomes' research is effecting a shift of interest away from what chaplains do with their patients (process) to how chaplains serve patients' health benefits (outcomes). Although the shift of emphasis may be subtle, its effect may lead to chaplains becoming less interested in our relationships and more focused on our interventions (Handzo *et al.* 2014). This may be imprudent, particularly if it leads to the instrumentalising of what we do. I don't think this will happen; chaplains are 'people persons', and we put high value on the relationships we have with those in our care. But, as this case of uncertain patient benefit shows, there is more to learn about the chaplain–patient relationship and how and why it works in ways that can be helpful. The fact that Kristof, an atheist academic who was prematurely dying, saw a relationship with a chaplain ('I'd like you to get to know about me') as a potential source of help to die well raises questions about our chaplain–patient relationship that invite further research. Equally, and despite the questionable effect of my work with him, the fact that Kristof used me to explore his belief in the Resurrection and find some sense of reassurance invites further research about the chaplain–patient relationship. Indeed, the fact that I feel I was ineffective and yet can observe there was some gain for Kristof, should question any wholesale turn to 'outcomes' research, especially if this threatens further examination of 'process'.

Conclusion

My objective in case study research is intrinsic (Stake 1994, p.237): I want to understand *how I might be of use to someone who is dying* (Nolan 2016). In this case, directed by my previous research (Nolan 2012), I wanted to look at how the quality of our relationship might have helped Kristof. I consider the quality of the case work was deficient in the sense that certain parallels between our stories caused me to over-identify with Kristof, which meant that I missed the opportunity to help him make sense of his life experience 'in relation to Christianity'. But despite this, Kristof was able to use me to explore his beliefs and find some sense of reassurance. He also affirmed that we had 'hit it off' and that he would continue using me as someone with whom he could talk about facing his own death.

References

Fitchett, G. (2011). 'Making our case(s).' *Journal of Health Care Chaplaincy*, 17, 1–2, 3–18.

Handzo, G., Cobb, M., Holmes, C., Kelly, E. and Sinclair, S. (2014). 'Outcomes for professional health care chaplaincy: An international call to action.' *Journal of Health Care Chaplaincy*, 20, 2, 43–53.

Nolan, S. (2012). *Spiritual Care at the End of Life: The Chaplain as a 'Hopeful Presence'.* London: Jessica Kingsley Publishers.

Nolan, S. (2016). '"He needs to talk!" – A chaplain's case study of non-religious spiritual care.' *Journal of Health Care Chaplaincy*, 22, 1, 1–16.

Nolan, S. (2017). 'Searching for Identity in Uncertain Professional Territory: Psycho-Spirituality as Discourse for Non-Religious Spiritual Care.' In G. Harrison (ed.) *Psycho-Spiritual Care in Health Care Practice* (pp.175–187). London: Jessica Kingsley Publishers.

Rowan, J. and Jacobs, M. (2002). *The Therapist's Use of Self.* Maidenhead: Open University Press.

Stake, R.E. (1994). 'Case Studies.' In N.K. Denzin and Y.S. Lincoln (eds) *The Handbook of Qualitative Research* (pp.236–247). Thousand Oaks, CA: Sage.

UKBHC (2015). *Spiritual and Religious Care Capabilities and Competences for Healthcare Chaplains Bands (or Levels) 5, 6, 7 & 8.* Cambridge: UK Board of Healthcare Chaplaincy. Available at www.ukbhc.org.uk/sites/default/files/ukbhc_spiritual_and_religious_capabilities_and_competences_bands_5_-_8_2017.pdf, accessed 14 January 2018.

Yalom, I.D. (2008). *Staring at the Sun: Overcoming the Dread of Death.* London: Piatkus.

Chapter 16

Critical Response to a Chaplain's Self-Reflexive Case Study

A Chaplain's Perspective

Cheryl Holmes

It has been many years since I have been involved in direct chaplaincy provision, although my work immerses me in this field. In my current role, I lead the development and promotion of spiritual care services in hospitals across Victoria in Australia. Thinking about spiritual care and its place within healthcare is the focus of my work. The opportunity to respond to this case study by Chaplain Nolan returns me again to the heart of this work and why I am passionate to see it take its place as an integral part of healthcare. Spiritual care is founded on the human capacity for vulnerability. For spiritual care to take place, one person must dare to reveal something of themselves to another, to allow themselves to be seen. But this is not a one-way interaction. The effectiveness of the chaplain requires that they are also a person with the capacity for vulnerability, with the courage to 'show up and be seen' (Brown 2010). The gift of the case study is that we see this interplay of vulnerability. As both patient and chaplain are revealed and 'seen', an encounter takes place, and we are offered the richness of their stories to learn from.

This case study shares reflections about a life in the context of an approaching death, not unusual in a hospice setting. What I became aware of alongside the life/death setting was the number of other opposites, or perhaps dualisms, recurring through the encounter and its assessment. Religions know a lot about dualistic thinking, for example good versus evil or heaven versus hell. This dualistic thinking has not served us well in navigating the complexities and messiness of life, where real lives are not so easily categorised. It is in this space that chaplains often find themselves, where identifying black and white or right and wrong is not so easy, and nor should it be. In my response to this case study, I will reflect on three areas where I was aware of this dualism: objectivity/subjectivity; logical/emotional; and process/outcomes. I hope that my responses might raise questions for consideration in both the wider healthcare context and for spiritual care in particular.

Objectivity/subjectivity

Chaplain Nolan introduces at the very beginning of the case study the idea of 'over-identification' as a critique of his response to Kristof. Further, he suggests that having a 'normal level of objectivity' would have improved the efficacy of his work with Kristof. It is interesting to think that, in other places where we engage with people, finding those things we hold in common is often the basis for sharing, mutuality and the formation of relationships. In fact, Kristof says, 'we seem to see things in the same way', which could be seen as an affirmation of the trust that is enabled when one 'identifies with' the other. For Kristof, it would seem that this identification with the chaplain is an enabler of their interaction, laying the foundations for the engagement that follows. This is in keeping with the shift occurring within healthcare to a focus on person-centred care and patient experience, an approach that is more than just expressions of empathy and presence. This focus seeks to engage patients as partners in their own healthcare and brings to the forefront the subjectivity inherent in the encounter.

What does this say about the professional–patient relationship and about professional boundaries? As patients and consumers take their place around the healthcare table, it seems that ideas about professional hierarchies and professional control are being challenged. From the very beginning of the case study, Kristof was very clear that he would 'welcome chaplaincy support'. He clearly identified in his first communication that he recognised the chaplain as someone who could help him. For Chaplain Nolan, the strong association with his professional role led to what was perhaps an unnecessary justification of his position. This raises some important questions. Is this perhaps where the 'over-identification' is apparent? What happens when chaplains over-identify with their professional role? When Chaplain Nolan 'shows up' by revealing something of himself, Kristof reveals more of his own working-class background and life history. There is a need for balance in thinking about objectivity/subjectivity in spiritual care. (How much should chaplains 'be seen'?) One of the outcomes of holding a level of objectivity can be the creation of distance between the professional and the patient. The professional is privileged with knowledge that the patient may not know they hold, in this case Kristof's failed suicide. This knowledge imbalance ensures that the professional is the one in control and is able to use this knowledge to lead the conversation. There are some significant questions raised by this case study. Who is most served by maintaining professional boundaries? What is the relationship between objectivity/subjectivity and power and control?

Logical/emotional

Internationally, the bio-medical model of healthcare has been found wanting. Medical and technological advances have saved lives but have not been the expected panacea for healthcare (Chan 2013). Somehow the centrality of people and relationships has been lost and, over the past decade, we have seen the resultant fallout. Moves towards reclaiming compassion in healthcare are bringing change (Firth-Cozens and Cornwell 2009; Puchalski *et al.* 2014). These overarching themes epitomise a logical/emotional dichotomy. The bio-medical model embodies a logical, rational approach, all of which might fall under the umbrella of the hard sciences. The move towards compassionate care, and indeed the integration of spiritual care, expresses a more emotional, sensitive approach, more often associated with the soft arts. There is often, too, a gendered overlay in these positions.

This dichotomy does not just occur at the systemic level, as Chaplain Nolan identifies in his case study. Understanding how we think and the inner resources used to shape the ways we make sense of the world is incumbent on all those working in spiritual care. This level of self-awareness (and self-reflexivity) is important as it can impact on how we are available to this work in the cause of another. In his honest assessment, Chaplain Nolan gains insight into the shift from the logical to the emotional realm for Kristof and identifies that he did not follow this movement. Was this due solely to over-identification with their shared similarities? When Chaplain Nolan asked about Kristof's research work, in response to his invitation 'to get to know about me', did this reflect, too, a need to stay within the logical/rational realm rather than enter the emotional space? Exploring the multiple layered reasons for why we take up certain positions is essential. Having the capacity to access both logical and emotional ways of understanding and meaning making is the path to whole-person care at all levels of healthcare.

Process/outcomes

These are somewhat different issues to those discussed above, as they do not represent opposite positions. Thinking about process and outcomes provides a way to look at the whole encounter, that is, what happened and what was the result. The process/outcomes framework structures the way we reflect on a case study, as Chaplain Nolan writes in his Introduction. In this specific incident, Chaplain Nolan is interested in the question of whether a case study can provide educational and research value. He raises questions about his process, that is, the nature and progression of his work with Kristof, and questions about the outcomes for Kristof, that is, the effectiveness and results of the work. It is obvious for me in reading the case study that the answer to the question of educational and research value is a resounding 'yes'. The richness of the material in both the case and Chaplain Nolan's reflection on it is dependent on the interplay between the process and the outcomes. These are in dynamic relationship. For me, this case highlights the limitations of considering this dynamic purely from the chaplain's perspective. I wonder how

Kristof would reflect on this process and how he might name the outcomes. I hear within the case some profound shifts in Kristof's reflections: 'And I think the one thing you have to admit, the one thing you have to believe in, is the Resurrection.' The patient's voice is needed if we are to gain greater understanding and knowledge of the chaplain–patient relationship, the process of spiritual care and the resultant outcomes. The work currently under way on spiritual care patient reported outcome measures is an important contribution in this area (Snowden and Telfer 2017). Which brings us to the question of research.

Chaplain Nolan raises process and outcomes in the context of research as though they represent opposite positions for research focus. As one of the authors of the article he references (Handzo *et al.* 2014), I find it appropriate to respond to this concern. The call to action on outcomes sought to address the increasing onus on chaplains to demonstrate the value of their contribution to healthcare. This requires that chaplains are able to demonstrate that their interventions result in measurable and meaningful outcomes. Both process and outcomes are important. Understanding the surgical process for a hip replacement is incredibly important but the process is only undertaken for a specific outcome, that is, to enable the patient to walk free of pain. What is the process for if not to effect an outcome? In spiritual care, we need to be able to answer the 'so what?' It is not enough to talk about our role as 'being present' and providing 'comfort and support'. Every healthcare worker is being challenged to think about the quality of the worker–patient relationship. This is why there has been such a growing emphasis on patient experience, and it is why we are seeing growing movements within healthcare for compassion and kindness (Youngson 2007; www. theschwartzcenter.org). Relationships in healthcare matter and this is not something that is the sole purview of spiritual care. So what difference does spiritual care make? What do chaplains do that contributes to positive patient experience, health outcomes and quality of care? Our capacity to answer these questions will depend on the research that addresses both process and outcomes.

Conclusion

A brief exploration of the dualisms that emerged from this case study has been a good reminder to me of how easy it is to take up certain ways of thinking and meaning making that serve to support particular positions. This is where Chaplain Nolan's emphasis on self-reflexivity is significant. The capacity to be in the midst of paradox and to hold the tensions without moving too quickly towards a position or an answer is one of the gifts of spiritual care.

References

Brown, B. (2010). *The Gifts of Imperfection*. Minneapolis, MN: Hazelden Information & Educational Services.

Chan, M. (2013). 'Maintaining the momentum for better health globally: Are innovation and technology game-changers for the future?' Keynote address at the 38th World Hospital Congress, Oslo, Norway (18 June). Available at www.who.int/dg/speeches/2013/world_hospital_congress_20130618/en, accessed 14 January 2018.

Firth-Cozens, J. and Cornwell, J. (2009). *The Point of Care: Enabling Compassionate Care in Acute Hospital Settings*. London: The King's Fund. Available at www.kingsfund.org.uk/sites/default/files/field/field_publication_file/poc-enabling-compassionate-care-hospital-settings-apr09.pdf, accessed 14 January 2018.

Handzo, G., Cobb, M., Holmes, C., Kelly, E. and Sinclair, S. (2014). 'Outcomes for professional health care chaplaincy: An international call to action.' *Journal of Health Care Chaplaincy*, 20, 2, 43–53.

Puchalski, C.M., Vitillo, R., Hull, S.K. and Reller, N. (2014). 'Improving the spiritual dimension of whole person care: Reaching national and international consensus.' *Journal of Palliative Medicine*, 17, 6, 642–656.

Snowden, A. and Telfer, I. (2017). 'Patient reported outcome measure of spiritual care as delivered by chaplains.' *Journal of Health Care Chaplaincy*, 23, 4, 131–155.

Youngson, R. (2007). 'The Organizational Domain of People-Centred Health Care.' In *People-Centred Health Care (Technical Papers)* (pp.35–50). International Symposium on People-Centred Health Care: Reorienting Health Systems in the 21st Century – The Tokyo International Forum (25 November). Available at www.wpro.who.int/health_services/people_at_the_centre_of_care/documents/PCItechPapers20Aug2008.pdf, accessed 14 January 2018.

Chapter 17

Critical Response to a Chaplain's Self-Reflexive Case Study

A Psychoanalyst's Perspective

Linda Emanuel

Chaplain Nolan is to be commended for doing something critical in clinical practice: engaging in candid self-reflection in print. This is critical for at least four big reasons. One is that candour includes entertaining one's own mistakes. Against the prevailing backdrop of ambitious professionals needing to show themselves as having positive outcomes for patients, it is common to lose the power of learning from mistakes. While some established leaders have been able to afford that power of humility (for instance, Charles Bosk wrote *Forgive and Remember* (Bosk 2003) and Arnold Goldberg wrote *The Analysis of Failure* (Goldberg 2012) late in their careers), it is so much harder for the less established and aspiring that we rarely see it in case reports. Since the less established and aspiring constitute the greater part of us, and since this is the time in our careers that we need most to learn from error as we refine our clinical skills, this is a serious matter. Failure to learn from mistakes is a major loss to optimal clinical practice. Mistakes are nothing to be ashamed of; pretences to infallibility and failure to take responsibility by learning from mistakes and improving are matters to be ashamed of. Chaplain Nolan helps us redress the culture that has failed to endorse that type of responsibility and that fertile source of learning.

The second reason is more specific to the type of work chaplains and psychologists do. Our work is inherently subjective and interpersonal; we use ourselves as an instrument of understanding and of change. It is not that we have magical personal properties but rather that we use awareness of what is happening in us in reference to the patient to gain insight into what is happening in the experience of our patient (countertransference). Then we use the intersubjective relationship between our self and the patient to identify old patterns from the patient that are transferred into our relationship to build new and better ways (Stefana 2017). Chaplain Nolan describes these for us and shows us how he uses them with candid self-reflection. Analysts rely a great deal on countertransference and building a different relational experience. If the analyst is feeling something towards the patient (anger, compassion, boredom, attraction or whatever), that is a clue to the patient's feelings (perhaps seeking incursion, emotional pain, defensive distancing, primitive need or whatever). Countertransference never gives us more than a good hypothesis but that often provides the start for fertile thought and engagement with the patient. Then the two build something healthy where the problem has been recreated in some fashion between the patient and therapist. Perhaps the patient feels betrayed or let down because the therapist has been late or failed to understand. The therapist can discover with the patient how that recreated old experiences. By identifying that source of amplified feeling and by forging a different outcome (for instance, adding the lost time to a future session or achieving and showing deep understanding or fostering the ability to live with the frustration, etc.), the therapist can create a new and healing experience with and for the patient.

Countertransference and intersubjective relational creation are not unique to the analytic setting; they are universal. Roughly, in day-to-day terms, countertransference is how we feel about the other person. But we usually translate that feeling into an attribute or a judgement about the other person (perhaps we decide the other person is invasive, needs a hug, is dangerous, inhibited, immature or whatever). In regular life, this can be plenty. In clinical work, it is a major part of what is healing – to understand the other person on their own terms and to create a new intersubjective relationship based on that understanding. Many people have suffered greatly for lack of having been understood and as a result not understanding themselves; they may have lived their lives trying to be, and believing they are, what they are asked to be or want to be. It comes as a great relief to be understood and appreciated for something they need no effort to be, and it is also an act of meaningful connection simply to be understood. People readily perceive the difference between being sized up and being appreciated at a deep level. As one of my mentors noted, when the workings of your purportedly insane patient make perfect sense to you and their mind has become a work of beauty in your mind, you are probably understanding them adequately to help them heal. The clinician who can do that has used countertransference to understand and become trustworthy to the patient, and the two can begin to create a healing interaction.

This delicate and intimate interaction depends on the clinician knowing themselves well – well enough to know when their issues (we all have our own unique issues; the only question is how well we know and handle them) are colouring the interaction. Often this undue colouring occurs when the clinician has an agenda. Since our professions rely on us having a kind of mission or calling to this difficult work, it can be a fine balance. We need to want our suffering clients' wellbeing enough, and we need to find fulfilment in wading into places of suffering enough, to be with them in their place of need. When does that become an unbalanced agenda?

Chaplain Nolan raises one example of where the balance can go awry: over-identification with the patient. We all have a powerful need to heal and advance ourselves, and we often try to do so by projection or sublimation or similar displacements. Knowing enough of that common-road-travelled and yet avoiding leaps to directive advice or presumption instead of gentle, wondering hypotheses is a tough balance. Advice is not always a bad thing but, for our professions, it is a hazardous thing; not only may we be wrong but, more importantly, we will have missed the mark, since our job is to help the patient understand what is at issue in their life and see a way forwards that comes from them. How do we know when we're off balance – more self-involved than other-involved?

By candid introspection. During clinical work, we must be constantly surveilling ourselves: do we feel more passionate than curious, more urgent than empathic, more ambitious than caring, more self-gratified than connected, or such like? The former of each of the foregoing counterpart feelings are perfectly fine things to feel for and about our own lives, but to feel them about another suggests we have felt as if we own them or they are part of us or we are part of them in a way that degrades them into a part of the clinician's agenda, rather than their own whole and precious person.

Did Chaplain Nolan let his issues colour his care of Kristof? I'm not sure. Partly, we cannot know because this assessment relies on Chaplain Nolan's own countertransference and self-reflection. So that is the third reason Chaplain Nolan's raising of the topic of candid self-reflection is so important. None can know a clinician's countertransference as sensitively as the clinician themselves. Self-regulating professionalism is nowhere more important than in this highly personal and subjective ingredient of effective healing care. Among analysts, it is normative – and I would assert should be required – to have consultation and ongoing personal analytic work throughout one's practising life. There is not a better way to help keep a sensitive perspective on this matter. I would hazard a guess that if such were required rather than merely normative, some of the more egregious transgressions of professional boundaries would have not occurred.

The fourth reason has to do with the nature of healthy relationships. As already alluded to, the therapist can foster healing by identifying old patterns of interaction that are not working and, finding them between the patient and therapist, forge a better interaction. Often these come about by tripping up on the old patterns. In other words, mistakes are made. Perhaps Chaplain Nolan offered advice too much informed by his own journey, with similar patterns of feeling, that he missed something unique and important about Kristof's. Or, in other cases, perhaps the therapist has what we refer to as an empathic break. For instance, the therapist may feel alienated when the patient has an angry outburst that is personally directed at the therapist and, instead of identifying the matter that made the patient angry, the therapist may get angry back. That would be a common mistake. But the therapist can then say something like: 'Oh, you found that what I did was similar in a way to what your uncle did back then; no wonder you were angry. And then I got angry, even more like your uncle. My mistake; I'm sorry.' Once the patient is understood perhaps they can also own the excessive response and learn to live with the frustration of whatever it was with a more modulated reaction. The therapist has demonstrated how to use self-understanding and empathic understanding, and how to use mistakes to further both. And, importantly, the therapist has demonstrated how to repair.

Kohut used the term 'optimal frustration' to describe the process of living with difficulties successfully so that growth occurs, and it is crucial to normal and reparative development (Kohut 1984). Mistakes can't be intentional, because then it is an altogether different set of matters, not least of which is the therapist attempting to create a controlled unwanted stimulus. But mistakes can be culled and used: Kohut referred more to frustrations dictated by circumstance but in our context we can say that he, in effect, asserts that mistakes must be culled and used, and I agree. So how can this be taught? Only by offering up our mistakes and how we used them clinically for peer discussion.

So Chaplain Nolan has made a major contribution, simply by raising the topic of having possibly erred. But did he? Chaplain Nolan acknowledges that he did some good things in his care for Kristof. He did assess, it seems accurately, that Kristof was expressing some concerns expected in someone facing death. Chaplain Nolan managed well to distinguish Kristof's desire to be pain-free even if it meant suicide from his existential suffering and a re-engagement with religion. Kristof was struggling to find, in the dialectic of his connection with Chaplain Nolan, if he could reconnect the dis-association that he had lived with for so long between his longing for continuity and spiritual embrace and his commitment to rationality, his affective and cognitive sources of knowing. Would he be able to heal his most important relationships before death? Would he be able to resolve things he felt guilty about or judged against, including his suicide attempt and plan, and the hurt he felt he had inflicted on one person, presumably his wife? Could he face death with a sense of peace because these things had been done well enough?

The task of a chaplain with a patient at this point in life can be seen as a fellow journeyer, as the patient does the growth and development of this last phase of life – a phase that colleagues and I have elsewhere termed existential maturity (Emanuel and Glasser Scandrett 2010). The journey entails being able to contemplate and think about the reality of mortality without decompensating; and when death is expected, it usually is accompanied by completing tasks of departure – making a will, preparing gifts, saying final words. Kristof had done these things. What he seemed to want from Chaplain Nolan was someone to accompany him as he moved beyond the ways of thinking that left him feeling judged and alienated (suicide is a sin; 'You-have-to-believe-what-you're-told') to a way of thinking that would allow him integrity within himself and a place in the afterlife he could imagine. He managed this well enough by believing in the Resurrection, which would logically entail believing in God after all but with a dose of empiricism – 'I'll find out in eight weeks.'

I suspect that Kristof's identification with Chaplain Nolan was at least as strong as Chaplain Nolan's with Kristof and that it was a facilitator of Kristof's resolution of his remaining dilemma. In the school of thought founded by Kohut, now called self-psychology, identification is a necessary part of healthy development (Kohut 1971). Kristof perhaps had his spiritual development stunted by the experiences he had that were alienating for him. Identification with Chaplain Nolan may have been just what he needed, and just in time. Chaplain Nolan had his own evolution in thought as he navigated his own spiritual and religious journey, and he had ways of articulating matters that Kristof needed but did not have time to discover alone any more. Chaplain Nolan offered Kristof these articulate thoughts at relevant times with a compassion that comes from personal experience, but I see no evidence that Chaplain Nolan pushed an agenda or made it difficult for Kristof.

So, while I thank Chaplain Nolan for raising the matter of using candid self-reflection, including on errors in case histories, I also thank Chaplain Nolan for illustrating how identification can facilitate existential maturity when it fits the patient's mode of psychological functioning and perhaps especially when time is short.

References

Bosk, C.L. (2003). *Forgive and Remember: Managing Medical Failure* (2nd edn). Chicago, IL: University of Chicago Press.

Emanuel, L. and Glasser Scandrett, K. (2010). 'Decisions at the end of life: Have we come of age?' *BMC Medicine*, 8, 1, 57. Available at https://bmcmedicine.biomedcentral. com/articles/10.1186/1741-7015-8-57, accessed 14 January 2018.

Goldberg, A. (2012). *The Analysis of Failure: An Investigation of Failed Cases in Psychoanalysis and Psychotherapy*. New York, NY; Hove, East Sussex: Routledge.

Kohut, H. (1971). *The Analysis of the Self: A Systematic Approach to the Psychoanalytic Treatment of Narcissistic Personality Disorders*. New York, NY: International Universities.

Kohut, H. (1984). *How Does Analysis Cure?* Chicago, IL: University of Chicago Press.

Stefana, A. (2017). *History of Countertransference: From Freud to the British Object Relations School*. Abingdon; New York, NY: Routledge.

Afterword

Case Studies and Chaplaincy Research

George Fitchett

Introduction

In describing the need for chaplain case studies, one of the arguments I have made is that chaplain case studies are important for advancing chaplaincy research (Fitchett 2011). In this Afterword, I will use the case studies in this book to explore two issues about chaplaincy research that are currently under discussion. The first issue is research about the outcomes associated with chaplaincy care. The second issue, which I will explore more briefly, is about how chaplains are responding to changes in religion and spirituality taking place in many societies.

An important preface to exploring these questions is to take note of the diversity in the cases in this book. The cases are least diverse in terms of the religious background of the patients/clients and chaplains. Eight of the patients are Christian or formerly Christian and all of their chaplains are Christian. In the ninth case, both the patient and the chaplain are Jewish. The cases are somewhat diverse in national context coming from the US, UK and Iceland. In terms of clinical context, the diversity in the cases expands considerably from general hospitals to specialty paediatric and veterans' hospitals to a nursing home, hospice and outpatient counselling. The diversity of who is being cared for in the cases mirrors the clinical contexts: infants, children, parents, veterans, elders, people with terminal illness and healthcare employees. There is remarkable diversity in the extent of the chaplains' relationships with the person cared for, from one session of an hour or less (Bratt Carle; Hanson), to several meetings over the course of several weeks (Ásgeirsdóttir;

Nolan), to many sessions over the course of several months (Bryson; Jinks; Sanders; Roberts), to a relationship that continued for nearly a year (Goodman and Baron). This diversity underscores the diversity of healthcare-related chaplains' work and the kinds of situations they are called on to address. It also points to a challenge for chaplaincy research: chaplains do many different things in many different contexts and their care may influence many different outcomes. As we proceed, we should remember that this group of cases was not chosen to be representative of chaplaincy in general or of chaplaincy in any specific context.

Research about chaplaincy outcomes

For a number of years, chaplaincy leaders around the world have described research about the outcomes of chaplaincy care as a priority for the profession (ENHC 2014; Handzo *et al.* 2014). There are two reasons why outcomes research is a priority for chaplains. The second reason, which is often uppermost in chaplains' minds, is that healthcare is an evidence-based activity, and unless chaplains working in healthcare can provide evidence for the benefits associated with their work, they will be marginalised. The first reason is at least as important: we need research to help us know if the care we are providing is having the effects we hope it will have. As Canadian chaplaincy researchers Tom O'Connor and Elizabeth Meakes wrote in 1998, in the first paper to use the term 'evidence-based pastoral care', 'Evidence from research needs to inform our pastoral care. To remove the evidence from pastoral care can create a ministry that is ineffective or possibly even harmful' (O'Connor and Meakes 1998, p.367).

As we consider this call for research about chaplaincy outcomes, it is important to note it is one of two ways of thinking about outcomes. This way of thinking focuses on formal research about outcomes. I will call this 'researching outcomes'. An example of this would be the study that found a positive association between higher levels of chaplain involvement with patients and their families in the ICU and the levels of satisfaction families whose loved one died in an ICU felt with treatment decision making and overall care for their loved one (Johnson *et al.*

2014). While researching outcomes is a new and challenging way of thinking for chaplains, there is a second way that is less formal and more integral to clinical practice in chaplaincy or any other profession. Good clinicians are always attentive to the effects of their efforts. Does the anxious patient seem more at peace; does the uncertain patient have a clear view of their next steps? I will call this 'observing outcomes'. An example of this in this book is the psychologist who was seeing Mrs Helen, the veteran who suffered military sexual trauma. The psychologist observed that her care was not helping Mrs Helen and as a result suggested a different course of action for Mrs Helen, speaking with Chaplain Sanders. In asking our case study authors to reflect on the outcomes of their care, we are asking them to be intentional about this aspect of good clinical practice.

What do we see when we examine what the chaplains write about observing outcomes in the 'Outcomes' section of their Discussions? The first thing that is evident is how brief they are, generally one or two paragraphs. Looking closely, we see that in several cases what the chaplains have written is not about outcomes but rather about the process of care or the aims for their care. In a few of the cases, information about outcomes can be found in the case itself or in other parts of the Discussion but the chaplains did not include it when they were writing about their outcomes. Why is this? For several of the cases in the book, it is genuinely hard to describe outcomes. I will return to that shortly, but first, it is important to note the influence of our training on our difficulty in describing the outcomes associated with our care. Learning to think about outcomes is only beginning to be included in chaplaincy education, and then not universally. Additionally, because thinking about outcomes is new, even motivated chaplain educators may have difficulty finding useful descriptions of chaplaincy outcomes (see Peery 2012; Snowden *et al.* 2013). Perhaps more importantly, for decades the emphasis in chaplain education has been on the process of chaplain care, frequently referred to as 'being present'. In this paradigm, focusing too intently on a plan or outcome is sometimes considered incompatible with a patient-centred focus on 'being present'.

When I look at the case studies in the book in light of a concern with outcomes, I see four groups of cases. In the first two groups, where the encounter is brief (Bratt Carle; Hanson) or where the patients' ability to communicate is limited (Bryson; Goodman and Baron), there are genuine challenges for both observing outcomes and researching outcomes. In some of these cases, the chaplains have observed behaviour that appears to be a positive response to their care: Mrs Pearlman, a woman with advanced dementia, moves her hands and head in time with the song sung by Rabbi Jacobs, she speaks a few words of familiar prayers with him, and she responds to his New Year's farewell with her own 'Shana Tovah'; Mark, an 11-year-old boy unable to communicate because of a stroke, was 'visibly thrilled with his stick doll and feelings card', interventions provided by Chaplain Bryson. In these cases, where circumstances limit observing outcomes, the chaplains sometimes add an interpretation for which the evidence is less clear. After observing that Mark was 'visibly thrilled', Chaplain Bryson writes, 'There was a sense of transcendent hope that was very present in this encounter.'

For these chaplains who were faced with limited opportunities to observe outcomes, describing the process of their care or the intentions in their care appeared to become a proxy for describing outcomes. At the end of her visit, the transgender veteran Vicki asks Chaplain Hanson, 'Do you really think God loves me like this?' 'Yes, I really do,' Chaplain Hanson tells her. Because the care in this case consists of this one encounter, Chaplain Hanson has limited ability to observe outcomes. Instead she describes the process of her care: Vicki 'left our session hearing she was blessed in God's eyes'. In her discussion of outcomes of her care with Mark, Chaplain Bryson also focuses on the process of her care. However, in this case, she is using an explicit set of spiritual care principles that have been developed by her team. This is an approach that should be considered for other contexts, especially where circumstances limit observing outcomes.

What can we say about researching outcomes about these four cases? I am not aware of any chaplaincy outcomes research for cases such as these. However, there is work being done to develop and use patient reported outcome measures (PROM) in chaplaincy care (Snowden and

Telfer 2017) that is relevant to the cases reported by Chaplains Bratt Carle and Hanson. The PROM consists of five items assessing feelings of anxiety, peace, hopefulness and sense of control. In a manner similar to the use of satisfaction measures in healthcare, chaplaincy departments might consider routinely sending the PROM to any clients that have been seen. An even stronger design, which might be difficult to use in a case like Chaplain Bratt Carle's but could be feasible in the context of a scheduled appointment such as with Chaplain Hanson, would be to have the patient complete the PROM items while waiting for their appointment and then at some point after the appointment.

Researching outcomes for cases like Mark is much more challenging and even more so for cases like Mrs Pearlman. The team at Birmingham Children's Hospital is committed to an evidence-based approach to developing and testing spiritual care interventions for children like Mark, and I look forward to the results of their work. For cases like Mrs Pearlman, what is needed are several teams that have the interest and capacity to identify appropriate outcomes for spiritual care with patients with advanced dementia and to begin to test interventions that address those outcomes.

The third group of cases is actually one case, the work of Chaplain Sanders with Mrs Helen, a woman troubled by memories of two instances of military sexual trauma, and especially the experience of being molested by a priest. As a case that involves outpatient pastoral counselling extending over several months, this case is unique among the others in this book. The ACT model that informs Chaplain Sanders's clinical work has an outcome focus built in: what is the client's committed action, the new behaviour they wish to enact? Her work with Chaplain Sanders helps Mrs Helen achieve some important goals, including sharing her angry feelings about her molester in the Roman Catholic Sacrament of Reconciliation and communicating her assault to church authorities. These are outcomes that are easily observable for both Chaplain Sanders and Mrs Helen. At the end of Chaplains Sanders's report, Mrs Helen is continuing counselling with Chaplain Sanders and with the counsellor at the MST clinic to address additional feelings associated with her experiences.

The fourth group of cases consists of the four cases where chaplains are providing care in the context of patient care at the end of life. In two of these cases (Ásgeirsdóttir; Jinks) the patients are at opposite ends of the life span but a similar issue – distrust of the medical team – emerges in both chaplains' very first meetings. In one case, Jessica, whose unborn child has been diagnosed with trisomy 18, tells Chaplain Jinks she is very fearful her baby will be born prematurely and that the staff will not follow her and her husband's wishes for everything to be done to care for their baby. After listening to Jessica and praying with her, Chaplain Jinks communicates Jessica's concern to the team. They respond by visiting Jessica and reassuring her that they will care for the baby in accordance with her wishes. Chaplain Jinks writes, 'Jessica later reported a much-improved level of trust in her care providers, which led to a significant improvement in her mood and positive coping.' (He includes this observation about outcomes in his report of the cases but doesn't mention it again when he writes about the outcomes of his care.) Similarly, when Jakob is transferred to palliative care, one of the first things Chaplain Ásgeirsdóttir learns is how upset his family is with the care he had previously received, which causes them to distrust the new palliative care team as well. The family also report that Jakob wants his new grandson to be baptised and they enquire about whether it can be done on the Unit. Chaplain Ásgeirsdóttir arranges for the baptism to be done the next day. This accommodation of their needs appears to improve the family's trust of the team, which 'resulted in better symptom care and influenced the mental status of the family members in a positive way'.

In both cases, the chaplains have observed and reported the impact of their care on important outcomes. The role of chaplains in facilitating communication between patients, their families and care teams in the end-of-life context is just beginning to be examined in chaplaincy research. A recent study of 382 US chaplains working in palliative care found that 46 per cent of them reported that they often facilitated such communication (Jeuland *et al.* 2017). As mentioned earlier, other research shows that chaplain involvement with patients who die in an ICU, and their families, is associated with greater family satisfaction with how treatment decisions were made during their loved one's ICU stay (Johnson *et al.* 2014). Studies of families whose loved one died in an ICU find a high proportion with serious emotional distress in the subsequent months; up to 20 per cent have been found to be depressed and between 14 per cent and 35 per cent to suffer from post-traumatic stress disorder (Anderson *et al.* 2008; Gries *et al.* 2010). This research points to possible wider implications of the positive effects of chaplains' interventions that improve communication between families and healthcare teams. Further research is needed to test this possibility.

In the other two cases involving a patient who dies (Roberts; Nolan), the chaplains observe an important outcome: whether the patient had a good death. Chaplain Roberts describes how her care facilitated a good death for Daisy, including maintaining her autonomy, which enabled Daisy to plan her funeral to be the way she wanted it to be. In her conversations with Chaplain Roberts, Daisy expresses grief about things she will not get to do. Chaplain Roberts also reassures Daisy that her suffering is not punishment for having been a 'bad person' and affirms Daisy's decision that it is okay to accept medication to ease her suffering. The heart of Chaplain Nolan's reflection is concerned with an outcome of his care for Kristof, specifically his concern that his over-identification with Kristof compromised his ability to help Kristof explore his life 'in relation to Christianity'. In his reflection, Chaplain Nolan notes the interesting possibility that despite this lapse, 'Kristof used me to explore his belief in the Resurrection and find some sense of reassurance'. In her comment on the case, Linda Emanuel observes that Chaplain Nolan 'had ways of articulating [religious] matters that Kristof needed but did not have time to discover alone'. The case raises the interesting possibility that patients can use chaplains to achieve outcomes despite limitations in our care.

Evaluating outcomes in care for people who are dying is a challenge for chaplains as well as all our colleagues who work in hospice and palliative care. The person who is the central focus of our care does not live to help us evaluate it and, in most cases, reaches a point where they are too ill to comment on it. Nonetheless, important research is being done about measuring quality in palliative care (Dy *et al.* 2015) and about spiritual care in palliative care (Balboni *et al.* 2017; Steinhauser *et al.* 2017). Chaplaincy outcomes research in the hospice and palliative care context can be informed by developing a consensus about what is meant by a good death. Linda Emanuel has written about helping patients develop existential maturity (Emanuel and Glasser Scandrett 2010). A number of other helpful models of good death have been described (for example, Leget 2017). There are rich opportunities for researching outcomes related to chaplaincy care at the end of life. Before leaving this topic, it should be noted that in many settings, such as hospice and palliative care, the care is provided by a team. For example, in the case of Kristof, many people are trying to help with pain control, and, to the extent he was experiencing existential pain – for example, about his life alienated from religion – the chaplain's care may have played a role in reducing his pain. In such cases, it is difficult to measure the effects on outcomes of one professional or discipline separately from the effects of care by the whole team.

To summarise, chaplains have not received education that helps them pay attention to the outcomes associated with their care. Nonetheless, good chaplains, like all good clinicians, are attentive to the effects of their care: they observe outcomes. The cutting edge for professional chaplaincy is developing research that can help us know if our care is having its intended effects and can help us communicate the benefits of our care to our healthcare colleagues.

Chaplaincy in a changing religious landscape

Changes in chaplaincy and changes in the religious landscape of many nations raise at least two questions about chaplaincy care that can be considered in light of the cases in this book. The first question is about the possibility of interfaith care, in which chaplains care for people from faith traditions that differ from their own. Interfaith chaplaincy is the norm for chaplaincy practice in many places; however, this approach has been questioned from two perspectives. From a conservative Christian theological perspective, this 'generic chaplaincy' is seen as incapable of providing authentic theological guidance in times of life and death when such guidance is most needed (Engelhardt 1998). From a very different perspective, sociologist Wendy Cadge studied what chaplains did when called on to provide interfaith spiritual care (Cadge and Sigalow 2013). She observed them 'neutralising', attempting to minimise differences by employing a broad language of spirituality. She also observed them 'code-switching', that is, attempting to use the language, symbols and rituals of the person being cared for. Cadge and Sigalow's observations of chaplains' use of these strategies to provide interfaith care left them with questions about its effectiveness.[1]

Three of the cases in this book (Jinks; Sanders; Bratt Carle) are examples of interdenominational care.

Over a period of many months, Chaplain Jinks, who is ordained in the Presbyterian Church (USA), provided care to Jessica, her newborn daughter Sarah, and members of her family. The family belonged to a Pentecostal church, and their religious beliefs played an important role in their decision not to terminate Jessica's pregnancy when they learned the baby had trisomy 18. Despite the differences in their religious backgrounds, Jessica and her family develop deep trust in Chaplain Jinks. It is unclear what strategies Chaplain Jinks uses to bridge the differences between his faith background and Jessica's, but it seems clear that he is effective in doing that. After Sarah dies, Jessica calls Chaplain Jinks and asks him to speak at her funeral. 'You were her pastor,' she tells him.

Mrs Helen's Roman Catholic faith was a central part of her life. Chaplain Sanders is ordained in the African Methodist Episcopal Church. As Chaplain Sanders's care was shaped by the principles of ACT, the issues of neutrality and code-switching do not seem central in this case. Their religious differences notwithstanding, Chaplain Sanders's care enabled Mrs Helen to follow through on her goal to confess her anger about her molestation to a priest in the Sacrament

---

1   For another very interesting critique of the concept of 'generic chaplaincy', see Pattison (2001).

of Reconciliation. As Chaplain Sanders writes, 'She experienced holding the pain of betrayal by one clergy member [with Chaplain Sanders] while taking the risk of trusting in another [the priest who heard her confession].' Would care for Mrs Helen have been more effective if the chaplain were also a Roman Catholic priest?

Chaplain Bratt Carle is a minister in the Reformed Church in America. Paul and his mother are Roman Catholic. Chaplain Bratt Carle and Paul's mother agree that a blessing is the preferred ritual as Paul is about to be transferred to the paediatric psychiatric hospital. It is unlikely there is a blessing in either a Roman Catholic or Reformed Church prayer book for precisely such an occasion. The blessing Chaplain Bratt Carle offers might be seen as an example of neutralising, appealing to a broad but not religiously specific view of God ('You never leave us alone, even when we feel like we are alone'). The mother's response is general, 'Thanks so much', and because the visit ends soon after that it is hard to evaluate the effectiveness of this instance of interfaith chaplaincy care.

The second issue for chaplaincy raised by the changing religious landscape is how best to provide care for the growing number of people who have no religious affiliation, many of whom identify themselves as 'spiritual but not religious'. This includes people who have been alienated by religious organisations or harmed by their leaders. Some observers suggest that, in light of these cultural changes, chaplains may become more essential as providers of spiritual care for people facing times of crisis and transition (Sullivan 2014). Four of the cases in the book (Hanson; Roberts; Ásgeirsdóttir; Nolan) fit this description. Vicki, the transgender veteran, comes to Chaplain Hanson in part because the Roman Catholic Church does not accept her. Chaplain Hanson is resourceful and provides Vicki with information that can help her find a parish that will accept her. Faith and fellowship seem important to Vicki, and perhaps this information and Chaplain Hanson's acceptance will help Vicki reconnect with the Catholic Church. As a child at school, Kristof, the hospice patient for whom Chaplain Nolan cared, 'was brought up with fire and brimstone sermons'. He 'rejected that as soon as possible' but he 'still think[s] religion is important'. Now that he is near death, he welcomes the opportunity to talk to a chaplain, 'to understand who

I've been, and to do that in relation to Christianity'. Chaplains Roberts and Ásgeirsdóttir, while working in two very different national contexts, provide care for patients (Roberts) or their families (Ásgeirsdóttir) who have minimal or no connection with religious institutions but who are very welcoming of a chaplain's solicitous concern, prayers and assistance with rituals.

These cases illustrate a variety of ways in which chaplains care for patients and families who are not connected to religious institutions but who, at times of crisis or need, still seek to locate themselves in relation to something transcendent and loving. They provide evidence that, as people become less connected to religious institutions, chaplains may become important sources of spiritual care.

Conclusion

As noted at the beginning of this chapter, I have argued that case studies play an important role as chaplaincy continues to become a research-informed profession (Fitchett 2011). Part of what I had in mind when I made that argument was that case studies would provide the detailed information about what chaplains do, which is needed to test the effects of chaplaincy interventions in randomised clinical trials and other research. Here, I have used the cases to reflect on issues in chaplaincy outcomes research and issues about chaplaincy in a changing religious landscape. Other chaplains are using case studies to conduct research, including chaplains in the Netherlands, whose Dutch Case Studies Project is designed to describe competent practice in chaplaincy in several sectors in addition to healthcare (Van Loenen *et al.*, 2017). The cases in this book add to a growing body of published chaplain case studies that form an important resource for research that can help us advance our profession.

References

Anderson, W.G., Arnold, R.M., Angus, D.C. and Bryce, C.L. (2008). 'Posttraumatic stress and complicated grief in family members of patients in the intensive care unit.' *Journal of General Internal Medicine*, 23, 11, 1871–1876.

Balboni, T.A., Fitchett, G., Handzo, G.F., Johnson, K.S. *et al.* (2017). 'State of the science of spirituality and palliative care research Part II: Screening, assessment, and interventions.' *Journal of Pain and Symptom Management*, 54, 3, 441–453.

Cadge, W. and Sigalow, E. (2013). 'Negotiating religious differences: The strategies of interfaith chaplains in healthcare.' *Journal for the Scientific Study of Religion*, 52, 146–158.

Dy, S.M., Kiley, K.B., Ast, K., Lupu, D. *et al.* (2015). 'Measuring what matters: Top-ranked quality indicators for hospice and palliative care from the American Academy of Hospice and Palliative Medicine and Hospice and Palliative Nurses Association.' *Journal of Pain and Symptom Management*, 49, 4, 773–781.

Emanuel, L. and Glasser Scandrett, K. (2010). 'Decisions at the end of life: Have we come of age?' *BMC Medicine*, 8, 1, 57. Available at https://bmcmedicine.biomedcentral.com/articles/10.1186/1741-7015-8-57, accessed 14 January 2018.

Engelhardt, H.T. (1998). 'Generic chaplaincy: Providing spiritual care in a post-Christian age.' *Christian Bioethics: Non-Ecumenical Studies in Medical Morality*, 4, 3, 231–238.

ENHC (2014). 'Statement – Healthcare chaplaincy in the midst of transition.' European Network of Healthcare Chaplaincy. Available at http://enhcc.eu/2014_salzburg_statement.pdf, accessed 14 January 2018.

Fitchett, G. (2011). 'Making our case(s).' *Journal of Health Care Chaplaincy*, 17, 1–2, 3–18.

Gries, C.J., Engelberg, R.A., Kross, E.K., Zatzick, D. *et al.* (2010). 'Predictors of symptoms of posttraumatic stress and depression in family members after patient death in the ICU.' *Chest*, 137, 2, 280–287.

Handzo, G., Cobb, M., Holmes, C., Kelly, E. and Sinclair, S. (2014). 'Outcomes for professional health care chaplaincy: An international call to action.' *Journal of Health Care Chaplaincy*, 20, 2, 43–53.

Jeuland, J., Fitchett, G., Schulman-Green, D. and Kapo, J. (2017). 'Chaplains working in palliative care: Who they are and what they do.' *Journal of Palliative Medicine*, 20, 5, 502–508.

Johnson, J.R., Engelberg, R.A., Nielsen, E.L., Kross, E.K. *et al.* (2014). 'The association of spiritual care providers' activities with family members' satisfaction with care after a death in the ICU.' *Critical Care Medicine*, 42, 9, 1991–2000.

Leget, C. (2017). *Art of Living, Art of Dying: Spiritual Care for a Good Death.* London; Philadelphia, PA: Jessica Kingsley Publishers.

O'Connor, T.S. and Meakes, E. (1998). 'Hope in the midst of challenge: Evidence-based pastoral care.' *Journal of Pastoral Care*, 52, 4, 359–367.

Pattison, S. (2001). 'Dumbing Down the Spirit.' In H. Orchard (ed.) *Spirituality in Health Care Contexts* (pp.33–46). London: Jessica Kingsley Publishers.

Peery, B. (2012). 'Outcome Oriented Chaplaincy: Intentional Caring.' In S.B. Roberts (ed.) *Professional Spiritual and Pastoral Care: A Practical Clergy and Chaplain's Handbook* (pp. 342–361). Woodstock, VT: Skylight Paths Publishing.

Snowden, A. and Telfer, I. (2017). 'Patient reported outcome measure of spiritual care as delivered by chaplains.' *Journal of Health Care Chaplaincy*, 23, 4, 131–155.

Snowden, A., Telfer, I., Kelly, E., Bunniss, S. and Mowat, H. (2013). 'The construction of the Lothian PROM.' *Scottish Journal of Healthcare Chaplaincy*, 16, 3–12.

Steinhauser, K.E., Fitchett, G., Handzo, G.F., Johnson, K.S. *et al.* (2017). 'State of the science of spirituality and palliative care research Part I: Definitions, measurement, and outcomes.' *Journal of Pain and Symptom Management*, 54, 3, 428–440.

Sullivan, W.F. (2014). *A Ministry of Presence: Chaplaincy, Spiritual Care, and the Law*. Chicago, IL: University of Chicago Press.

Van Leonen, G., Körver, J., Walton, M. and DeVries, R. (In press). 'Case Study of "Moral Injury": Format Dutch Case Studies Project.' *Health and Social Care Chaplaincy*, 5, 2, 281–296.

Contributors

Herbert Anderson, PhD, is a Lutheran pastor and retired professor of pastoral care and practical theology. He was a parish pastor and a hospital chaplain before beginning his teaching career at Princeton Theological Seminary in 1969. Dr Anderson has authored or co-authored over 100 articles and 13 books, including *All Our Losses, All Our Griefs*, a classic in grief literature. His most recent work is *The Divine Art of Dying: How to Live Well While Dying*, co-authored with Karen Speerstra. He received the 2015 Lifetime Achievement Award from the International Congress in Pastoral Care and Counselling.

Guðlaug Helga Ásgeirsdóttir, Dr. theol., is a family therapist, an ordained pastor in the National Church of Iceland, and a hospital chaplain at Landspitali, The National University Hospital, Iceland. A specialist in palliative care, she participated in developing the first specialised palliative care unit in Iceland. She is Chair of Lífið, The Icelandic Association for Palliative Care, and Chair of the Icelandic Christian Healthcare Fellowship Organization. She has been Chair of the Young Women's Christian Association in Iceland and a member of many boards of various organisations. Dr Ásgeirsdóttir has lectured at the University of Iceland.

Jennifer Baird, PhD, MPH, MSW, RN, CPN, is the Director of the Institute for Nursing and Interprofessional Research at Children's Hospital, Los Angeles, California. She holds a doctorate in nursing from the University of California, San Francisco, USA, a master's in social work from Virginia Commonwealth University, and a master's in public health from the Harvard T.H. Chan School of Public Health. Dr Baird's clinical practice in the paediatric intensive care unit informed her research interests in care for children with medical complexity. Her programme of research focuses on parent/provider communication and the design and implementation of family-centred care environments.

Joel Baron, a hospice chaplain at Hebrew SeniorLife, had a successful career in scientific and medical publishing. Now devoting the second phase of his work life to comforting end-of-life patients and their families, he provides spiritual and emotional support to the sick and dying, Jews and non-Jews alike; he likens counselling his patients to 'standing on holy ground'. Rabbi Baron served as Program Director of the Certificate Program in Spiritual Care at the End of Life, Hebrew College, part of the school's expanded focus on pastoral education. He is co-author of *Deathbed Wisdom of the Hasidic Masters* (Jewish Lights 2016).

Jessica Bratt Carle, MDiv, BCC, is a chaplain at Spectrum Health and Helen DeVos Children's Hospital in Grand Rapids, Michigan, USA. She completed chaplaincy training at the National Institutes of Health and Yale New Haven Hospital and has also worked at Boston Children's Hospital, Monroe Carell Jr. Children's Hospital at Vanderbilt, Saint Thomas Health in Nashville and St Jude Children's Research Hospital. She is a doctoral candidate in religion, psychology and culture at Vanderbilt University. She is a member of the Association of Professional Chaplains and the Pediatric Chaplains Network and is deeply grateful for their collegiality and resources.

Liz Bryson has a postgraduate certificate in paediatric chaplaincy through the Institute for Children, Youth and Mission and Staffordshire University. She has a background in education and taught students (aged 11–18), including those with additional needs. She has been part of pastoral care and leadership teams in faith communities. Since 2012, she has worked as a part-time, unpaid member of the chaplaincy team at Birmingham Children's Hospital. For 17 years, she was the carer for her eldest daughter, who, from age 10, lived with disability following brain surgery and cancer treatment and died from a second brain tumour aged 27.

Mark Cobb, BSc, MA, PhD, is a Clinical Director and Honorary Senior Chaplain at Sheffield Teaching Hospitals, UK. He holds honorary academic appointments at the University of Liverpool, the University of Sheffield and Sheffield Hallam University. Dr Cobb's specialist field of practice and research is palliative care, and his previous publications include *A Handbook of Chaplaincy Studies* (Routledge) and the *Oxford Textbook of Spirituality in Healthcare* (Oxford University Press).

Linda Emanuel, MD, PhD, is a Professor of Medicine, Psychiatry and Behavioral Sciences at Feinberg School of Medicine, Northwestern University, Chicago, Illinois, USA. Dr Emanuel started her career as a neurophysiologist, being fascinated by the human mind. Finding that area too restrictive, she went into medicine where, for several decades, she practised as an internist, researcher and educator in palliative and end-of-life care. Eventually, convinced of the need for understanding human experience person by person, she added training as a psychoanalyst. She now provides psychoanalytic therapy for people facing cancer or serious illness in themselves or a loved one.

Hans Evers, MA, BCC, works at the Leiden University Medical Center (Netherlands). As chaplain, he is responsible for the paediatric departments and the intensive care departments. He previously worked as an episcopal delegate and as a chaplain for students from the Diocese of Rotterdam, and as a research assistant at the University for Theology and Pastoral Care in Heerlen/Nijmegen. He teaches pastoral and moral counselling and contemplative listening.

George Fitchett, DMin, PhD, is Professor and Director of Research at the Department of Religion, Health and Human Values, Rush University Medical Center, Chicago, Illinois, USA. Trained as a chaplain and a researcher (epidemiology), he leads a programme of research focused on the role of religion/spirituality in coping with illness and the development of a research-informed approach to chaplaincy care. He is co-director, with Wendy Cadge, of the Transforming Chaplaincy project (www.transformchaplaincy.org).

Amy E. Goodman is Rabbinic Director for Hebrew SeniorLife (HSL) Hospice Care, with administrative responsibilities for spiritual, bereavement, and complementary care as well as volunteer services for HSL's Jewish hospice programme. She frequently speaks on Jewish hospice and palliative care, spirituality at the end of life, and Jewish traditions and practices at the end of life. Previously, she was a Development Director for MJHS Foundation and Director for the Center for Jewish End of Life Care. Rabbi Goodman graduated with distinction from the University of Michigan, Ann Arbor, and received her rabbinic ordination from Hebrew Union College – Jewish Institute of Religion.

Janet Hanson, MDiv, is a CPE certified educator and chaplain and teaches in the Clinical Pastoral Education programme at the Veterans Affairs (VA) Portland Health Care System. She supervises CPE interns, residents and post-traumatic stress disorder (PTSD)/mental health/ palliative care Fellows and co-leads PTSD, moral injury and women's spirituality groups, along with providing individual spiritual support to outpatients. Chaplain Hanson is a faculty member with the Mental Health Integration for Chaplaincy Services training programme, teaching VA and military chaplains evidence-based principles and fostering multidisciplinary collaboration. She is also a member of the Sexual Orientation and Gender Identity Advisory Group interdisciplinary team of providers at the VA.

Cheryl Holmes, OAM, BAppSc, DipPastMin, Grad Cert, MAppSocSc, has been the Chief Executive Officer for Spiritual Health Victoria in Australia since 2002. She has had extensive training and professional experience in healthcare, spiritual care and organisational change and management. She completed a master's degree in 2014 focused on management and leadership and commenced a PhD in 2016 at La Trobe University, Melbourne, Australia, exploring the narratives shaping spiritual care in public hospitals. She was awarded an Order of Australia Medal for her spiritual care roles in the health sector on Australia Day 2015.

Patrick Jinks, MDiv, BCC, is the Coordinator of Spiritual Care at the Children's Hospital of Greenville Health System, Greenville, South Carolina, USA. Chaplain Jinks is an ordained minister in the Presbyterian Church (USA) and is board certified by the Association of Professional Chaplains. He serves as teaching faculty for the Pediatric Chaplains Institute and is an active member of the Pediatric Chaplains Network. Patrick's clinical interests include medical ethics, research literacy and integration, paediatric palliative care, bereavement, and the spiritual care of children and their families.

Paul Nash is Senior Chaplain at Birmingham Children's Hospital; co-founder and convener of the Paediatric Chaplaincy Network; founder of the Centre for Paediatric Spiritual Care, including Red Balloon Resources; member of the UK Board of Healthcare Chaplaincy; member of the National Institute for Health and Care Excellence (NICE) Centre for Guidelines Expert Advisors Panel; Chaplaincy Services Advisory Committee member, Health Care Chaplaincy Network (USA); and tutor in chaplaincy, ethics, ministry and practical theology for the Midlands Institute for Children, Youth and Mission. Paul has published books and articles on paediatric chaplaincy, bereavement, spiritual care, multifaith care, ethics, ministry and work with young people.

Sally Nash, PhD, is the research lead for the Centre for Paediatric Spiritual Care and the Birmingham Children's Hospital Chaplaincy Team; and Director of the Midlands Institute for Children, Youth and Mission at St John's College, Nottingham. She coordinates the Centre for Chaplaincy with Children and Young People and is Associate Minister at Hodge Hill Church in Birmingham. She has completed two doctorates in practical theology and a master's in education, and has published a range of books and journal articles in the fields of work with children and young people, spirituality, shame, ministry, reflective practice and spiritual care.

Jason A. Nieuwsma, PhD, is a clinical psychologist, and Associate Professor in the Department of Psychiatry and Behavioral Sciences at Duke University Medical Center, and serves as the Associate Director for Mental Health and Chaplaincy in the Department of Veterans Affairs. He has conducted extensive research, education and clinical quality improvement work in the area of integrating mental health and chaplain services, including tailoring research-informed psychosocial approaches for utilisation within chaplaincy. Dr Nieuwsma has authored dozens of peer-reviewed journal articles and is a co-editor of the book *ACT for Clergy and Pastoral Counselors* (New Harbinger 2016).

Steve Nolan, PhD, is chaplain at Princess Alice Hospice, Esher, UK, and a Visiting Research Fellow at the University of Winchester, Hampshire, UK. He holds a PhD from the University of Manchester and is dual qualified as a British Association for Counselling and Psychotherapy accredited counsellor/therapist. He has published on chaplaincy, spiritual care and counselling therapy. Previous books include: *Spiritual Care at the End of Life: The Chaplain as a 'Hopeful Presence'* (Jessica Kingsley Publishers 2012); (with Margaret Holloway) *A–Z of Spirituality* (Palgrave-Macmillan 2014); and (with George Fitchett) *Spiritual Care in Practice: Case Studies in Healthcare Chaplaincy* (Jessica Kingsley Publishers 2015).

Patricia Roberts directs the Chaplain Service at the James A. Haley Veterans' Hospital, Tampa, Florida, USA. She is an Associate CPE Educator who received her training via the US Army. She has served as a chaplain since 2005, with a primary chaplain specialty in mental health. She has also served as a local pastor in Oklahoma, Nova Scotia and Iowa, and is ordained and endorsed by the Christian Church (Disciples of Christ). She received her Master of Divinity from Phillips Theological Seminary.

Valerie C. Sanders, DMin, LMFT, earned her Master of Divinity from The Howard University, School of Divinity in Washington, DC and her Doctor of Ministry from Columbia Theological Seminary in Decatur, Georgia. She has over 20 years' professional pastoral care experience, primarily as a clinical chaplain and as a marriage and family therapist. Chaplain Sanders currently serves as a staff chaplain at the Atlanta VA Medical Center, providing spiritual support to veterans living with PTSD and moral injury.

Andrew Todd, PhD, is Coordinator of the Centre for Contemporary Spirituality, Sarum College, Salisbury, UK. He was previously Director of the Cardiff Centre for Chaplaincy Studies. Publications include: Chris Swift, Mark Cobb and Andrew Todd (eds) *A Handbook of Chaplaincy Studies* (2015); Jonathan Pye, Peter Sedgwick and Andrew Todd (eds) *Critical Care: Delivering Spiritual Care in Healthcare Contexts* (2015); Andrew Todd (ed.) *Military Chaplaincy in Contention: Chaplains, Churches, and the Morality of Conflict* (2013). He is a practical theologian and ethnographer, with particular interests in contemporary religion and spirituality. He is also an Honorary Research Fellow of Cardiff University.

Index